'This book offers the reader a variety of philosophical ideas and approaches to spur reflection on taken for granted assumptions about what entrepreneurship is and the ways entrepreneurship scholars understand this phenomenon. The chapters in this book go beyond critiquing current ideas and perspectives, rather, the book opens up important lines of inquiry in such topic areas as: uncertainty, the imagination, social construction, critical realism, and the nature of failure. I expect that many of the insights from this book will provide directions for major avenues of entrepreneurship scholarship over the next decade. Scholars who want clues about the future direction of the entrepreneurship field would be wise to explore this book.'

–**William B. Gartner,** *Bertarelli Foundation Distinguished Professor of Family Entrepreneurship*

Philosophical Reflexivity and Entrepreneurship Research

Entrepreneurship research attracts scholars from a wide spectrum of disciplines. Yet the field is multi-paradigmatic and lacking consensus, even on the nature of core entrepreneurial phenomena. What is recognized is that it is characterized by dynamic and emergent processes – a complex interplay between actors, processes and contexts. As a result, post-positivistic approaches are gaining traction in a field long dominated by positivistic philosophies.

This book reflects on the fundamental philosophical basis of entrepreneurship scholarship. It explores the shifting meanings of entrepreneur and entrepreneurship, the unexamined assumptions which lie behind the established discourses which legitimize or dismiss the possibilities for scholarship. Contributing scholars adopt a reflexive approach to entrepreneurship research challenging readers to question their approaches and assumptions and explicitly defend them against competing alternatives.

Building on this critical reflection, this book provides space for philosophical reflexivity in the conduct and publication of scholarly enquiry and will be of great interest to scholars, researchers and advanced students in all aspect of entrepreneurship study.

Alain Fayolle is Professor of entrepreneurship, the founder and Director of the Entrepreneurship Research Centre at EM Lyon Business School, France. Alain published thirty-five books and over 100 articles.

Stratos Ramoglou is Associate Professor of Strategy, Innovation and Entrepreneurship at the University of Southampton, UK. He holds a PhD from the University of Cambridge, and his research interests include entrepreneurship, organization theory and philosophy of science.

Mine Karatas-Ozkan is Professor of Strategy and Entrepreneurship at Southampton Business School. Her research focuses on social and diversity dimensions of entrepreneurship.

Katerina Nicolopoulou is Senior Lecturer at Strathclyde Business School, UK. Her research focuses on social, sustainable and diversity-based forms of entrepreneurship as well as on the concept of cosmopolitanism as a disposition for developing entrepreneurship.

Routledge Rethinking Entrepreneurship Research
Edited by Alain Fayolle and Philippe Riot

The current focus on entrepreneurship as a purely market-based phenomenon and an unquestionably desirable economic and profitable activity leads to undervaluing and under-researching important issues in relation to power, ideology or phenomenology. New postures, new theoretical lenses and new approaches are needed to study entrepreneurship as a contextualized and socially embedded phenomenon. The objective of this series therefore is to adopt a critical and constructive posture towards the theories, methods, epistemologies, assumptions and beliefs which dominate mainstream thinking. It aims to provide a forum for scholarship which questions the prevailing assumptions and beliefs currently dominating entrepreneurship research and invites contributions from a wide range of different communities of scholars, which focus on novelty, diversity and critique.

Rethinking Entrepreneurship
Debating research orientations
Edited by Alain Fayolle and Philippe Riot

Family Entrepreneurship
Rethinking the research agenda
Kathleen Randerson, Cristina Bettinelli, Alain Fayolle and Giovanna Dossena

Challenging Entrepreneurship Research
Edited by Hans Landström, Annaleena Parankangas, Alain Fayolle and Philippe Riot

Revitalizing Entrepreneurship Education
Adopting a critical approach in the classroom
Karin Berglund and Karen Verduijn

Philosophical Reflexivity and Entrepreneurship Research
Edited by Alain Fayolle, Stratos Ramoglou, Mine Karatas-Ozkan and Katerina Nicolopoulou

For more information about this series, please visit: www.routledge.com

Philosophical Reflexivity and Entrepreneurship Research

Edited by Alain Fayolle,
Stratos Ramoglou,
Mine Karatas-Ozkan and
Katerina Nicolopoulou

Routledge
Taylor & Francis Group

LONDON AND NEW YORK

First published 2018 by Routledge

2 Park Square, Milton Park, Abingdon, Oxon, OX14 4RN
605 Third Avenue, New York, NY 10017

Routledge is an imprint of the Taylor & Francis Group, an informa business

First issued in paperback 2020

British Library Cataloguing-in-Publication Data
A catalogue record for this book is available from the British Library

Library of Congress Cataloging-in-Publication Data
A catalog record for this book has been requested

ISBN: 978-1-138-65029-9 (hbk)
ISBN: 978-0-367-73455-8 (pbk)

Typeset in Times New Roman
by Apex CoVantage, LLC

Contents

Illustrations

Figures

Table

1 Introduction

Reflecting on our philosophical journey

Stratos Ramoglou, Mine Karatas-Ozkan and Alain Fayolle

There will be some fundamental assumptions, which adherents of all variant systems within the epoch unconsciously presuppose. Such assumptions appear so obvious that people do not know what they are assuming because no other way of putting things has ever occurred to them.

A. N. Whitehead

As entrepreneurship researchers, we also adhere to some fundamental assumptions about the nature of the entrepreneurial phenomenon (ontological assumptions) and ways of knowing it (epistemological assumptions). Moreover, the multidisciplinary nature of entrepreneurship research entails that there is no single set of such assumptions. Different philosophical traditions are silently affecting the evolution of academic debate – regardless of whether we are ever aware of them or the exact ways through which they facilitate or constrain our scholarly imagination (Wittgenstein, 1958).

In fact, even the most "hardcore" empirical researcher – keen to dismiss the relevance of philosophy – would philosophize in her very dismissal of philosophy (van Fraassen, 1995). The only genuine difference is that her conclusions would be the result of unexamined philosophical preoccupations. She would also be a philosopher, yet unreflective of the precise nature of her philosophical preoccupations and the manner in which they affect her research practice.

Philosophy is inescapable. The only genuine choice lies in the kind of philosophies that we will trust in our scholarly journey. This volume emerged from an invitation to entrepreneurship researchers to detect and reflect upon prevalent philosophical assumptions underlying scholarly practice. The motivation for this invitation emerged from the conviction that our field cannot make sufficient progress without standing back to seriously and patiently reflect upon the most fundamental assumptions underpinning empirical research. There is no doubt that empirical inquiry is fundamental for the possibility of scientific progress (Alvarez, Barney, McBride, & Wuebker, 2017; Davidsson, 2016). However, it is doubtful that headway can be made without sufficient reflection about the direction of the empirical journey. There are fundamental questions that simply cannot be tackled by means of empirical scrutiny (Ramoglou & Tsang, 2017a, 2017b). These are philosophical questions that can be addressed only by means of careful reflection and argumentation.

Needless to say, the philosophical journey does not have a final stop in sight. So long as we are interested in the thoughtful study of entrepreneurial phenomena, it is inescapable that conceptual confusions will emerge and profound questions will beg our attention. Yet this does not mean that it is not a journey worth traveling. Actually, even the dead-ends of such a journey should be welcomed. For the least of reasons, they alert us to the wrong turns that future scholarship should better avoid. More importantly perhaps, we cannot avoid taking this journey for the reason that we are already on this journey. And enhancing the levels of reflexivity may only help us improve the "philosophical maps" guiding the direction of the travel.

Against this backdrop, the second chapter opens the debate on philosophy and the social sciences. McBride raises some fundamental questions that we must consider before beginning the examination of philosophical assumptions and approaches to entrepreneurship. He suggests that the foundational building block of the social sciences is that they are inherently social and distinctive from physical phenomena, to discuss the implications that the explicit appreciation of this distinction entails regarding the explanatory frameworks that should guide entrepreneurship research. McBride concludes his chapter confronting entrepreneurship scholars with a fundamental social ontological question: how do beliefs blend in a social environment such that one becomes established and "real"? It is answers to such fundamental questions that should form the foundation of a well-grounded understanding of the social sciences in general, and entrepreneurship in particular.

In the third chapter, Arend critically examines the idea of progress in entrepreneurship research by testing recently proposed theories (bricolage, effectuation and creation opportunities). Arend's verdict is that they are not sufficiently new. He argues that entrepreneurship, as a relatively nascent and vulnerable field, lacks a strong, sufficiently different and indigenous theory. In addition, Arend demonstrates that entrepreneurship research tends to attract the kind of theories that are not necessarily new and novel but presented as such. This practice hinders the healthy development of the field; thus, Arend calls for more responsible scholarship that relies on more critical analyses of allegedly "new" theories. By critiquing the already popular theories of "bricolage", "effectuation" and "creation opportunities" Arend provides us the means for testing the originality and contribution of more "novel" theories to come, and urges us to take more seriously the process of theory development in entrepreneurship research.

The fourth chapter by Pittaway, Aïssaoui and Fox presents social constructionism as a meta-theory and defends its philosophical potential for entrepreneurship research. Pittaway et al. critique the overwhelming nature and use of functionalist approaches in the study of entrepreneurship. They argue that such assumptions create various problems, e.g., they solidify the conviction that entrepreneurship is an individual rather than societal phenomenon. Applying a social constructionist approach to studying entrepreneurial opportunity as a specific domain of entrepreneurship research, Pittaway et al. try to delineate how the opposing camps (the discovery versus creation perspective of opportunities) are linked to different dimensions of social constructionist epistemology. In doing so, they argue that social constructionism can accommodate diverse views and forms of entrepreneurship.

In the fifth chapter, Martin and Wilson put forward a competing meta-theoretical perspective that stresses the value of realist philosophy. They make the case for serious realist philosophical approaches that, inter alia, demonstrate theory and practice inconsistencies and facilitate action. Their point of departure is that whilst entrepreneurship is a distinctively pragmatic domain, it is incorrect to think that matters of doing (making it work) should be prior to theoretical matters (understanding why it works). They especially draw attention to the under-theorized "entrepreneurial project" as the means through which entrepreneurial opportunities are realized, and highlight how understanding the conditions that enable such projects to develop can form the basis of an applied theory of entrepreneurial opportunity development. Moreover, Martin and Wilson make a convincing case of the practical value of realist theorizing in providing the background structure necessary for informed decisions about entrepreneurial projects.

Reinforcing the case for critical realism made by Martin and Wilson, in the sixth chapter, Kitching proposes critical realism as a philosophically superior approach to the major alternatives, viz., positivism, social constructionism and pragmatism. He explains that critical realism is a facilitating philosophy for entrepreneurship and small business research as it channels attention to the condition of possibility of particular business practices. More specifically, Kitching points out the distinctive value of critical realist research in allowing for generating insights into entrepreneurship as experienced by disadvantaged groups. A key point stemming from a critical realist approach of identity and entrepreneurship is the emphasis on entrepreneurs' positioning within particular social relations.

The seventh chapter, authored by Kaasila-Pakanen and Puhakka, takes the debate further by reflecting on the use of postcolonial deconstruction for enhancing our understanding of the diverse meanings and sides of entrepreneurship. They argue that as entrepreneurship scholars, we should be prepared to take responsibility of our complicity in webs of power through the explicit acknowledgement of our epistemological positioning. Taking a postcolonial deconstructionist view entails self-reflexivity as to the role of the researcher and author in sustaining dominant social relations. It also implies questioning deeper philosophical underpinnings of entrepreneurship research as to the nature of entrepreneurship, the borders and taken for granted assumptions of entrepreneurship research, as well as the inclusion and exclusion criteria to be applied.

In the eighth chapter, Slutskaya, Mallett and Borgerson explore entrepreneurial attachment to success ethics (i.e. a system of legitimation that prioritizes norms and actions consistent with institutionalized notion of success) as generated by a cluster of promises of the enterprise culture. Drawing on empirical insights, their chapter reveals a dark side of entrepreneurship. They especially highlight the role of cruel optimism in the context of failure as a result of the pressure towards entrepreneurial success along with the demand for entrepreneurial identities to function smoothly. Their findings reveal that entrepreneurs demonstrate a paradoxical desire to belong to and participate in the very normative entrepreneurial culture that has failed them. This chapter makes an important contribution to ongoing debates on reflexivity in entrepreneurship research through the problematization of the concept of failure through a novel critique of the ideological underpinnings of the normative enterprise culture.

The ninth chapter applies this reflexivity to the concept of "entrepreneurial imagination". Thompson points out that, though the concept has a long history in heterodox economics and is recurrently used in references to the entrepreneurial process, we lack a critical review of the uses of the concept – let alone a reflective analysis of the philosophical underpinnings of perspectives of the "entrepreneurial imagination". This chapter therefore presents an important contribution on this front. Thompson brings to the open common assumptions underlying the use of imagination in entrepreneurship research. He puts forward a three-pronged critique that touches on the processual, relational and aesthetic aspects of imagination; to explain how extant conceptualizations constrict the potential of the concept to illuminate the entrepreneurial process in a more complete and dynamic manner. This critique offers the springboard on which Thompson turns to redirect entrepreneurship research toward renewed theoretical perspectives that benefit from hitherto unutilized developments in the philosophy of imagination.

In the tenth chapter, Nicolopoulou and Samy address some of the noted gaps in the established philosophical outlooks of entrepreneurship by incorporating perspectives from the social sciences. In particular, they examine the concepts of cosmopolitanism and orientalism as part of the conceptualization of disposition and context in entrepreneurship research. This chapter helps us delve into complex social science-informed constructs and flesh out potential implications for the further development of the field. The authors maintain that such an interdisciplinary focus can facilitate the emergence of multiple lines of inquiry, narrative and interpretation toward the creation of pathways that can inform help us address the contemporary "grand challenges".

In the eleventh chapter, Gordon and McBride take us through a scholarly journey suggesting that we should rethink some of our core assumptions, definitions and constructs in entrepreneurship studies. They study the nature of the firm in entrepreneurship research, and highlight the importance of getting the ontology right. Without sufficient clarity about the nature of the firm as an organized social entity, we simply cannot generate meaningful theories and explanations. Given that a necessary component of any entrepreneurial venture is the dynamic, ongoing effort to design and build the vehicle that creates and captures economic and social value – the firm – Gordon and McBride offer us a reconceptualization of this vehicle through a deontic architecture view.

Our final chapter, authored by Dimov, encourages us to rethink basic assumptions. Entrepreneurship is action in the face of uncertainty, and this mantra is routinely repeated in entrepreneurship research. Dimov stands back to reflectively wonder what we mean when we say that entrepreneurs bear uncertainty. In fact, through an original analysis of the concept he is led to the conclusion that "those who truly bear the uncertainty, do not really exist", to suggest that uncertainty-bearing is essentially an academic construct, detached from the realities of acting entrepreneurs. Against this backdrop, he moves to ground uncertainty firmly in the real-world experience of enterprise. In this effort, Dimov guides us through colorful thought experiments, excursions in process philosophy, and autobiographical accounts, to recommend that we should fundamentally reconsider the nature of entrepreneurship. Instead of ruminating that entrepreneurship is action in the face of uncertainty, Dimov concludes that, at a deeper ontological level, entrepreneurship is the enactment of purpose. It is the attachment to this that, in turn, generates uncertainty – though, in the absence of philosophical reflexivity, it is tempting to frame the bearing of uncertainty as the essence of entrepreneurship.

We trust that the chapters of this volume contain some potentially valuable contributions in the direction of improving the levels of our collective reflexivity on some of the most important questions animating entrepreneurship research.

References

Alvarez, S. A., Barney, J. B., McBride, R., & Wuebker, R. (2017). On opportunities: Philosophical and empirical implications. *Academy of Management Review*, forthcoming.

Davidsson, P. (2016). *Researching entrepreneurship: Conceptualization and design* (2nd ed.). New York: Springer.

Ramoglou, S., & Tsang, E. W. K. (2017a). In defense of common sense in entrepreneurship theory: Beyond philosophical extremities and linguistic abuses. *Academy of Management Review*, in press.

Ramoglou, S., & Tsang, E. W. K. (2017b). Accepting the unknowables of entrepreneurship and overcoming philosophical obstacles to scientific progress. *Journal of Business Venturing Insights*, *8*, 71–77.

van Fraassen, B. C. (1995). Against naturalized empiricism. In P. Leonardi & M. Santambrogio (Eds.), *On Quine* (pp. 68–88). Cambridge: Cambridge University Press.

Wittgenstein, L. (1958). *Philosophical investigations* (2nd ed.). Oxford: Basil Blackwell.

2 Applying philosophy to entrepreneurship and the social sciences

Russ McBride

Philosophy

There are ongoing efforts to apply philosophy to research in entrepreneurship theory, and not only entrepreneurship of course, but all the business sciences – strategy, organizational behavior, management, finance, etc. Some of these efforts have been successful, some unsuccessful, and others nonsensical. In what follows, I want to look at what it means to apply philosophy, some formalisms for how to do it (and not do it), and describe the best path forward for those interested in applying philosophy to questions in entrepreneurship and the social sciences in general.

Let's start with the obvious question. What is philosophy? At dinner parties, one of my undergraduate philosophy professors would respond to this question tongue-in-cheek by saying, "Would you like the four-hour response or the long answer?" Funny, but I never liked that response very much because, as another one of my mentors, my dissertation advisor John Searle, used to say, "If you can't say it clearly then you don't understand it yourself", and I think all of us do actually understand what philosophy is and it doesn't require a four-hour-long explanation. Rather, it's quite simple. On my take, philosophy is reasoned talk about fundamental questions. That's it. So, talking about one's favorite color or what movie one wants to see doesn't count as philosophy because neither are foundational nor fundamental topics. Neither is haggling over the cost of a car repair. And although haggling over the cost of a car repair is not philosophy, discussing the question of what makes an economic exchange an economic exchange is philosophy, if it is discussed in a "reasoned" manner.

So, philosophy, then, on this view, is: a) first, an activity, the activity of talking or discussing, whether in person or print. Not just any talk, but talk that is performed in a certain manner and directed toward certain topics. b) Specifically, it gravitates around topics involving foundational or fundamental questions. And c) the discussion unfolds in the manner of good reasoning. Some professional philosophers would disagree with this definition, but I think it captures most of what we would want to call philosophy'.[1]

Philosophy, then, extends well beyond the traditional categories of logic, ethics, metaphysics, epistemology, and aesthetics because if you're exploring the fundamentals of any topic in a reasoned manner then that's philosophy. You can discuss the philosophy of X where X is almost anything – biology, language, sport, economics, physics, entrepreneurship, etc. This coheres nicely with the use of the term in advanced academic studies and with the history of human knowledge. A Ph.D., we often forget, is a "doctorate of philosophy" because one (presumably) spent time exploring fundamentals in one's field of study. "Natural philosophy" was for centuries the term for the reasoned study of fundamental questions of the natural (physical) world, which is why Newton termed his (1687) work, *Philosophiae Naturalis Principia Mathematica*, or, *Mathematical Principles of Natural Philosophy*.

It wasn't until there was enough agreement about the basics of the physical world, with enough evidence in support of those basic answers, that physics branched off from philosophy and matured into a field of its own. And this is how specialized knowledge arose. The fundamental questions began as pure philosophy and when they gained enough theoretical structure they left the nest and moved out on their own. This happened to biology, chemistry, physics, psychology, anthropology, and the rest of the natural sciences.[2] Insofar as there are still fundamental questions at the core of these fields, it is still possible to do philosophy of physics, philosophy of biology, philosophy of psychology, etc., and many careers are built around searching for answers to the fundamental questions inside one's chosen field. Many people work on a philosophy-of-X topic either from the philosophy side or the X side. Scholars working on fundamental questions in the business sciences do this too.

What does 'fundamental' mean? An issue that's fundamental is one that is conceptually prior, more general, or about something's essential nature. For example, the question of what the actual units of genetic selection are is more fundamental than the question of whether birds descended from reptiles, though both questions are important questions in biology. And the question of what constitutes a social entity is prior to, and a more fundamental question than, the question of what specific incorporated legal entity provides the best tax advantages. Most of us agree about whether a question is fundamental or foundational even without hard metrics for quantifying the precise degree to which it is fundamental.

Reasoning and logic

If philosophy is *reasoned* talk about such fundamental issues, then it's important to understand what 'reasoned' means. Logic is the study of the methods of good and bad reasoning and in the Western world we take logic to be the compass that guides us toward good reasoning. Logic is the language of philosophy, as math is the language of physics. Indeed, a well-trained philosopher might have limited empirical understanding of any particular topic but typically possesses well-honed powers of logical reasoning and analysis. This is why philosophy majors typically get the top, or near-top, spots in graduate exams like the LSAT, GRE, and MCAT (APA report, 2014)[3] and have the highest rates of acceptance into medical school and law school. They've had lots of practice doing conceptual analysis and reasoning their way through analytic problems of the kind contained in such entrance exams.

Doing philosophy, on the account presented here, requires a discussion that unfolds in the manner of good reasoning and it is here where the business journals need the most help and where philosophy can pay the biggest dividends. The fundamental principle of good reasoning is that there must be a reason, or reasons, in support of a conclusion, either reasons that purport to support a claim conclusively (a deductive argument) or with some inconclusive degree of probabilistic support (an inductive argument).[4] A well-reasoned discussion, like the discussion in a paper, should offer a clear thesis as a conclusion supported by a series of relevant reasons that together form the core argument. That is the framework around which the fabric of the discussion is spun.

Somehow, this fundamental tenet of good reasoning sometimes goes missing in contemporary business journals and, when lost, dysfunctional substitutes appear. A thesis "that's interesting" (Davis, 1971) is no substitute for a claim properly supported by reasons. Here's an example of an interesting thesis: aliens from planet Zyborg control Earth's interest rates by means of telekinesis. That's certainly "interesting" but not worth reading if no plausible reasons are offered in support of it.

Another thing that fails to provide a genuine reason in support of a claim is a citation. Yes, that's right. Someone believing your claim is not a logical reason in support of that claim. Just the opposite. To justify your claim on the basis of another's belief in it is a well-known informal logical fallacy called 'appeal to authority', or 'appeal to the masses'. Somewhere during the growth of the business sciences we began to confuse two things – the use of a citation as a way of helping a reader understand where discussants stand (and confirming that your statement is relevant to that discussion), and the use of a citation as logical support for a claim. Having a thousand citations for your claim is no logical reason for it anymore than a thousand people believing the Earth is flat is a reason the Earth is flat.

A third substitute that fails is a *merely related idea*. If I'm arguing that combustion engines are the best kind of engines and in support of that I say that lawnmowers have combustion engines, I have offered no reason at all for why combustion engines are the best; I have offered a *merely related idea*. Providing nothing but a collection of merely related ideas that orbit around a thesis is to merely gesticulate around a claim without offering any real, logical reason in support of that claim. This is perhaps the single most commonly occurring failure of logic today.

In sum, the central edict of good reasoning is to provide reasons in support of a thesis. There are at least three ways to *fail* to provide reasons, and so three ways to fail to provide a logically coherent discussion: 1) to think that you've provided a reason for your thesis because your thesis is "interesting"; 2) to think that you've provided a reason for your thesis because you've provided a citation (or 1,000 citations) in support of it; 3) to think that you've provided a reason for your thesis because you've provided an idea that is merely related to it.

Crafting a good definition

Before moving on to the topic of philosophical *content*, I would like to discuss one last formalism used in the application of philosophy to the business sciences, and that is the formal definition. A lack of careful conceptual analysis reveals itself readily in a poor definition. There are many kinds of definitions but at the most general level there are a) intensional (conceptual) definitions that state the essential character of something (usually by stating its necessary and sufficient conditions or through genus-differentia), there are b) extensional definitions that simply list all the members of the defined category, and there are c) operational definitions that specify a technique for determining the members of an extensional category. One can get an intentional (conceptual) definition wrong by mis-specifying the concept. One can get an extensional definition wrong by identifying the wrong members. And one can get an operational definition wrong by specifying a technique that identifies the wrong members.

The real trouble is the rampant proliferation of poorly constructed definitions in theory papers where a genuine understanding of the core constructs is critical and cannot be sidelined or avoided. Getting the concept right in the first place not only corrects a bad conceptual definition but increases the likelihood of getting the operational and extensional definitions right too. In this sense, it can be argued that the conceptual definition is perhaps primary, so we shall focus on the it, though, in reality, each type of definition affects the others in the give-and-take process, like staking down the corners of an tarp. It's sometimes said that formal conceptual definitions are irrelevant or unimportant, but this is true only if having a concise statement of the essential nature of something is irrelevant or unimportant. If philosophy is the discussion of the essential nature of some phenomenon, then an accurate conceptual definition is a little bit of bedrock of pure philosophy upon which a theory can be successfully built.

Why do we find so many broken definitions in theory papers? There are two reasons. The first is that any definition requires deep reflection. In fact, if Plato knew one thing, he knew that making minced meat out of a poorly constructed definition was easy.[5] Definitions are important for the same reason that they are hard to get right – they force one to think through the nature of something, be explicit, and clarify exactly what its essential structure is. And it just takes a single counterexample to refute a definition, which is why the prime directive for every practicing philosopher since 300 BC is "never offer an explicit definition". A favorite Philosophy 101 first-class-of-the-semester pastime is to start by asking the students to define "chair" and then mercilessly dismantle the definitions. "Something with four legs that you sit on". Counterexample: a log-stump chair or a bean-bag chair. "O.K., something you sit on." Counterexample: "Well you can sit on a tranquilized tiger and that's not a chair. . . ." And on it goes until the poor undergraduate is left with the feeling that, first, composing a definition (a definiens) is basically impossible, and second, that philosophy is a waste of time, a feeling echoed by many in the business sciences.

'Entrepreneurship' definition examples

Still, theory papers must provide better conceptual definitions. But if it's not easy to formulate a definition, even for something seemingly as easy and concrete as 'chair', how is one supposed to come up with a definition for a deeply contentious phenomenon like 'entrepreneurship'? Sentiments run deep here: "If we waited for arm-chair speculators to agree on the definition of 'entrepreneurship', nothing would've gotten done in the last 50 years! Work must go on! Besides we've repeatedly tried and never made progress on a definition!" For most researchers in entrepreneurship, working on their field's definition is about as much fun as reliving the scene of a multi-victim car crash. Still, other fields can quite easily state what they study. Strategy? The study of competitive advantage in firms. History? The study of past events. Physics? The study of matter. Psychology? The study of human behavior and mind. Shouldn't entrepreneurship scholars be able to at least state what the nature of their field's study is too?

I shall be forthright and suggest my own definition of entrepreneurship:

> Taking action with the intention to generate economic value under conditions that are uncertain or novel for the agent.

The first thing to notice about this formulation is that entrepreneurship is an activity. The second thing to notice is that what counts as entrepreneurial activity is relativized to the knowledge and experience of the agent such that two people can be engaged in the very same activity and it be entrepreneurial for one but not for the other. This 'agent relativization' solves a number of puzzles that have plagued the field over the years and coheres nicely with how we think about entrepreneurship in daily life.

Here's one apparent contradiction it resolves. Imagine a life-long janitor who buys his first McDonalds fast food franchise and compare this to a life-long franchisee who buys his thousandth McDonalds. There is of course a question of whether buying a franchise is a real case of entrepreneurship at all, but more than 98% of us believe that the janitor is acting *more entrepreneurially* than the professional franchisee (McBride, 2017). But if they are both purchasing the same McDonalds, there is no distinction to be made in the product or the business itself. Nor is there any difference in the degree of innovativeness. Neither is innovative. The discrepancy in the evaluation of the two cases seems like a contradiction. It's not. The difference is due to a difference *in the agents*. The janitor is engaged in a novel activity; the professional isn't. A relativized conception of entrepreneurship handles this deftly. Non-relativized approaches don't. The approaches that define entrepreneurship as, simply, innovation, or starting a new venture, or economic activity, are absolute definitions that don't take the agent's background knowledge or experience into consideration. But that knowledge and experience determines whether the conditions within which the agent is acting are novel and uncertain for the agent or not. Buying one's thousandth McDonalds is not novel for the experienced professional; it is for the janitor.

An investigation into this conception of entrepreneurship requires a large treatment of its own and the purpose here is to instead explore the application of philosophy to entrepreneurship, within which definitions are merely one prominent methodological tool. But there are a few implications of this definition that are worth noting before moving on to some definitions that don't work so well. The first is that firms *can* act entrepreneurially insofar as they are moving into novel and unknown areas – e.g., a completely new product or service offering. The second is that, given that the essential context is one of uncertainty and novelty, the essential activity is one of navigating and reducing uncertainty and deploying creative problem solving because the agent lacks the experience and knowledge for routine problem decomposition. The third is that, insofar as the goal is economic value generation and 'economic value' is an inherently *social phenomenon*, entrepreneurship itself is inherently a social phenomenon. This shouldn't be surprising since entrepreneurship is, after all, just one of the social sciences, like economics, sociology, management, strategy, political science, etc. But this simple point – that entrepreneurship is *social* – is a critically important point, confusion about which has caused endless problems over the decades, so we will cycle back to it later and I will repeat it again here: *entrepreneurship is a social phenomenon.*

So what should one do if one wants better definitions of a theoretical construct? Well, one needs to pay attention to those pesky counterexamples. Plato taught us this a couple of millennia ago. The power of the counterexample is that it points out a "rotten member" in the extension of members that would be there if one were to operationalize the conceptual definition. It therefore serves to detect problems across all three species of definition types in one fell swoop.

Let's look at some obvious counterexamples to recently offered definitions of 'entrepreneurship'. On one definition, entrepreneurship is that which causes economic change. It should be clear that this is a pretty broad definition open to endless counterexamples. A tsunami that rolls over Japan causes lots of economic change but none of us want to say that the tsunami is an entrepreneur. Again, it takes only one counterexample to torpedo a definition. You can no longer say "that's O.K., that's still a good definition because . . .". Rather you've got only two options. The first option is to admit the damage and modify your definition to avoid it. "Yes, that counterexample illustrates that not *any* form of economic change involves entrepreneurship. Let me modify the definition to, e.g., *human-caused* economic change." Whether this modified definition works is a separate question, but at least the objection was handled. The second option is to try to show why the counterexample doesn't really apply. To do this one might say, "No, a tsunami causes only physical damage, but never economic change so this counterexample doesn't apply." This would be a hard argument to make, in my opinion, but it at least acknowledges the force of the counterexample and attempts to defuse it. To ignore the force of a legitimate counterexample is to reject the basic principles of reason which form the bedrock of intellectual work.

Another often-cited definition of entrepreneurship is "the formation of a new venture". There are low-hanging counterexamples here too: a multi-national starts a new venture to sell a red widget instead of the white ones that it's sold for the last 20 years. Is that entrepreneurship? Most are inclined to say, 'no', so that seems like a legitimate counterexample. Or if I walk down to the Department of Corporations, hand over a form and the $100 necessary to get a C-corp, and never do anything with that firm, and never make or sell any product or service, is that entrepreneurship, since there is a newly formed venture? Again, this seems like a counterexample. There are moves available here too. You could suggest that, though there is a new firm, there's no new *venture*. This would require some fiddling with the concepts of 'firm' and 'venture' to find way of distinguishing them. And you might respond to the first counterexample by suggesting that merely offering a new color of the same widget is not truly a *new* venture so the counterexample carries no weight. These responses may or may not actually work, but again, at least they are attempts to grapple with the counterexamples.

A final example. If you take entrepreneurship to be essentially some kind of social phenomena but suggest that entrepreneurship is essentially "the making of judgments about the allocation of scarce resources" (notice the similarity to the standard definition of 'economics') then I'm going to call foul because there exist glaring counterexamples. A lone survivor on an otherwise deserted island trying to decide whether to save or eat one of his last remaining coconuts is, on this definition, a genuine entrepreneur. Faced with this counterexample you have to either bite the bullet and accept the implication that entrepreneurship is *not essentially social* (since a lone individual making judgments apart from any society can be an entrepreneur), or the definition must be modified. To take *neither* path is, well, to act in a way that is irrational. Those who like this definition of entrepreneurship usually bite the bullet and accept such counterexamples and the implication that entrepreneurship is *not essentially social*. This would be a very peculiar result if one of the social sciences itself turned out to not be social, so I don't think this move works and it's worth delving into exactly why this is wrong, why it doesn't work, and why entrepreneurship is, as we in fact already know, inherently social.

We must first, however, work through the second reason why it's so hard to build a robust formal definition. The first reason, recall, is simply that a good definition requires considered reflection to get right, as Plato showed. The second reason is deeper. In exploring the second reason we move away from our discussion of philosophic formalisms and into a discussion of the philosophical foundation of entrepreneurship, and the social sciences in general.

The social sciences lack a unified theory

A good definition, as we noted, forces one to carefully state something's essential nature. This is difficult to do, and it is more difficult in the social sciences. By 'social sciences', again, I mean: sociology, social psychology, anthropology, economics, entrepreneurship, strategy, political science, finance, organizational behavior, management science, etc. Why is it so much more difficult to state something's essential nature in the social sciences than in the physical sciences? Because, unlike physics, in which one can clearly state the composition of, e.g., a chunk of rock (molecules comprised of atoms and ultimately smaller particles in fields of force), the social sciences have not so far been able to state the composition of a 'chunk' of social reality. They have so far been unable to say what a social entity (or a social fact) *actually is*! We have not, as it were, yet found the *atoms* of the social world!

We see a rift in the social sciences between theoretical work and empirical work with few bridges between the two. The bulk of the work done is empirical, statistical work. And when there is theoretical work we rarely see 'deep' foundational theory but rather localized theories with a narrow range of application to the particular specialized field. We see work on, e.g., transaction cost economics or the resource-based view, rather than work on the connection between transaction costs and the fundamental structure of social entities themselves. And we don't see this work because there simply hasn't been work done that clearly identifies *what the fundamental structure of a social entity is in the first place.*

We have, in other words, evidence across all the social sciences that points to one inescapable and difficult-to-swallow fact, a fact which most who work in the social sciences (me included) would much rather ignore, pretend is not true, or postpone for a future generation of scholars to confront, and that fact is the following: There is no unified theoretical framework that underlies the social sciences. And there is no unified framework because we do not understand what a social entity is, at heart. We do not know what a team, a government, or a firm really is. And if we do not yet know what it is, it's very hard to *state* what it is or offer definitions for social phenomena that ultimately depend on 'the social atoms' of the world, whatever they are, as all social phenomena ultimately do.

The natural sciences are distinctly different on this point. They have a broad collection of overlapping and unified theories that support one another in a vast web of coherent knowledge. Physics informs chemistry and biology. Neurobiology rests on principles of physics, chemistry, and biology, etc. *In contrast, the fundamental truth of the social sciences is that we do not yet know the fundamental truth.* We do not have anything resembling a unified theory; we don't know what the structure of social reality is; we can't describe the principles by which social reality changes; nor do we have anything resembling agreement about what the fundamental units of social reality might be.

> Research programs in the social sciences are built on a shaky understanding of the most fundamental question of all: *what are the social sciences **about**?* Or more specifically, *what **are** social facts, social objects, and social phenomena* – these things that the social sciences aim to model and explain?
> (Epstein, 2015)

These questions *should* have been the responsibility of sociology as the broadest study of these fields, but sociology was, rather, founded by Durkheim on what sociology *is not*. It was founded on the claim by fiat that sociology is *not* psychology, as a way of declaring its independence from the one field to which it had the most obvious ties. It didn't develop to a reasonable point of maturity first, like each of the natural sciences, which built a core framework of facts about the basic principles of its domain before moving out onto their own.

One might think that *there is a fundamental truth of the social world* and it is that social entities are *made of people*. Indeed, the methodological individualists claim that social entities ultimately 'reduce' to individual humans, and most economists agree. But many disagree. Epstein (2015) refers to this false belief as "the ant trap". Sociologists believe that there are attributes of social entities that cannot be explained by their individual members, hence the age-old debate between the methodological individualists and the structuralists. This debate is now mirrored in a debate in strategy between those who advocate 'microfoundations' (methodological individualism) and those who reject it. But even if the structuralists are correct that the social level holds important powers and facts that cannot be explained by the individuals that comprise a social group, it doesn't explain *why*, and still doesn't amount to anything resembling a foundational theory. The hard-to-swallow truth is that we simply have almost no understanding of what social reality consists, how social structures are born and die, and by what 'laws' they change. And this collection of core problems is distinct from the recognized problem, already well accepted, that the social sciences, and economics in particular, have failed miserably at predicting critically important events, like the Great Depression or the financial meltdown of 2008.

Four options: social ontology, social evolutionary theory, institutional theory, and critical realism

The core foundation for the social sciences in general is missing. It turns out, however, that recent decades have seen a surge of work on the core problem by theorists studying what is called 'social ontology' (or sometimes, 'collective intentionality'). Social ontology's raison d'être is the study of the core problem – the question of what a social entity is – and there has been relentless pursuit of an answer in recent decades, for example: Bratman (1987, 2014); Gilbert (1992, 2015); Petit and List (2013); Searle (1995, 2010); Tuomela (2002, 2007, 2013); and Epstein (2015) among others.

There have also been at least a few other camps working on the core problem – social evolutionary theory (sometimes called, "universal Darwinism"), institutional theory, and critical realism. Social evolutionary theory suggests that the very mechanisms of evolution are not unique to biology but applicable universally, including to the social world. The Achilles heel of this view is that, where biological evolution has a clear unit over which an organism's attributes vary and are inherited – DNA – there is no agreed-upon unit of variance, inheritance, or mechanism of selection in the social world. We don't have the analogical "DNA" to make the theory work in the social sphere (McBride, 2016).

Neither institutional theorists nor critical realists hold a unified position, respectively. In fact, 'institutional theory' at this point is taken to refer to almost any social theoretical work, roughly since Marx (Scott, 2015). And the only consistent position held among critical realists is their rejection of postmodernism. In both schools there is intermittent, but regular, discussion of the physical sciences and frequent discussion of philosophy of science as if the natural sciences are in any way, shape, or form relevant to the social sciences. They are not. The Achilles heel of these positions is the claim that the social world should be studied through philosophy of science, because it is fundamentally similar to the physical sciences. And this is false (McBride, 2018).

In some importance sense perhaps "everything is physical". But, even if true, this does not imply that *every field* must use the methods and principles of physics anymore than it makes sense to break out an electron microscope and infrared goggles to see the source of price fluctuations in the NASDAQ. Or to use the Hubble Space Telescope to locate the trend toward more conservative-leaning political parties in Europe. Different phenomena require different explanatory structures, and, though there is only one world, nothing is more different than physical phenomena and the social phenomena. Physical phenomena include molecules and atoms and quarks and muons and gravity; social phenomena include firms and unemployment and football teams and options derivatives. It's true that social entities, like Microsoft, e.g., own a physical building and physical resources. But what makes Microsoft, Microsoft is not its buildings. If it were, then a firm that left its building would cease to exist before coming back into existence in a new building.

Social ontology offers a more flexible path forward, not hitching its horse to the single post of evolutionary theory (like social evolutionary theory) or Roy Bhaskar's work (like critical realism), and insofar as it is oriented around attempts to solve the core problem, unlike institutional theory which roams broadly, it is free to deftly navigate obstacles as they arise. And it does not commit the fundamental error of conflating the physical world with the social world. Further, it has the greatest number researchers, and the most diverse and the most active research currently. So my suggestion is that the best path forward is probably some variant of work that has the greatest recent successes behind it – social ontology – without the obvious flaws just mentioned. But it would be far too great a task to delve into a thorough exploration of social ontology, or compare in detail the four theoretical options here, or adjudicate the debate about methodological individualism, or attempt to justify my claim that social ontology affords the best hope for a unified theory of the social sciences. Instead, to conclude, I would like to offer my suggestion for what the first philosophical building block of entrepreneurship and the social sciences must be, regardless of your theoretical allegiance.

The first building block for theoretical work in the social sciences

The most basic building block, I suggest, and you can guess by now, is that the social sciences are, in general, *inherently social*. This might seem banal, or like an irrelevant generalization, but the failure to get this basic issue right has caused an enormous amount of problems, missteps, and unnecessary hurdles for the progress of the social sciences. And, as suggested, it's the most common error at the heart of the social evolutionary views, institutional theory, critical realism, and the anti-social stance of the "judgment view". So getting this first block in the foundation correct eliminates an enormous variety of "shaky structures".

Why is the seemingly boring, analytic fact that the social sciences are – surprise! – *social* so important and why should we care? First, as mentioned, it forces an appreciation of the distinction between physical phenomena and social phenomena. It's no exaggeration to note that the conflation of the physical and the social is the greatest, and longest running, error in the history of social theory (McBride, 2018). The physical world and the social world are very different things and, as such, demand different explanatory frameworks – one 'all purpose' theory will do a good job of neither. Physical facts (e.g., that hydrogen atoms have one proton) are radically different from social facts (e.g., that Paris is the capital of France). Non-linear colliders and electron microscopes help discover the first fact. But I cannot point a microscope at the Eiffel Tower to determine France's capital. Similarly, if I study property rights and I decide to take my pint of beer and send it to the CERN laboratory for analysis, telling the technicians that "I want you to find the type-identifying chemical configuration that determines the beer to be *my beer* and no one else's", they will politely explain to me that I am deeply confused (Searle, 2010). Why? Because there is nothing in the chemical constitution of that pint, or any other possession, that makes it *my property*. Property, like any other social phenomena – an employment contract, a recession, the government of the Maldives, a chess match, a start-up venture – is not what it is because of any attributes of the physical world. It's what it is because of its *social properties*. Exactly what makes something distinctly *social* remains to be seen, but it is crucial to first, before any more work is done, cull away considerations of *physical explanations*. Avogadro's number can shed light on firm performance about as well as double entry bookkeeping can shed light on nuclear fission.

Second, given this very rudimentary distinction between the physical and the social, we can actually begin to make progress on the core problem of understanding what makes a social entity *social*. Let's compare the physical fact that 'hydrogen atoms have one proton' to the social fact that 'Paris is the capital of France'. The former is true regardless of whether anyone is alive to acknowledge it. The latter, somewhat shockingly, is true only because of what people *believe* to be the case. If everyone on the planet awoke tomorrow believing that Lyon was the capital of France then Lyon would, *in reality*, be the capital of France. By contrast, if everyone awoke believing that the hydrogen atom has ten protons, that would not make it the case that the hydrogen atom has ten protons. This seemingly innocuous distinction is a breakthrough discovery: social facts *depend on the minds of people*; physical facts do not! The important conclusion from this is that, in some very important sense, social reality is socially constructed in a way that physical reality is not (McBride, 2018).

There are common misconceptions here that must be blocked. Though it's true that the activity of understanding the physical world is a social activity – it takes teams of experts and analysts to build, run, and analyze the results from a non-linear particle collider, e.g. – the actual structure of the physical world is independent from what we think about it. Indeed, if the human race were wiped out, the laws of nature and the facts of the physical world, like the fact that a hydrogen atom has one proton, would remain as stable and robust as ever. Though the work of *knowledge accumulation* is typically done in coordination with other people, such knowledge points to facts about the world itself that are independent of such efforts.

To use philosophy jargon, the physical world is *ontologically objective*. The social world is *ontologically subjective* (Searle, 2010). This is just shorthand for saying what we already said, that the very nature of the physical world is objective and independent of what we think about it, while the social world is not. In fact, all of entrepreneurship, strategy, management, organizational behavior, institutional theory, and every other social science is fundamentally different from the physical sciences in that the social sciences all study ontologically subjective social phenomena. It's only the "natural sciences", like chemistry, physics, and astronomy, on the other hand, that study ontologically objective phenomena. The role of a CEO, your bank account balance, the capital of France, and the current stock price of IBM are all *social* phenomena.

There is another misconception that must be blocked. The above truth does not mean that social phenomena are somehow "not real" (as critical realists are quick to note). They are quite real. The fact that social phenomena are socially constructed by the beliefs of those who make them real doesn't mean that "anything goes" or "it's all relative". Still, if your bank account balance is real, it must be real in a very different sense from the reality of the fact that a hydrogen atom has one proton – and it is. Where the stability of the laws of the physical world establish the stability of the fact that a hydrogen atom has one proton, the stability and consistency of people's beliefs establish the stability of the fact that Paris is the capital of France. Another way of saying this is that such social phenomena are objective in the sense that they are *epistemologically objective*. Put simply, this just means that France's capital is a relatively stable fact because the beliefs of people on this topic are relatively stable. Of course, human beliefs are much less permanent than the physical laws of the universe and when people's beliefs change en masse, as they did during a twenty-year period of hyperinflation in Zimbabwe leaving the Zimbabwean dollar, which people formerly believed worth 1.47 U.S. dollars, later believed to be worth about one millionth of a U.S. dollar.

There is always a misconception about how the social world, being subjective in the sense that it is dependent on beliefs in the minds of people, can also be at the same time so . . . objective. It seems like a paradox. People spend their entire careers fighting against some objective firmament of their society they want changed. Your bank has very rigid rules that prevent you from rewriting your account balance with a collection of zeros to the end of your current balance. How can such a social fact be subjective but so objective and fixed at the same time? It turns out that there is no deep mystery here. We already see that the simple answer is that it can be both *ontologically subjective* because it depends on people's beliefs for its existence, but *epistemologically objective* because such knowledge and beliefs are relatively stable and consistent. It turns out that there is no real paradox. There are just different kinds of objectivity.

Given that the very structure of the physical world is entirely different from the structure of the social world, it should now be clear that taking explanations that work well for the physical world and applying them haphazardly to the social world can lead to disaster. These are distinct phenomena that require radically distinct explanatory frameworks. Facts of the physical world are grounded by the physical world itself. Facts of the social world are grounded in the beliefs, attitudes, and habits of people. Intuitively, we already knew this insofar as we knew that, e.g., the stock market is driven by a "herd mentality", i.e., that the prices are driven by the beliefs and sentiments of people. This implies that those theories which borrow techniques from the physical sciences and apply them to social phenomena, will not often work. They are taking successful explanatory techniques and applying them to the wrong domain, like taking banana tree farming to the Artic Sea.

But this seemingly obvious distinction between the physical and the social makes it possible to gain traction on the core question – *what is a social entity?* We can now see how to begin to answer it. A social entity, whatever it is, is constituted by the beliefs and attitudes in the minds of people. The hard work, then, lies in explaining *exactly how* it is constituted by the beliefs and attitudes in the minds of people. Investigating this question requires a deep, fascinating investigation.

It is important to note now, though, that a single individual's belief can't constitute a genuinely social entity. My mistaken belief upon landing in France that Lyon is the capital has absolutely no effect on what the actual capital of France is. Neither does my belief that Apple's stock price is $1M make it the case. Economic value is a social phenomenon, so it is more like the capital of France or Apple's stock price than it is like a baseball or a coconut. If it is a social phenomenon, then it requires beliefs in the minds of more than one person. But, if this is true, then neither can it be the case that a lone survivor on a desert island can be engaged in any kind of *social* phenomenon and so he can't be engaged in any kind of *economic activity* or *entrepreneurship* even if he is engaged in making various judgments about what to do on a daily basis to survive his mishap. A pile of coconuts may be *valuable* for his efforts to survive, but they don't have *economic* value. So, the judgment theory of entrepreneurship can't be correct in this case.

But there is something critically correct about the importance of an individual's beliefs, judgments, attitudes, and habits in the formation of social phenomena. What happens when a raft of shipwreck victims wash up on our lone survivor's shore? They might trade medical supplies or food bars for some of the lone survivor's coconuts and, at that point, economic value is established based on the group's beliefs about worth of the coconuts. How is that worth determined? And what aspects of the individual's cognition are relevant in determining that worth? These are deep questions.

Future investigations will have to answer exactly how such beliefs *blend* in a social environment such that one belief becomes established and "real" – that, e.g., Paris really is the capital of France. What kinds of beliefs and attitudes work to do this, and what exactly is their structure? These are important questions that will require a lot of work to sort through, but at least we are now on the right path forward and have the most basic piece of the foundation for a well-grounded understanding of the structure of social reality, and with it, a well-grounded understanding of the social sciences and hope, one day, for a unified theory for them, perhaps even one as coherent and integrated as the physical sciences.

Notes

1 Since roughly the middle of the twentieth century the so-called linguistic turn has dominated Western philosophy departments, leaving an approach called 'analytic philosophy' dominant. Analytic philosophy is a methodology that relies primarily on the analysis of language used in the discussion of the problem at hand. Analytic philosophy, then, is a specification *of the methods* by which such fundamental problems are discussed and, as such, is not incompatible with the definition suggested here. Analytic philosophy has afforded both huge advances in the last century and created huge problems, but a discussion of it here would take us too far astray.
2 Interestingly, this isn't how the business sciences arose.
3 http://c.ymcdn.com/sites/www.apaonline.org/resource/resmgr/Data_on_Profession/2014_Philosophy_Performance_.pdf
   www1.wne.edu/arts-and-sciences/departments/arts-and-humanities/why-philosophy.cfm
4 And to set the record straight, Sherlock Holmes, despite Watson always saying, "That was a brilliant deduction Mr. Holmes!" never did deductive work. He always reasoned from evidence that pointed, *with some degree of likelihood*, that, e.g., the butler was the killer. Sherlock Holmes always did *induction*, not *deduction*.
5 Well, every definition except one. Where today we believe that we understand everything except love, Plato (well, Socrates – it's hard to tell where one's beliefs begin and the other's ends) seemed to believe that he understood nothing . . . except the definition of love. What was Plato's secret to love, you ask? Well, his definition of love is: that which you desire in another that you do not yourself possess.

References

Bratman, M. (1987). *Intentions, plans, and practical reason*. Harvard University Press.
Bratman, M. (2014). *Shared agency: A planning theory of acting together*. Oxford University Press.
Davis, M. S. (1971). That's interesting: Towards a phenomenology of sociology and a sociology of phenomenology. *Philosophy of the Social Sciences*, *1*(4), 309.
Epstein, B. (2015). *The ant trap: Rebuilding the foundations of the social sciences*. Oxford: Oxford University Press.
Foss, N. J., & Klein, P. G. (2012). *Organizing entrepreneurial judgment: A new approach to the firm*. Cambridge: Cambridge University Press.
Gilbert, M. (1992). *On social facts*. Princeton University Press.
Gilbert, M. (2015). *Joint commitment: How we make the social world*. Oxford University Press.
McBride, R. (2016). The missing DNA of social reality. Paper presented at *WINIR*, 2016, Boston, MA.
McBride, R. (2017). An ordinary language analysis of 'entrepreneurship'. *UC Merced*, Working paper.
McBride, R. (2018). Hazards of socio-economic theorizing: are opportunities objective? Manuscript submitted for publication.

Petit, P., & List, C. (2011). *Group agency: The possibility, design, and status of corporate agents*. New York: Oxford University Press.

Scott, R. W. (2015). *Institutions and organizations: Ideas, interests, and identities* (4th ed.). Los Angeles: Sage Publications Ltd.

Searle, J. R. (1995). *Construction of Social Reality*. New York: Free Press.

Searle, J. R. (2010). *Making the social world: The structure of human civilization*. Oxford: Oxford University Press.

Tuomela, R. (2002). *The philosophy of social practices: A collective acceptance view*. Cambridge University Press.

Tuomela, R. (2007). *The philosophy of sociality*. Oxford University Press.

Tuomela, R. (2013). *Social ontology: collective intentionality and group agents*. New York: Oxford University Press.

3 New partial theory in entrepreneurship

Explanation, examination, exploitation, and exemplification

Richard J. Arend

Capitalism is a virtuous cycle fueled by the reinvestment of profits into *entrepreneurial activity* – an activity that promises to increase current profits (e.g., by decreasing costs, by increasing volume, or by increasing priced value) – where a part of that increase in profits is reinvested. The attraction of such profit growth is evident in capitalist economies; for example, where in the US about half-a-million for-profit new ventures start up each month (Fairlie, 2014). That activity also holds attraction to academia; with significant increases in entrepreneurship-related theorizing, data analysis, and publications in the past decades (Ireland, Reutzel, & Webb, 2005). In fact, it appears that there has been a recent spike in proposed new entrepreneurship theory since 2000, with concepts like business models and bricolage shifting the focus of the field away from individuals and towards opportunities and processes. When such spikes occur, it is often useful to stop and reflect, with a critical perspective, in order to provide balance to the exuberance. Such an exercise may help mitigate the unnecessary cannibalization of existing explanations and models when spurious proposed *gaps* in the literature are newly addressed. We provide that reflection here, by challenging several recently proposed *partial theories*[1] over their novelty, and then offering a counter-proposal for contrast. We do so with the intention of strengthening this field, and in so doing, also providing a template for the critical examination of theoretical novelty for other developing fields in management.

We consider the following set of research questions: *Is what has been proposed as new partial theory in entrepreneurship actually new? If not, how has it been accepted as new, and what then is an example of partial theory that is actually new?* We answer these questions by proceeding through a set of related steps: i) we summarize the relevant model that exists in our field in order to establish a baseline to test the newness of proposed partial theory; ii) we then put the newness of recently proposed partial theories to the test; iii) we provide likely explanations for why something may look new regardless if it fails the test; and iv) we outline one example of the kind of entrepreneurship partial theory that passes the test. By addressing the research questions, we re-establish the baseline model in the field, and we provide several unique contributions: We provide a test for novelty that has not existed in our field. We make explicit the ways in which the newness test is avoided by proposed conceptualization in order to make it harder to do so in the future. We provide an example of where the field could go that is new. And we open debate on a specific set of contentious issues (i.e., those involved in items i to iii) that, once resolved, will form a basis for moving the field forward in theory-building.

Explaining entrepreneurship

To many in the field, at its core, the phenomenon of *entrepreneurship* captures a basic process that is almost as ubiquitous as evolution. The basic process involves the realization of new value (e.g., by constructing new lower cost processes) resulting from action. That action can be both mental (e.g., involving the construction of beliefs, making decisions, and learning) and physical (e.g., involving searching and prototyping). That action is sparked by some change in the environment (e.g., an exogenous shock that changes the information available to the market). Of course, such a process is *not* exclusive to entrepreneurship, or to technological progress, or even to humans. It is a process also considered in fields like technology innovation management, in creative outlets beyond the technological, and in non-human biological systems (although that outside research – e.g., in biology – is seldom cited in the entrepreneurship literature).[2]

One existing, common and core explanatory model that depicts the basic process in entrepreneurship phenomena consists of three related pieces: 1) a *way* (or the belief of a way) *to increase profits*; 2) a *market imperfection* (e.g., any condition impeding the increase of efficiency or of value in supplying a good) that is addressed by that way; and 3) a *specific entrepreneur* who embodies some heterogeneity in her differentiated ability to address that market imperfection. We detail this basic process on pp. 23–28 by providing a relevant context, by defining the terms involved, by clarifying the drivers, and by stripping away all of the excess in order to re-establish what academics who study entrepreneurship focus on.

The basic process labeled as *entrepreneurial activity* (or entrepreneurship) is *not* new or exclusively commercial or human-specific. Market imperfections (referred to as *MIs*) have existed throughout time and space, and continue to do so, and are developed and exploited by differentiated entities. That basic process, as the most important part of the engine of capitalism, explains how most recent and successful empires were built. That basic process occurred in the first ancient exploitation of the giant species in Australia by *homo sapiens* – where giant mammals (mainly marsupials) did not know the dangers of the newly arrived species of man.[3] That basic process has even been applied by less-intentioned parties (e.g., the wheat plant, and the canine animal) to exploit the preferences of the genes of mankind, resulting at times in the centuries-long detriment to the living conditions of an average person for the gain of an increase in the population of certain genes (Harari, 2015). In other words, the basic process of an entity trying to improve its existence by exploiting an MI using its differentiation (i.e., its heterogeneous advantages) is a *natural* one, and does not require a human or a monetize-able opportunity to exist.

The main newness test

Thus, even though the basic process at the core of the entrepreneurship field does *not* differentiate the field, *proving separation from that basic explanatory model forms the most important test for newness for any proposed partial theory*. Recently proposed contributions we consider here each focus on a certain kind of activity in a specific context in order to argue the case for their own newness. For example, a focus on the ability of some firms to *bricolage* – to create something newly valuable from existing factors (Levi-Strauss, 1966) – appears to be a restatement of the basic process. It is a story about how a differentiated entity exploits an MI underlying the mispriced value of a set of available factors.[4]

We realize that our proposed test for newness is likely to be contentious, but it is clear and it is fair. If a proposed partial theory is going to present a set of ideas akin to Dubin's (1969) theory-building requirements (e.g., new units, new laws, new propositions, and so on), then those need to be substantially different from the existing units, laws, boundaries, and states of the model we have described on pp. 23–28. To be clear, the proposed partial theories we test have not defined themselves as a level above the general phenomenon (e.g., at the level of utility theory) nor have they defined themselves as a level below the general phenomenon (e.g., at the level of transaction governance choice); each has defined itself as describing a version of entrepreneurial activity at the level where the basic process already provides an explanation. Thus, the applicable test is against the established model.

Definitions and explanations

Drawing on the description of the core explanatory model underlying existing entrepreneurship activity, we now define the important terms of that process, and further describe its elements that are referred to in recently proposed partial theory (and, that given these are widely understood terms or straightforward logical statements, we state them without fanfare, understanding that some scholars will not be in agreement even if citations were provided). Figure 3.1 depicts the summary of terms explaining the basic process (as commonly understood in the field).

The definition of entrepreneurship: Under the basic process that defines the core of the field, entrepreneurship can be defined and explained (unoriginally) as *heterogeneously addressed market imperfections*. The MI provides the possibility to *increase profits*.[5] The heterogeneity provides the basis for a competitive advantage to the focal unique entity. Together, these form the basis for a belief (or a natural programming for non-humans) that underlies the intention of an entity to act to appropriate some part of that profit.[6]

For-profit MI types: One of the most important identity relationships in business is that *profit equals margin times quantity sold less fixed costs*. It is our field's touchstone, much like, in physics, force equals mass times acceleration. Entrepreneurial activity, as an engine of capitalism, seeks to increase profits in two main ways: i) for an existing good – by lowering costs (variable or fixed), by increasing price, or by growing quantity sold [or some net positive combination of these

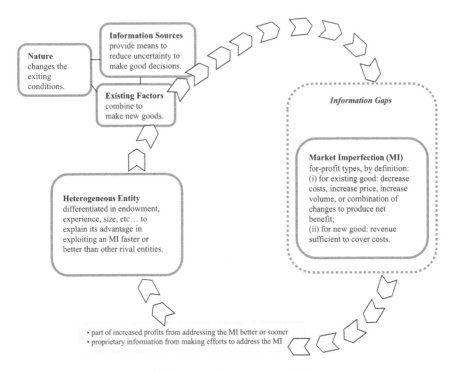

Figure 3.1 Basic process underlying existing entrepreneurship theory

variables]; or ii) for a new good, by having sufficient net income to cover fixed cost investments. Thus, every for-profit MI involves possibilities and actions relevant to either i) or ii). The entrepreneur seeks to increase profits in order to capture some profits privately (or, for social entrepreneurs, to increase in value for its intended targets). The entrepreneur faces some level of uncertainty that necessarily comes from newness and from the changes that are supposed to lead to the increase in profitability (where the uncertainty can entail unknowns regarding technical success, market demand, rival reaction, and competency in the new venture to gain legitimacy and deliver). With success, the entrepreneur and her investors reinvest some of the increased profits in further attempts to increase future profits, thus keeping the virtuous cycle of capitalism driving.

The origins spurring entrepreneurial activity: There exist only two MI origins – those directly based on unforeseeable shocks, and those that are not. In the former case, the entity that profits is differentiated in its speed or effectiveness in responding to the external shock's effects on profitable possibilities (e.g., in exploiting a new technology to lower manufacturing costs of an existing good). In the latter case, the focal entity's actions expose a new profit possibility (e.g., in the firm's experiments with existing technologies), where such actions are based ultimately upon endowed beliefs or abilities that were then leveraged in experiences that the entity had with its environment (some of which may have involved stochastic processes). Note in either case, the MI arises directly or indirectly from shocks or endowments that were exogenous.

The heterogeneity of the entity: The heterogeneity that differentiates the entity trying to address the MI can take many forms. Consider the heterogeneity captured in the form most commonly associated with human entrepreneurial activity – the differential advantage of a *new venture* relative to an incumbent. For the focal new venture to have an advantage, incumbency must be detrimental. Incumbency must involve relative disadvantages due to sunk costs, commitments that lock them out of new technologies, outdated mental maps, slow bureaucracies, cannibalization concerns, and so on. Additionally, it must be the case that the focal new venture can pursue its course while being able to sidestep those existing *traps* (i.e., the ones the incumbents cannot avoid) to make different choices and take different actions. Furthermore, the focal new venture must be able to do so without the requirement for much legitimacy, complementary assets, experience, brand, supply chain, and so on. And, still further, that focal new venture must be able to do so in a context where the parties in the relevant industry value chain (especially the customers) understand the new, alternative offering provided by that venture quickly and pain-lessly (e.g., without prohibitive switching costs, training, disposal costs, and so on). In other words, the heterogeneity involved in this process is multi-dimensional, and involves several affected parties; it is not simply that the entity differs from others, but it is how and to whom those differences matter (as well as possibly why, when, and where those differences matter).[7]

Endogeneity and exogeneity: It is important not only to define the MI and the heterogeneity in the core process that defines entrepreneurial activity, but also to be explicit about other terms related to the process, as these have been used as wedges to promote proposed new concepts. One such clarification that is important to make relates to the endogeneity and exogeneity involved in the process. No entrepreneurial activity is an island; all such activity involves *both* exogenous and endogenous influences. Endogeneity is implied by the heterogeneity part of the core process, where a differentiated entity (internally) takes actions to address the MI. Exogeneity is implied in both the external origins of the entity's *heterogeneity* (i.e., in some endowment) and in the spark (i.e., external shock) that identifies the MI is now ready for the entity to act upon. Thus, entrepreneurial activity defined as *heterogeneously addressed market imperfections* is a combination of both an internal and an external driver at work in the process. (It is a definition that recognizes that entrepreneurship is a complex process, open to a wide variety of factor influences – both hard and soft – combining in interdependent ways and sequences.)

Factor types: Another clarification to make relates to the *nature* of the factors involved in providing the increase in value: specifically, relating to the way such factors exist – e.g., objectively, subjectively, or otherwise. Recent proposed theorizing sets this question up as a choice between objective reality and social construction. While objective reality is readily understood, social construction is a more complicated idea. Social construction is best understood in an evolutionary, historic perspective; it is an integrating, cooperative method for humans to collectively imagine *a thing* (i.e., to believe in it) so that they can operate efficiently and effectively in large numbers (i.e., at over the 150-person tribe size – see Harari, 2015). The most useful and obvious example *thing* is money – where specific objects (e.g., metal disks or shells or paper) represented *transferrable general value* that many people who wanted to trade other goods accepted in exchange (e.g., money for labor units, for crops, for spices, etc.). Money is a thing that provided the basis for geographically wide trade, for the separation of people from business in the form of a limited liability company, and so on (Harari, 2015). Socially constructed things are *real* given that others believe in them and even buttress those beliefs by force (e.g., by force of the crown who backed the value of the coins). Two consequences of social construction should be noted then: First, it does not apply to small groups – like an entrepreneur and her initial partners and customers – where a common set of beliefs can be supported through personal trust rather than through constructs that rely on external enforcement. In other words, the beliefs in the focal things that are not immediately tangible are sufficiently real within that group to be considered tangible, given that the minds that can touch them are housed in touchable members of that small group. Second, even when the relevant group gets big, and the idea of socially constructed things actually applies, those things (e.g., money, loans, stock, wave-particle duality, etc.) are sufficiently real to the entrepreneurs to have equivalence to tangible things. For example, even if the entrepreneur suddenly does not believe in money because it is *socially constructed*, she will still be thrown in a very tangible jail if she steals some. Her ability to combine a set of existing factors – whether those factors are tangible things or not – in order to address an MI is the *only* important issue in the process. A philosophical debate about the immediately tangible nature of the factors is a secondary concern, at best, to real entrepreneurs.

Existing factors are combined: To be clear, the process that the heterogeneous entity takes to address an MI involves decisions and actions. Those actions involve combining existing factors in new ways to increase profits. Those factors can be existing tangible things (e.g., materials), or existing intangible things (e.g., knowledge). No matter what, however, they must already exist somewhere or they would not be available to be combined anew. Every new invention uses existing factors. A confusion may arise when there are multiple steps involved, where intermediate newly created factors are used to get to the final combination of factors embodying the final product that addresses the MI. In that case, the focus can then be shifted to the existing things that were combined to produce the intermediate factors. In other words, no new thing can be created from nothing (i.e., a vacuum); a new thing must be created by combining existing things. The point is that those existing things (that are later combined in new ways to address the MI) are all real in the same sense to the entrepreneur – all exist sufficiently in the entrepreneur's mind to apply, regardless of their immediate tangibility. And, given that all combinations involve knowledge – an intangible thing – *all* entrepreneurial activity involves some form of subjective reality.

Informational gaps: The process that the heterogeneous entity takes to address an MI involves decisions and actions that take place where vital information is *not* immediately available (or no MI would exist, as it would be known as would be its solution). The assumed heterogeneity across entities implies that not everyone knows everything that everyone else knows. In the real world, any shock will create ripples of informational updates from *those who know what is new* to *those who want to know what is new*, and so on. The process that allows some differentiated entities to combine existing factors into something new to address a new MI is messy, dynamic and complex. One of the details not well understood is the sub-process involving identifying which factors to combine and how (and when and where and why). This is a sub-process that involves teasing information out of others in order for the focal entity to translate contextual ambiguity into risk, and addresses a set of informational gaps and asymmetry problems in order to move from a position where not all states and their probabilities are known (i.e., ambiguity) to a position where the states and their probabilities are known (i.e., risk). Only under the latter state can optimal decisions be made.

From ambiguity to risk: This translation from ambiguity to risk that the entrepreneur must undertake to make the decisions to combine the factors to address the MI involves getting *nature* (e.g., its physical properties in terms of technological possibilities, like super-conductance, or its deposits of materials, like oil) and *people* (e.g., customers, investors, suppliers, and so on) to respond with answers to the actions taken that represent the entrepreneur's hypotheses and questions. Obviously, better answers are more likely when something is at stake for the respondent (e.g., an attractive product behind the offered prototype) and when the offering being presented is more complete (so the respondent does not have to use as much imagination and can focus on specifics). When nature and people provide feedback, then the possible states and their probabilities become increasingly known to the entrepreneur. Essentially, the informational gaps that need to be filled involve information that nature and people hold (e.g., involving technological feasibility and market demand levels) that the entrepreneur tries to pry from them using certain actions (e.g., testing prototypes for performance and asking for pre-order commitments). Given that it is standard to assume that, *over time*, firms end up making decisions under risk, it must be that ambiguities over such commercial opportunities are always resolvable once nature and people provide that initially missing information. In other words, the standard assumption is that ambiguity can always be translated into risk by drawing out the *existing* needed information from nature and people. Successful entrepreneurs seem to do this earlier and then to exploit the first-mover advantages involved.

Note that we are arguing that *all* entrepreneurial activity, given its necessary condition of *doing something new* entails gathering new information from nature and from people to formulate a risk-based decision. Regardless of whether the underlying innovation is incremental (i.e., with few unknowns to resolve) or radical (i.e., with many unknowns to resolve), *the process is the same*. Any separation of entrepreneurial activity based on how many unknowns need to be resolved alone does not appear warranted at first blush.

The divide between ambiguity and risk: It is a standard assumption that there is a clear division between ambiguity and risk, even though (in our literature) ambiguity always reduces to risk over time (except in the special cases, like those of wicked problems). That assumption implies that the only challenge is whether ambiguity can be reduced to risk before it is ready to be so reduced. (The challenge is met through the mechanism of nature and people providing feedback to actions to provide the missing states and their probabilities.) But is that a false or artificial challenge? It is simple to prove that *any* ambiguous context can be reduced to a risky one even *without* any significant action by the entrepreneur. Given the power to choose the states, an entrepreneur can always choose the currently known *knowable* state of the *status quo* (given she has experience with this), with the alternative state of *not status quo* covering all else, and be able to assign a probability to each. Thus, that divide is not a natural one; it is an artificial one. (On the other extreme, one could argue that all possible states of a real world can never be known down to the sub-atomic level, and so risk is never possible either.) In fact, the important divide has to do with the application to the real world, and the idea that the real world effectively chooses the level of detail of the states (and not the entrepreneur, although she may try to). It is the *level of the decision* that defines the necessary level of detail of the states (e.g., one needs to know rain or not rain if one cares about the decision to take an umbrella, whereas one needs to know more detail like the inches of precipitation over a set of hours in a specific geographic location if one needs to plan for flooding, and so on). The real world alone should define the decision levels that are useful and the states that need to be known. (Given that the decision level may depend on the possible states, it is likely that this uncovering of information is a co-evolving process, but that is not the point here. The point is that the divide between ambiguity and risk is artificial in a specific way – i.e., contingent on the decision – and, as such, any proposed theory that uses such a divide as a wedge is likely to be standing on shaky ground.)

It may be helpful to envision a *theoretical world* where the process unfolds, one much like Kirzner implies (1973, 1979). It is a world full of possible combinations of existing factors along different sequences, some of which can lead to new profits. To identify those few in the latter category, the entrepreneur needs to ask the right questions of information-holders to get their attention and motivation and reaction, at a specific time. There is no lasting *ambiguity* but instead it is a lack of specific knowledge at any one time about un-addressed MIs (where quality effort in quantity is needed to shed light on a particular corner of that unknown space to determine if it can be profitable and how so). But, the entrepreneur cannot just try any combinations at hand without knowing somewhat deeply *what is being tried* or she is unlikely to learn the right lessons to progress. The learning approach is captured in humankind's recent *cognitive revolution* where ignorance is finally seen as a kind of *truth* (i.e., knowing the unknowns), and as opportunity (i.e., to make those identified unknowns then known).

The choice of how to explain entrepreneurial activity

Prior to testing the newness of recently proposed partial theories, it is useful to describe the main approaches for explaining phenomena used in the social sciences. Burrell and Morgan (1979) provide some guidance here regarding the choices along ontological, epistemological, methodological, and *human nature* dimensions, where one consistent approach is considered subjectivist (defined by nominalism, anti-positivism, ideography, and voluntarism), while its contrasting consistent approach is considered objectivist (defined by realism, positivism, nomothety, and determinism). If the core model has been traditionally described in terms of one approach (objectivist), while the proposed partial theories all take the contrasting approach (subjectivist), then that *cross-approach translation issue* might explain why tests for newness have been lacking.

Theory is valuable because it provides the understanding behind science's purpose *as a means to understand, predict, and control phenomena*. Theory explains the *how* and the *why* focal outcomes occur (e.g., outcomes between variables, or along a process sequence), as well as how, when, where, and who. Once the theory is provided, humankind can then act to influence the phenomena to its benefit (e.g., by directing the outcomes, or by preparing for the outcomes given an accurate prediction). Influencing the phenomena, however, means adding some specificity to the description, and that is done through explanation. The explanatory model specifies, in applicable and explicit terms, what is controlled for, what variables or events are focal, what the boundaries of applicability are, and so on. The explanatory model provides an academic, and often a practical, context where the theory should work. For convenience, let's consider the explanatory model as the means of identifying the assumptions, drivers, outcomes, relationships, controllable levers, dangers, and so on of the partial theory.

The approaches for explanation are many, but are anchored by two choices, objectivist and subjectivist. The objectivist approach maximizes simplicity while capturing the focal relationship that is theorized. It is abstract yet robust and tends to provide maximally explicit (mathematical) definitions of all terms, assumptions, and mechanics in a simplified version of what is supposed to be the real world. The subjectivist approach maximizes reality, attempting to capture the full complexity, messiness, and unknowns involved in the focal phenomenon. Its description is based on small sample experience, and is informed by heuristics (e.g., gained through trial-and-error). The objectivist approach provides a maximum understanding (e.g., a set of mathematical equations) of a minimal set of factors (e.g., variables and events). This is done in an assumed ideal laboratory setting where items that are uncontrollable in the real world are assumed controlled in this theoretical world. It is mostly deductive. The latter anchor provides at least a minimally useful understanding of a maximum set of factors combining. This is done in a real-world setting where an attempt is made to build theory based on trying to recognize patterns in that world. In is mostly inductive (although sometimes abductive).

Based on the descriptions of the approaches, it follows that each approach has its limitations. Each involves a trade-off between how much reality to capture and how simply the focal relationship can be described. The more frictions and second-order effects and variables that are captured in the explanatory model, the more complex and difficult to optimize (or difficult to predict) the focal relationships become. A problem arises when one approach is held up as a *straw man* to argue for the other approach's superiority as an explanation (e.g., without noting its own limitations). Unfortunately, that problem seems to manifest itself in several recently proposed partial theories.

Given that most of the theory in entrepreneurship uses one of the two approaches, we focus on the contrast between them. It is a choice between the mathematical, abstracted explanatory model of the objectivist approach, and the experiential, real-world explanatory model of the subjectivist approach. The objectivist approach often provides mathematical precision – e.g., explicit definitions, simplifying assumptions, and a focus on mostly isolated single relationships. The value of this approach is that it is very testable, accessible, and understandable, and provides a clearly bounded benchmark for further works (Such further work would add complexities in an orderly fashion, say, by considering specific contingencies to the focal relationship.) The limitations of this approach mainly involve its forced simplicity, based on explicitly excluding real-world complexities like additional variables and their interactions with the focal relationships. Thus, this model cannot provide a holistic understanding of a phenomenon. That said, it is an approach that is universally used in science, is precise, is objective, and isolates the hypothesized primary drivers of a phenomenon. By contrast, the subjectivist approach often involves experiential, descriptive richness of a real phenomenon as observed in the field. The value of this approach is that it provides detail, qualitative information, patterns at multiple system levels, and a big picture of a noisy phenomenon. The limitations of this approach mainly involve small sample size, subjectivity, possible interference with the system through the act of observation, susceptibility to noise, potential lack of immediate generalizability, imprecise definitions, unexplained *black boxes*, and imprecise boundaries.[8] That said, it is an approach that is common in social science, provides a more holistic version of the phenomenon, and is more relatable to the practitioner.[9]

Of the two approaches, the subjectivist, experiential approach appears to hold the most danger of being exploited (although any data supporting either approach could be falsified). Description of a phenomenon is useful, but it is *not* scientific theory; it is only data (Whetten, 1989). Unless that description is translated into a story of relationships among factors (or sequences of events), no theoretical contribution exists. Besides the danger of never explaining *the why* of the focal relationships over describing *the how*, there is the danger of the subjective specification of the story based on what is normally proprietary data. This experiential approach is more susceptible to exploitation because it is often inductive and, thus, involves an open system, with imprecision and no immediate validation checks on the initial observations (e.g., Denzin & Lincoln, 2000). It involves a relatively younger methodology, making it more susceptible to unexposed issues.[10] Further, the approach may be accompanied by a type of salesmanship that cannot be applied to an objectivist, more mathematical and deductive approach. The experiential modeling is often accompanied by rich details of the initial observations that appeal to senses rather than to cold scientific logic. This approach appears to leave open a temptation to describe a magic show rather than to explain the mechanics of the illusion behind it (e.g., the *art* of core skills in DCV micro-foundations as described by

Teece, 2007). And that temptation is strong because the data from which proposed inductive theory is drawn are difficult to replicate and to test independently. As such, it is relatively more likely for less scrupulous researchers to let their self-interests guide the field observations they report, the strong patterns they find, and the novel explanations they propose. Such temptation appears more likely when the lead researchers accept a cultish position of the person who is an expert on the initial observations that led to the new proposed theory. Such *cultishness* is less likely in an objectivist, mathematical approach because there is a cleaner break of model from modeler, given that the premises used are almost always standard, accepted assumptions and, if not, are argued by drawing upon a wide set of empirically tested results where the modeler would not usually have absolute personal influence.[11]

Testing proposed theories

We test three different types of recently proposed partial theories for newness based upon what is known about entrepreneurial activity and explanatory approach choices. We do so focusing on each type's recent example in the literature, while commenting on why each has been considered as new theory and why. To be clear, the test for newness we conduct is *not* a test for contribution. Research that fleshes out an existing theory can be a contribution. (It could introduce an interesting contingency, or fill in some missing steps in a process, though, but it would not serve to differentiate the field).

We test *bricolage, effectuation*, and *creation opportunities* as the examples of the three different types of proposed theories. The first type details *one MI variant occurring under a specific context*. For bricolage, it is the underpricing of internally available factors (and/or their combinations). Bricolage occurs when the entrepreneurs uncover those arbitrage possibilities – the ones embodied in new, though often temporary, uses for those available factors – under conditions of necessity, as being the mother of invention. The second type of proposed theory details *an individual's journey in finding her MI to address*, focusing on ambiguous contexts, and suggesting helpful heuristics to use in those contexts (e.g., heuristics for risk-mitigation, for information access, for adaptability, and so on). Effectuation is presented as a more realistic journey than that reflected in the simplified model of the existing basic process. The third type of proposed theory leverages the link between the MI and the heterogeneous entity, focusing on contexts characterized by higher levels of informational uncertainties. In contrast to the second type, there is less focus on any individual's story and more focus on *generalizable actions for the entrepreneur to take in her social world* (i.e., the world made up of real people and their beliefs as consumers, suppliers, investors, partners, and so on). The partial theory of *creation opportunities* provides a contrast to the existing model in a different way than the other two types. It challenges the *discovery* assumptions of the basic process of entrepreneurial activity (e.g., that factors underlying MIs are objectively real and searches for them are optimizable).

While all three types of proposed partial theories differ in significant respects, they also share several common characteristics that helped make each of them highly marketable: First, they all confound their processes with the wicked research area of *creativity*. This is problematic for numerous reasons, including that creativity is an area of study that is much wider than commercial entrepreneurship, and so does little to help define the field. As well, creativity entails its own golden rule precluding optimization – i.e., that creativity can never be fully understood or else it would no longer be creativity (because everyone would do it and nothing would then stand out as creative). Thus, any proposed theory centered on the black box of creativity is likely to be widely interesting but also very unlikely to provide clear differentiation for our field. Second, they all choose the more inductive, observation-based, realism-rich subjectivist approach to explain the phenomena – i.e., where small samples are drawn upon to find discernable patterns of actions and outcomes. This leads to interesting narrative stories of active heroes who confront surprising obstacles on their paths to successes. Unfortunately, that may lead to a capturing of the process pieces and patterns based on surprise rather than on strategic importance. Third, they all sell their proposals by contrasting them to a straw-man super-rational model of the basic process, often keying in on the known limitations of such an abstract approach. This can lead to a downplaying of the limitations of the subjectivist approach, and even to some selective – and sometimes inaccurate – characterizations of existing explanations (e.g., to create theory as *gap-filling*). It may also indicate that the proposed theory cannot stand on its own merits under its own theorized boundaries. Fourth, all provide seductive new labels for their constructs or process steps that give an appearance of having more understanding of the unknown issues – like creativity – than is warranted. The admission of ignorance of such issues (i.e., of the creativity process) would be more helpful in guiding future research, but may hinder the marketing of the new proposals. Fifth, in the end, all redescribe the existing basic process outlined on pp. 23–28 – where an MI is addressed by a heterogeneous entity. None of the proposals provides propositions that lie outside this known story.

Prior to testing those proposed types of partial theories, we describe a set of premises that formalize relevant parts of the *existing* explanations that we can then draw upon to explain specific testing analyses (again, based on existing, common understandings in the field).

Premise 1: *one cannot make something from nothing* – addressing any MI entails combining existing factors, regardless of whether those factors are easy or difficult to find, or are tangible or intangible.

Premise 2: *all for-profit MIs are of known types* – addressing MIs for profit, by definition, entails known types of goals – i.e., to reduce costs, to increase price or quantity, or to combine of these activities to produce new monetized value.

Premise 3: *entrepreneurial success is explained through the relationship between the addressed MI and the focal heterogeneous entity* – a specific success must rely on some recognizable differentiated advantage of the pursuer of the MI that allows that MI to be addressed in a manner that provides new profits in a competitive environment.

Premise 4: *all MIs are addressable by several entities ex post, using existing factors* – in order to be economically commercializable at a reasonable scale by the entrepreneur's firm or licensee, the ability to address the MI must be replicable by others, or able to be routinized.[12]

Testing the first type of proposed theory, using the example of bricolage: this is the most straightforward test, given that the concept of bricolage is admittedly an established idea (Baker & Nelson, 2005; Levi-Strauss, 1966). Providing details about the process of how a specific type of MI is addressed in a specific context (i.e., a permissive one) by differentiated entities (i.e., through enacting) is a contribution, but it does *not* constitute a new *theory*. Further, the underlying creativity involved in combining immediately available factors to make something new, spurred by necessity, remains a black box. Although the entrepreneur is more active in discovering and exploiting the arbitrage opportunity than in a traditional, simplified model, the pieces and relationships don't change regardless of whether the story has become more exciting from references to successful visible cases (e.g., the Danish wind turbine industry – Garud & Karnøe, 2003).

Testing the second type of proposed theory, using the example of effectuation: given this proposed theory has been recently comprehensively critiqued regarding its contributions to the entrepreneurship field (Arend, Sarooghi, & Burkemper, 2015), we will keep the testing here relatively short. Effectuation applies an interesting wedge involving Premise 3 to leverage the necessary link between the MI and the individual (Sarasvathy, 2001). It does so to support the notion that *every* addressed MI emerges only because an individual took action. Under that notion, effectuation can then logically focus on the individual herself and her unique path to actively finding her own MI, which makes for some very interesting and marketable stories. Unfortunately, it does not make for *new theory* given that the basic process remains the same as captured in the existing model. There may be some contribution in the focus on ambiguous contexts, where traditional, simplified decision-making rules do not initially apply, but where heuristics and alternative approaches like experimentation are more applicable to reduce the uncertainty into risk. However, there may also be some confusion in the approach. The implicit assumption that every individual has her own guaranteed profitable MI is actually not implied by the premise that every profitable MI has its individual. Further, the creativity involved in how the individuals successfully exploit contingencies to make a new artifact remains a black box, regardless of the risk-mitigation, cooperation-focused heuristics prescribed. There do not appear to be any propositions emerging from the proposed theory that conflict with the existing basic process of an MI being addressed by a heterogeneous entity. Effectuation describes different prescriptions to use in more uncertain environments than in more certain ones, but that is not new (e.g., experimentation is a well-known approach to reduce uncertainty), nor does that alter the pieces of the basic process or the relationships involved regardless of whether the individuals seem more involved in uncovering the relevant information to address the MI.

Testing the third type of proposed theory, using the example of creation opportunities: this example is not old like bricolage, nor has it been comprehensively critiqued like effectuation, and so we focus more attention on it here. This example also applies the Premise 3 wedge to link the individual to the MI, but does so for a different reason. It does so to focus on the importance of the *social interactions* of the entrepreneurs to other relevant people in identifying and addressing MIs (Alvarez & Barney, 2007). This also means less of a focus on personal utility as an outcome and more of a focus on profitability (i.e., on the goals outlined in Premise 2) compared to effectuation, making this type of proposed theory closer to the existing model. Despite that proximity, the proposed theory argues its differentiation based on a questionable assumption that violates Premise 1. The assumption is that different factors and relationships describe the basic process when an MI is more difficult to address – i.e., when the informational requirements are harder to uncover through social interactions, when there are more factors that are needed to combine and some of these are intangible, and so on. Essentially, the assumption is that a different theory is needed to explain the basic entrepreneurial process when it involves creating an online community-based brokerage like *eBay* than when it involves wild-cat drilling to discover oil (i.e., a different theory is needed to create something from not quite nothing – from intangibles or from harder-to-do tasks). The main explanation is a philosophical one – one that may resonate with academics but would be meaningless to practitioners (which poses somewhat of an irony for a proposed theory that is supposed to be more realistic). The explanation is that, while contrasting MIs labeled *discovery* are based on *objectively real* factors (e.g., existing oil deposits), those labeled *creativity* are based on *socially constructed* factors (e.g., on belief-based transaction-supporting systems and factors like currency and stocks). Of course, all of these factors are equally real to the real entrepreneur; she knows that her digitized money will buy other goods just like her analog oil will.

While philosophical differences may exist over types of factors, those do not translate into the necessity for either a different process or a different theory (Ramoglou, 2013). The process is the same because all MIs are addressed by individuals (Premise 3) and thus all involve social interaction and reliance on socially constructed factors. In other words, a continuum exists that describes the characteristics of the factors and steps involved in the process, but it remains as only one process of combining existing factors to address an MI in a differentiated fashion. While some MIs may involve a more complex combination of factors, and more intermediate steps to reduce the informational gaps (e.g., through experimenting in order to reduce uncertainties into risks), the pieces and relationships remain the same. There is *no* new theory in the example of creation opportunities.

As with the other types of proposed theory, a subjectivist approach has been used effectively to provide rich, marketable stories of entrepreneurial journeys and to identify patterns in the complex actions taken (although with more deductive and philosophical discussion than with effectuation). As with the other examples, the *black box of creativity* remains unopened, although this example highlights the type of ingenuity used by entrepreneurs in their social activities to alter the beliefs of others to market their products and to solicit the true beliefs of others to understand the possible states and probabilities of new commercial territories. Although unopened, the patina of a greater understanding of creativity is provided in the labeling of the shocks that initiate this process as endogenous versus exogenous (Barreto, 2012). As explained previously, such a division is unjustified, as both internal and external changes drive all attempts to address an MI when it is actually addressed. The creativity is hidden in the suggestion that the entrepreneur manufactures the shock through her own actions, endogenously, to uncover the MI. That relabeling of creativity is unhelpful, and confuses types of factor characteristics (e.g., factor tangibility) with effort characteristics (e.g., their physical, social or mental dimensions; their informational load; and, so on). And, as with the other examples, there is a contrasting straw man version of existing theory to compare against – here, of so-called *discovery* opportunities (i.e., those based solely on objectively real factors).

If there is some contribution to existing explanations provided by this example, it is in the detailing of the deeper issues involved in the MIs (and the factors) that take more effort, are less obvious, have greater informational problems, and so on. However, any such contribution appears to be based on some shaky ground. First, as noted earlier, the reference to the term *social construction* is unusual because the *size of the society* needed to share beliefs initially to address the MI is likely small. Regardless, building shared mental models within a network is *not* a new phenomenon and it only draws on existing theory (e.g., sociology). Second, the proposed contrast to *discovery* appears to be inaccurate at best. The Austrian economists (e.g., Hayek, Kirzner, Schumpeter) who describe versions of the concept all appear to describe a process that is not the rote search procedure alluded to in the creation opportunities literature, but instead a process that is more creative (Kor, Mahoney, & Michael, 2007). For example, as Kirzner (1997, p. 72) explains: "*the notion of discovery, midway between that of the deliberately produced information in standard search theory, and that of sheer windfall gain generated by pure chance, is central.*" In other words, this type of proposed theory may be more effective in providing a contribution to existing theory by specifying what its boundaries are (e.g., regarding the reality of factor types involved) and by accurately using existing labels (e.g., about what discovery is, what social construction is, and what an opportunity versus a business idea is).

Discussion

We now discuss the preceding testing of proposed theories in entrepreneurship. We comment upon the potential for harm to the field's theory-building when newness is misidentified (e.g., lost legitimacy), and propose possible ways to mitigate the occurrence of such misidentification (e.g., acid tests for newness that editors could apply). We suggest alternative approaches for creating new theory, and we provide an example to prove that this feat can be accomplished. Table 3.1 summarizes the testing of the three proposed theories we explained on p. xxx, and the differences of the new theory example we describe on p. xxx.

Table 3.1 Proposed theory characteristics and testing

Type of Proposed Theory	Example	Defining Characteristic	Questionable Assumption	Goal Assumed	Newness
Specific MI addressed in a specific context, with entity defined by context.	Bricolage	Immediately available factors are always under-priced over the complete range of their possible uses (in combination) some of which arise from holding the resources.	Arbitrage opportunities involving immediately available (internal) factors exist for entities under pressure.	Meet an immediately necessary internal need as at least a temporary next step for firm survival, or meet external need for a profitable market demand.	No.
Focal entity's active journey in a highly uncertain context to create a new artifact to address her own MI.	Effectuation	Focus on individual path to success in ambiguous contexts, using risk-mitigation heuristics (e.g., cooperation, experimentation, adaptability).	A feasible MI exists for every focal individual at the time the entrepreneur begins her journey.	Artifact creation by the focal individual; or, at least, their education about themselves as entrepreneurs.	No.
Pursuit of for-profit MIs by entities actively engaging in social construction in contexts with high levels of informational gaps.	Creation opportunities	Heavy use of socially construction as necessary to address more significant MIs.	MIs (and their addressing factors) that involve more efforts (involving people, information, intangibles), require different skills and steps to address than those involving less such efforts.	Addressing a for-profit MI by acting through social construction to address necessary information gaps in the markets.	No.
Exploitation by deceiving parties engaged in the existing entrepreneurial process.	Example	Legal exploitation of the existing process of capitalistic entrepreneurial activity, at tolerable risk.	Entrepreneur can meet the necessary conditions to deceive others, legally, and this be an attractive option to her.	Rent-shifting; monetizing the deception-as-new-market-friction added to the basic entrepreneurial process.	Yes.

Are there harms from popularizing the proposed partial theories as new when they are not? While all three types of proposed partial theories, as illustrated by their recent examples, provide contributions to the existing model, none provide a new, alternative theory. So, while each provides value to the field, it should be noted that each may also entail harm when any one of them is mistaken as an alternative theory. First, there may be harm caused by adding confusion about the basic process. That may lead to misallocations of research resources, to cannibalistic relabeling of concepts, and to misleading prescriptions to practice. Second, there may be harm to the legitimacy of the field when such *false starts* occur repeatedly. Outsiders start to question the motivations and abilities of the gatekeepers, critics and academic bodies to do their job to properly vet new proposals. This may lead to questions about who *owns* the field if no one seems responsible for, at a minimum, ensuring proper critical debate over new proposals. To be clear, the continued proposal of new partial theories is healthy for the field, as it provides potential contributions to existing theory and also possibly leads to alternative views. However, it needs to be tempered with timely, multi-perspective and critical reviewing in order to help test each proposed theory's differences and to identify the true contributions. And, this seems especially necessary for inductive theory proposals where the main assumptions and relationships are relatively less clearly defined and entail less historic methodological context.

Possible solutions: To avoid the unjustified promotion of proposed new theory, two things need to exist: i) a fair acid test to vet new theory; and ii) a set of responsible parties in the field to apply the test early. To simplify the testing, any proposed new theory needs to be presented in a form that clearly states its differences (in propositions), its foci (of core relationships), its boundaries, its assumptions, its detailed definitions, its modeling choice, how it should be tested, and how it stands alone as an alternative explanation of relevant phenomena. Prior to allowing its authors to repeat its message (versus to test it) in subsequent outlets, at least one critical assessment (beyond what the reviewers and editorial team did) should be published by independent scholars. The acid tests should involve ensuring that the proposed theory meets the criteria for standard theory-building (e.g., Dubin, 1969), and that it provides clearly differentiated relationships, some of which are in the form of propositions that conflict with existing theory. As for responsible parties, perhaps there is a need for an explicit code to be written and then followed in the field by those with more power (e.g., journal editors), enforced through peer pressure. In other words, instead of moving the field, through the use of power, towards a particular view or model choice, instead we should at least agree on a framework for the process for debating (and evaluating) the viable options proposed for that movement.

An example alternative

We now illustrate that a proposed theory can be significantly differentiated from existing theory. Further, we argue that such proposals may form a viable path forward for delineating the field. Consider the following differentiated entrepreneurial process – instead of a rehash of the story of a *heterogeneously addressed market imperfection*, we focus on a new process that exploits that story. The new process leverages the market frictions inherent in the basic process that exist because of the informational asymmetries and uncertainties involved in it. The new process is unlikely to provide net benefits (in contrast to the basic process), because it is parasitic in nature (i.e., with rent-shifting as its focus). The entrepreneurs in this new process play a different game; it is one where they lower the risk to themselves in an attempt to capture monetize-able value flowing through the basic process. They do so by attempting to disguise themselves as legitimate actors. They pose as motivated entrepreneurs in order to fleece investors, partners and customers using false promises of new products. And, they also pose as interested investors, partners and customers and in order to misappropriate valuable ideas from motivated entrepreneurs.[13]

This process differs significantly from existing model in entrepreneurship. It also differs from existing theory in economics (or in deceptive phenomena). It does not involve an illegal act, as the deception used is in a context where the rules outlawing these specific entrepreneurial acts have yet to be written, or where the proof of that deception (beyond a reasonable doubt) is lacking due to the inherent uncertainties involved (e.g., in technology, in the market, and so on). It does not involve a standard information asymmetry problem, as it is neither adverse selection nor moral hazard because of types of unknowns assumed. For example, without knowing the proper production or demand functions, it is impossible to know the right quality or level of effort to use as inputs, or even what the best output should be or its value (i.e., those unknowns make the standard economic models and their solutions inapplicable). The proposed theory also does not involve a standard lie, or fraud, because that would entail knowing the future state of a promised entrepreneurial activity with certainty, and that is ruled out by the focal context assumed here. (At the same time, the deception we are interested in for this proposed theory cannot be based on an *in*feasible future, as such deception could not sway sophisticated investors.) Thus, the proposed theory is differentiated by its context (e.g., commercial transactions under uncertainty where others are pursuing feasible opportunities) and its focus on a type of rent-shifting behavior characterized by the active manufacture of a new market friction that can be exploited selfishly.

In the existing process, there is a focus on the positive entrepreneurial story where individuals aim to appropriate some piece of a new, big, risky *value pie*. In this proposed process, there is a focus on a more negative story where individuals aim to take some large piece of a small, non-risky value pie, where that latter pie is sold as a version of the former to outsiders. These deceptive entrepreneurs take their part of the pie through salary, expenses, nepotism, and consulting. These deceptive entrepreneurs sell their promises through various schemes, including misrepresentations of early success – e.g., through friendly rankings and Ponzi-like pyramids. As with other proposed new theory, there is also a focus here on the social relationships, but instead of that involving the building of new mutually beneficial beliefs, it involves the exploitation of the optimistic prior beliefs that investors and partners have built up based on the good interactions they have had with true entrepreneurs in the past. There is also a difference in what supports the stability of this proposed process. In existing entrepreneurial theory, the stability is supported by the promise and realization of mutual benefits within the virtuous cycle of capitalism. In this newly proposed theory, the stability is supported by a lack of an effective solution to the new market friction and by a lack of motivation by the parties negatively affected to police it. None of these parties appear to be powerful enough, or harmed sufficiently, to affect change to remove what is essentially the small tax on the primary process that this proposed secondary parasitic process entails. In summary, this example proposed partial theory (and phenomenon) is new, as it includes: new pieces (e.g., an added market friction); new conditions (e.g., that allow deception that is legal); and, a new process (i.e., that is parasitic on the existing process, where information gaps are not reduced but manipulated).

We have described one example of a proposed theory can be different from the existing theory. We now suggest that such proposed theories delineate possible ways to differentiate the field, especially when the new processes described are specific to human, commercial, uncertain, and unusual (e.g., parasitic) activities. We have provided only one illustration of the type of proposed theory upon which the field could progress. It needs further detailing, and study, and testing. That is left for future work because the ability to perform this new activity is not trivial, as several conditions on how the deception is built and sold and yet not punished exist that are conflicting and complex in nature. And, this opening up of the field to proposed theories of a negative nature provides some very interesting possibilities. For example, the phenomenon where a technology is *dual-use* – one use of which is a negative one in that it pushes existing ethical boundaries while the other is an acceptable one with clear benefits – may be exploited in that the supporters of the latter use may overcome those opposing the former use (e.g., in technologies that affect security, lifespan, and so on). In other words, the pursuit of new theory to explain unusual, often unpopular, phenomena (e.g., phenomena that involve negative outcomes) may be an effective strategy to differentiating the field given its past focus on the big, positive, ubiquitous activity has not.

Conclusions

The progression of theory in social science is fragile, as illustrated by our analysis and discussion of the recent attempts to build new partial theory in entrepreneurship. We live in an imperfect world in social science, where market failures exist, and so the *best* ideas are not always published, recognized, rewarded, and otherwise supported. Our *markets for ideas* fail sometimes because of the influences of politics, organizational power struggles, business interests (e.g., in consulting), ideologies, private interests, and so on. Such failures persist because there are few laws or means-of-investigation or means-of-enforcement in academia, other than peer-pressure and reputational interests, to see that things are done right. But, as history has shown, when no independent judiciary exists, then power will corrupt, market failures will allow and even reward corruption, and such outcomes usually do not end well for the majority of interested parties. It may not be that any one field in management is at that point yet, but we all should be vigilant and active in protecting the integrity of our fields.

Particularly vulnerable are fields, like entrepreneurship, that are newer, lack a strong differentiating theory, focus on phenomena that draw in alternative explanations from diverse, self-interested external areas of study, and have failed to build a powerful core of proponents who primarily identify with the new field. We have illustrated here that such a field can attract the kind of proposed theories that are not-really-new-but-are-sold-as-such, and that that can lead to harm. We have tried to argue that a response is required. That response relies on critical analyses that draw attention to possible issues in proposed partial theorizing so they may be understood, possibly investigated further, and then possibly acted upon. Unfortunately, we have not seen much of this comprehensive critical response forthcoming, other than that done at micro-levels, where interesting debates occur but often remain unresolved (due to differences in definitions or philosophies). Unfortunately, such incomplete debates can have the *opposite* effect as to what is needed, when such debating instead legitimizes a new partial theory by recognizing it and responding to it, without providing a way to test it and then either accept it or dismiss it. To address how such testing can be done, we have critiqued three recently proposed entrepreneurship theories here and found them each lacking in newness. We have also provided an example of what new is, in order to show that such testing can be passed. We hope that such illustrations can shed light on how to reduce the failures we have in our idea-markets so that more theories that can pass the novelty tests are recognized and used to improve management understanding and practice.

Notes

1   Here, *partial theory* entails any form of a set of relational statements among variables or process steps that is normally attributed the label *theory* in science, but has also been referred to as *logics*, *mid-range theory*, *processes*, *models*, and so on in our literature.

2   The explanation of entrepreneurship provided, and the definition of the phenomenon of entrepreneurship used, are by no means universally agreed upon inside or outside the field. No amount of citations or cases will be sufficient to satisfy scholars who come at the field from alternative philosophies, experiences and motivations, that these are the only explanations and definitions. That said, we assume these are sufficiently widely held, existing (i.e., not original) understandings. Thus, we acknowledge that criticism (applicable to all work in the field), understand it as a limitation, and we move on with our arguments, standing on the shoulders of the giants who preceded us (e.g., Kirzner).

3   Such historic examples also prove that short-term opportunity exploitation can have significant long-term costs, so much so that the net effects of some applications of the process may not be beneficial – e.g., by driving a species extinction which then causes famine in the community.

4   If it is just a restatement or specific example, then it is *not* new theory; it needs to be treated appropriately at its level of intended contribution in the field. To our knowledge,

the only *tests for newness* that exist in our field are focused on empirical tests rather than theory-content tests (e.g., Leavitt, Mitchell, & Peterson, 2010), and we believe we need the latter type as well.

5　By *increase profits* we intend to cover all organizations; in other words, for incumbents it is increase profits, but for new firms it is generate profits, and for other organizations it is increase value.

6　Although the individual-opportunity nexus model (Shane & Venkatarman, 2000) remains the most-cited work in entrepreneurship, it was written to direct further work rather than to establish a general core process for the field (although the opportunity can be understood as the MI and the individual as the heterogeneous entity in the base model we have described). It was written to open the field up to certain other fields (e.g., psychology) and shut it down to others (e.g., strategic management) in order to flesh out a Venn diagram where individuals-as-sets-of-characteristics and opportunities-as-types-of-commercial-progress overlap. That work did not define a *new* phenomenon or a *new* theory explaining differentiated relationships and processes. And, unfortunately, the terms defined in that model were not sufficiently specified to avoid the recent debates about just what an opportunity is.

7　This issue of heterogeneity, as explaining which entities pursue which MIs, falls into the purview of other fields, such as the innovation, where the focus is on who innovates and how (and why, where, and when). Books on innovation, such as Afuah's (1998), provide a solid history of the progress of the understanding of the different innovation and innovator types in the modern academic era – e.g., from Schumpeter on, and through incremental, radical, architectural, and disruptive innovations, to those involving production functions, market expansions, supply chains, and so on. The idea that the basic process at the core of entrepreneurial activity is *not* the sole property of the field is important to note because it increases the hurdle for any new, proposed theoretical contribution to entrepreneurship, as it must then be that the proposal must also be new to all of the related fields as well.

8　The relative lack of precision in the subjectivist approach raises the danger in *not knowing what you don't know*. This seems less problematic with the objectivist approach that is often explicit about *what you know*.

9　The contrast in models parallels that between deductive and inductive approaches. In a deductive approach, if the premises are true then the conclusions reached by drawing on them are also true in the closed domain of discourse. In the inductive approach, if the observations are true then the patterns of relationships extrapolated from them are also likely to be true. Either way, the value of the theory written is based on faith in the validity of the foundation and of the skills and objectivity of the theory-builder.

10　Qualitative research (i.e., as the more inductive, subjectivist approach) started in the 1920s at the Chicago School, had a reformist movement in the 1970s and transformed in the 1990s, and remains open-ended in nature (Denzin & Lincoln, 2000). It includes positivism, postpositivism, and several other approaches, but remains focused on empirical methods to study individual lives, and follows the scientific paradigm of: research design, data gathering, analysis and interpretation. It answers the how question behind social experience, and is more explicit about the influence of researcher values than quantitative research, which also is susceptible to the influence of such values.

11　It is relatively straightforward to list the characteristics of someone who would be more likely to be successful with the exploitation of the experiential model choice given the reliance on trusting the person as a reliable source of the initial observations. For example, that person would be more likely to have a powerful position.

12 This premise should not be surprising, although it detracts from the lore of the individual genius of entrepreneurs pursuing crazy ideas. Few, if any, commercial discoveries emerge in isolation, without any competition. It is almost always the case that rivals are working on decreasing costs, or adding differentiated features, using similarly available factors, in order to generate new profits. There is little that Apple, Microsoft, Facebook, Google or Intel did that was radically different from rivals at their inceptions.

13 This is an outline of a proposed new partial theory, not a full description of it (as that would involve a completely new paper). It is provided to prove that such new partial theory can exist to pass our fair test. This proposed theory captures acts of guileful agents in innovative product markets to shift rents, and not acts of earnest agents pursuing alternative ideas that they believe will add value.

References

Afuah, A. (1998). *Innovation management: Strategies, implementation and profits*. New York: Oxford University Press.

Alvarez, S. A., & Barney, J. B. (2007). Discovery and creation: Alternative theories of entrepreneurial action. *Strategic Entrepreneurship Journal, 1*, 11–26.

Arend, R. J., Sarooghi, H., & Burkemper, A. (2015). Effectuation as ineffectual? Applying the 3E theory-assessment framework to a proposed new theory of entrepreneurship. *Academy of Management Review, 40*(4), 630–651.

Baker, T., & Nelson, R. E. (2005). Creating something from nothing: Resource construction through entrepreneurial bricolage. *Administrative Science Quarterly, 50*, 329–366.

Barreto, I. (2012). Solving the entrepreneurial puzzle: The role of entrepreneurial interpretation in opportunity formation and related processes. *Journal of Management Studies, 49*(2), 356–380.

Burrell, G., & Morgan, G. (1979). *Sociological paradigms and organizational analysis: Elements of the sociology of corporate life*. London: Heinemann.

Denzin, N. K., & Lincoln, Y. S. (2000). *Handbook of qualitative research* (2nd ed.). Thousand Oaks, CA: Sage Publications Inc.

Dubin, R. (1969). *Theory building*. New York: Free Press.

Fairlie, R. W. (2014). *Kauffman index of entrepreneurial activity, 1996–2013*. Kansas City: Ewing Marion Kauffman Foundation.

Garud, R., & Karnøe, P. (2003). Bricolage versus breakthrough: Distributed and embedded agency in technology entrepreneurship. *Research Policy, 32*, 277–300.

Harari, Y. N. (2015). *Sapiens*. New York: HarperCollins.

Ireland, R. D., Reutzel, C. R., & Webb, J. W. (2005). Entrepreneurship research in AMJ: What has been published, and what might the future hold? *Academy of Management Journal, 48*(4), 557–564.

Kirzner, I. M. (1973). *Competition and entrepreneurship*. Chicago: University of Chicago Press.

Kirzner, I. M. (1979). *Perception, opportunity, and profit: Studies in the theory of entrepreneurship*. Chicago: University of Chicago Press.

Kirzner, I. M. (1997). Entrepreneurial discovery and the competitive market process: An Austrian approach. *Journal of Economic Literature, 35*, 60–85.

Kor, Y. Y., Mahoney, J. T., & Michael, S. C. (2007). Resources, capabilities and entrepreneurial perceptions. *Journal of Management Studies, 44*(7), 1187–1212.

Leavitt, K., Mitchell, T. R., & Peterson, J. (2010). Theory pruning: Strategies to reduce our dense theoretical landscape. *Organizational Research Methods, 13*(4), 644–667.

Levi-Strauss, C. (1966). *The savage mind*. Chicago: University of Chicago Press.

Ramoglou, S. (2013). On the misuse of realism in the study of entrepreneurship. *Academy of Management Review, 38*(3), 463–465.

Sarasvathy, S. D. (2001). Causation and effectuation: Toward a theoretical shift from economic inevitability to entrepreneurial contingency. *Academy of Management Review, 26*, 243–263.

Shane, S., & Venkataraman, S. (2000). The promise of entrepreneurship as a field of research. *Academy of Management Review, 25*, 217–226.

Teece, D. J. (2007). Explicating dynamic capabilities: The nature and microfoundations of (sustainable) enterprise performance. *Strategic Management Journal, 28*(13), 1319–1350.

Whetten, D. A. (1989). What constitutes a theoretical contribution? *Academy of Management Review, 14*, 490–495.

4 Social constructionism and entrepreneurial opportunity

Luke Pittaway, Rachida Aïssaoui and Joe Fox

Introduction

The role of imagination and deliberate choices in the creation of future realities through entrepreneurial endeavor is, we contend, a surprisingly under-researched subject (Pittaway & Tunstall, 2016). Approaches that take an explicit 'voluntaristic' stance on human behavior and humankind's ability to influence, mold and build the future in an explicit and deliberate way have not taken central stage in research on entrepreneurship (Grant & Perren, 2002). Studies reviewing underlying philosophies of research in the field of entrepreneurship have shown a number common features that have guided an overwhelming majority of studies (Pittaway, 2005; Pittaway & Tunstall, 2016). These assumptions are drawn predominantly from the functionalist paradigm of social science inquiry (Burrell & Morgan, 1979). They imply a realist ontology that social reality exists outside of the individual's interaction with it and can be 'discovered'. Applied to entrepreneurship, such approaches often perceive that opportunity exists in the marketplace and entrepreneurs must first 'discover' these opportunities. Typically, approaches in the functionalist paradigm use positivist epistemological assumptions and assume that knowledge needs to be constructed through scientific methods applied to social science. In entrepreneurship, this assumption drives 'hypothesis driven' methods that collect large volumes of data, engage in structural equation modeling and seek to generalize and predict, in order to aid knowledge construction. Approaches in the functionalist paradigm are also dominated by deterministic assumptions about human behavior. Here behavior is viewed to be a function of factors beyond the control of the individual, such as, their personality, their immediate context and their family history and so forth (Carland, Hoy, & Carland, 1988; Gartner, 1989). In entrepreneurship, such assumptions guide research that seeks to understand what factors support entrepreneurial endeavor rather than what leads a person to choose an entrepreneurial life course and seeks to appreciate how they might learn as they practice entrepreneurship (Bygrave, 1989; Gibb, 1996). The functionalist paradigm also makes 'social order' based assumptions regarding the nature of society, that it changes slowly and incrementally rather than suddenly and disruptively (Burrell & Morgan, 1979). In entrepreneurship, this assumption can lead researchers to underappreciate the nature of disruptive change and innovation as articulated by Schumpeter (Kilby,

1971; Pittaway, 2005). The overwhelming nature and use of functionalist assumptions in the study of entrepreneurship has led to a number of traps into which entrepreneurship research has fallen (Pittaway & Tunstall, 2016). Trap one posits that entrepreneurship research has been lured into aiming to be too scientific, that it is not recognizing that the domain is social scientific. Trap two suggests that the domain has largely ignored social systems and structures and has been too psychological in its focus. Trap three argues that it has applied an 'individualistic' axiom to the subject and largely assumed that entrepreneurship is an individual (rather than a group or societal) phenomenon. We argue here that a social constructionist approach to the study of entrepreneurship, along with other non-functionalist approaches such as critical realism and structuration theory, offers paths out of these traps for entrepreneurship research.

In the first part of the chapter, we introduce social constructionism. Here we focus on its ontological and epistemological nature. We also explore underlying assumptions about human behavior and perceptions of human interaction with society more widely. In the next part of the chapter, we introduce a contemporary debate in the entrepreneurship domain and show how a social constructionist frame can be useful in understanding that debate. Specifically, we focus on recent discussions about the nature of entrepreneurial opportunities. The debate is at its root an ontological disagreement and so it is ripe for illustrating the value of social constructionism.

Social constructionism

Social constructionism, particularly in social psychology, is not simply one thing and assumptions vary between approaches particularly regarding the relativism-realism debate about the nature of reality (Nightingale & Cromby, 1999; Parker, 1998). Indeed, there is also some distinction between what is regarded as a *constructivist* framework and other approaches that have been described as *constructionist* frameworks (Chell & Rhodes, 1999; Martin & Sugarman, 1996). Martin and Sugarman (1996), for example, indicate that cognitive constructivism has its roots in the psychology of the individual examining internal mental processes while social constructionism has its roots in the sociology of the public and social world examining the external world of social phenomena. Other such disagreements about the nature of the appropriate underlying assumptions in social constructionism can be found in virtually all debates in social psychology (Parker, 1998). In fact, it has been argued that such debate has overwhelmed contemporary thought and itself endangers the utility of social constructionism for applied research (Stainton-Rogers & Stainton-Rogers, 1999). Social constructionism, however, has made it possible for psychology to introduce a more critical reflexive approach to theory and practice which has moved psychology away from the study of mental characteristics toward a more socially embedded and historically situated study of human action and experience (Parker, 1998). In order to understand social constructionism and some of its internal debates, we introduce some of the key underlying assumptions.

The social construction of reality (ontology)

What is reality? This is a question that has been posed for as long as human thought has existed and also dominates debate in social constructionism (Parker, 1998). Berger and Luckmann's (1967) *'The social construction of reality'* is one attempt to present assumptions about reality that are social constructionist. In this view, reality is multifaceted, there are 'multiple realities': dreams, the imagined future, sensations, observed materiality, unobserved materiality, heuristics and language are a few. All these forms of 'reality' pose important questions, and understanding of them inevitably leads to different forms and types of knowledge. 'Common-sense' reality is the form of reality that imposes itself on our everyday activity (Berger & Luckmann, 1967). We apprehend this reality in everything we do. It is inescapable because it is what we encounter as we interpret it. The materiality of it is there in our experience, accessible through our senses and the meaning ascribed to it is categorized for us by our language. This is what can be described as 'common-sense' reality; it is that which is experienced, however subjectively, that has an already constructed meaning that may be 'taken for granted'. This everyday reality is described as 'common-sense' reality because the reality experienced in everyday life is ordered.

> *Its phenomena are prearranged in patterns that seem to be independent of my apprehension of them and that impose themselves upon the latter. The reality of everyday life appears already objectified, that is, constituted by an order of objects that have been designated as objects before my appearance on the scene.*
> (Berger & Luckmann, 1967, p. 35)

Social constructionism accepts a degree of realism but only in the sense that objectification (assumed realism) exists in the very nature of experience and that such reality is based on its historical construction, which predates an individual's experience. The point being that language is inherited and provides a continuous and ever-changing link between the objects, contexts and people one experiences and one's own consciousness. Objectifications (or concepts) embedded in language and that are learnt through the course of human interaction enable an individual to make sense and order their everyday existence. The experiences of the individual, for which the objectifications are central, enable an individual to construct their existing perceptions of social reality. As such, an individual's subjective consciousness is interacting constantly with the objectifications and experiences that make up their objective reality. The social construction of reality is thus based on three core principles:

i) All individuals have a 'subjective' reality because they must interpret their own social and physical context.
ii) There is an 'objective' reality existing outside the individual human being comprised of objects (materiality), other people and one's own physical being (embodiment). Understanding of this 'objective' reality is a relative process depending on the senses and sensual experience.

iii) Humans also share reality through the use of verbal and non-verbal communication, symbols and behavior. Such sharing enables the existence of a sense of both relativist and realist qualities because language can be common to all, ordering and structuring experience and interpretive, being dependent on the individual's interpretation.

Clearly, this ontology cannot be described as simply being either relativist or realist. When comparing societies and groups it is also evident that this 'common-sense reality', while 'real' to the individual, is not necessarily 'real' to other individuals who do not share the same 'common-sense' reality. In other words, there are multiple common-sense realities (Berger & Luckmann, 1967, p. 35). As a consequence, this form of social constructionism leads to relativist epistemology that has features of realism for those experiencing particular 'common-sense' realities. This occurs because both the subjective and objective dimensions of reality are dependent on the shared dimension. Such social relativity suggests that the total 'reality' of one individual is different from the total 'reality' of another. For example, when one meets a group of people who work together and they discuss work in one's presence there are always words, euphemisms and abbreviations that are understood by the group but not by the individual who is not a member of the group. The individual often misses the meaning and the reality behind what is being discussed. Words and abbreviations are constructed by groups to enable them to share efficiently the phenomena they seek to discuss and they work in much the same way that language works. Thus, if one does not understand the language of the group, one will find it difficult to understand the meaning.

There are two further dimensions that influence the relativity of what is 'real' to groups and individuals: the temporal and the spatial dimensions of the social context (Bird, 1988; Bird & West, 1997; Fischer, Reuber, Hababou, Johnson, & Lee, 1997; Shackle, 1955; West & Meyer, 1997).

> *The reality of everyday life is organized around the 'here' of my body and the 'now' of my present.*
>
> (Berger & Luckmann, 1967, p. 36)

Time has an impact in two ways. First, time impacts on an individual's ability to understand past human society and human interaction (Clark, 1985; Giddens, 1984). By separating an individual's experience from the context, the relativity to the individual of the historic past is increased. Second, time has an impact on an individual's present reality (Bird, 1992; Butler, 1995; Clark, 1985). Individuals exist only in the present and thus 'knowledge' accrued from the past is important in constructing one's current view of 'reality'. Individuals also interpret the 'knowledge' they gather, select, reject and accept some of it, forget much of it and unconsciously use 'knowledge' they sought to reject. The imprecise nature of this process indicates that every individual's subjective reality is unique to some degree. As a consequence, therefore, reality for any individual is inextricably bound with the 'now' of their social context, their personal history and their access to common knowledge through language. The spatial dimension of reality also plays a similar role (Berger & Luckmann, 1967; Giddens, 1976). The relativity of 'common-sense' reality is increased because individuals experience everyday life only at the 'here' of the space surrounding their body. It is only possible for an individual to directly experience one space at one time; although clearly technology can play a part in widening a person's access beyond their immediate spatial context.

The reality of everyday life, however, is not limited purely by these spatial and temporal contexts but embraces phenomena that are not present 'here and now'. The shared dimension of reality enables us to transfer understanding and escape the spatial and temporal constraints of the subjective dimension. For example, language enables a person to transfer to another ideas and concepts about reality. People are able to understand and share this knowledge because they share an understanding of the symbols used. The implication is that we use language and symbols to escape the temporal and spatial features of our subjective reality. In doing so, however, an individual's remoteness to a reality in which they were not directly involved is increased. In other words, experience in everyday life has different degrees of closeness and remoteness to different social realities (Butler, 1995). To conclude, there are a number propositions that define the social construction of reality.

i) There are three dimensions of reality, the subjective reality, the objective reality and the shared reality (Berger & Luckmann, 1967).

ii) An individual's subjective reality is completely unique because each individual will experience different times and spaces (Butler, 1995).

iii) There is an objective 'material' and 'embodied' reality but our understanding of it is limited by our senses (Schutz, 1967).

iv) There is no objective 'social' reality because it is constructed from the objectifications used in language. This means that what appears to be objective in the social world is in fact a symbolic construct used to explain categories created by us to order our experiences (Garfinkel, 1967).

v) Language, symbols and other mechanisms enable human beings to transcend, to some degree, the spatial and temporal features of subjective reality (Blumer, 1969) leading to some feelings of objectiveness in our 'common-sense' reality.

vi) Remoteness or closeness in time and space to social reality will have an impact on how social situations are interpreted.

vii) Individual human beings experience many social realities.

viii) Significant relativity exists between everyday social realities.

ix) Human groups and societies use language, symbols and other forms of communication to reduce the relativity that exists between everyday social realities (Berger & Luckmann, 1967) by creating collective interpretations.

Social construction of knowledge (epistemology)

The complexity of this position with regard to 'common-sense' reality inevitably leads to a relatively complex position regarding epistemology. In the social construction of knowledge, as applied here, the shared dimension of reality is the most important (Berger & Luckmann, 1967; Weick, 1969, 1995). Language is thus considered to be the repository of 'knowledge', although knowledge itself maintains its social and historical relativity (Garfinkel, 1967; Schutz, 1967). The first element of language is considered to be typificatory schemes that are shared by groups and can be transferred between generations. The transference of meaning through typifications also enables language to transcend the 'here and now' of face-to-face situations. This occurs because the anonymity of a typification increases with its distance from the 'here and now', its intimacy to the user and its individualization. For example, a work colleague can be typified as 'a friend', 'a colleague', 'a lecturer', 'a man' and 'a happy type'. Each typification about the same person varies in relation to its anonymity. This creates the mechanism that allows language to escape the purely 'here and now' of face-to-face interaction because a person can talk about a 'man' and this can refer to a type that does not have to relate to the 'here and now' of a current social context. It can also enable language to convey 'knowledge' because the typification 'man' collects a group of observations together in a label. The label then allows these observations to be shared by the group in a habitual way. In other words, the observations enter into the group's 'common-sense' reality and are accepted as taken for granted (Isabella, 1990). The construction of language is the repository of 'knowledge' because it builds increasingly complex typifications that can become more general and more specific. The combining of labels, from which habitual 'knowledge' has been acquired, enables language to transfer 'knowledge' to individuals who have no experiential 'knowledge' of something. As well as the introduction of new forms of typification into language, these labels can change meaning, depart from the common stock of a group's 'knowledge' and have dual meanings and, as such, have a dynamic nature. 'Knowledge' about objective reality is thus held in language and learnt habitually by the members of a group or society who use that common language. There are a number of implications of this stance that can be highlighted (Schutz, 1967).

i) 'Common-sense knowledge' is dependent on a group's shared typifactory schemes, which are a form of 'intersubjective' reality.
ii) These schemes are dynamic, undergo constant change and are dependent on the group's usage (Isabella, 1990).
iii) The vast majority of human 'knowledge' about objective reality is deposited in these typifactory schema (Blumer, 1969).
iv) Most 'knowledge' is acquired in this habitual way. In using particular typifications, an individual acquires the human groups past observations and ideas without needing to be consciously aware of it.

   v) Typifactory schema allow human 'knowledge' to transcend the 'here and now' of an individual's experience.

   vi) The complexity of typifactory schemes allows new 'knowledge' to be created from a combination of labels in a new way.

The second element of language that contributes to the construction of knowledge is the use of objects to signify the subjective state (Chell & Pittaway, 1998). The fact that an internal state can be objectified and communicated to others is also important; such objectifications can become signs. For example, the signs hot and irritable allow a person to communicate knowledge about their subjective state and these signs are detachable from the 'here and now' of their current context. Such signs and groups of signs, therefore, enable the internal state of an individual to be shared. A number further implications can be highlighted.

   i) Humans use objects to symbolize the subjective state (Blumer, 1969).

   ii) These objectifications have allowed the development of signs and symbols that represent the inner feelings, beliefs and thoughts of individuals (Pfeffer, 1993).

   iii) By developing such symbols humans have been able to detach individual internal 'knowledge' from its immediate context. Thus enabling 'knowledge' from an individual's subjective reality to be available to others in the social group (Berger & Luckmann, 1967).

   iv) This detachment also enables an individual's unique 'knowledge' to be capable of transcending their immediate social situation (Bougon et al., 1977).

In the social construction of knowledge these two principles allow knowledge to flow between the objective, subjective and shared realities and across time and space. First, *typifications* are observations of the external (objective) world that are grouped into types, categories and labels, and that transfer habitual knowledge between individuals and across generations. Second, *significations* are signs that communicate internal (subjective) feelings, emotions, ideas, beliefs and thoughts, and that enable an individual's subjective reality to be available to others and across time and space. These two types allow 'knowledge' about objective and subjective reality to be shared and, therefore, the assumption made by the social construction of knowledge is that *knowledge resides in language, in the construction of language and in its use* (Weick, 1969, 1995).

This assumption suggests that knowledge is both relative and universal (real). Knowledge is relative for two reasons. First, all individuals will have experienced different spatial and temporal contexts and will have drawn knowledge from these contexts differently. This knowledge and experience is processed by individuals, which adds further relativity, and is shared with the human group (the process of communication also adds a degree of relativity). Second, knowledge is relative because the typifications and significations used by a human group will be unique to that group.[1] To a degree, knowledge is also universal because typifications and significations enable us to share knowledge habitually (and consciously). 'Knowledge' that resides in language (habitual knowledge), therefore, is automatically available to all members of a social group who share the same language and hence universal to the members of that community.

The social construction of human behavior

As a consequence of assumptions made about reality and knowledge, a number of principles about the social construction of human behavior can be identified. Such assumptions about behavior can be developed from work on the social construction of personality (Hampson, 1982), ideas about the nature of choice (Shackle, 1979) and implications from other works on social constructionism (Berger & Luckmann, 1967; Fischer et al., 1997; Garfinkel, 1967; Giddens, 1976; Isabella, 1990; Nightingale & Cromby, 1999; Parker, 1998; Pfeffer, 1993; Schutz, 1967; Weick, 1995).

The three dimensions of reality highlighted have a differential impact on assumptions about human behavior. The subjective dimension leads to assumptions from psychology and economic psychology about the nature of internal processes, including modes of thought, the acquisition of belief systems and the processes involved in individual choice. The objective dimension leads to assumptions about how individuals observe and interpret the external world including theories about the senses. The shared dimension leads to assumptions derived from social psychology, sociology, ethnography and linguistics and includes views about how individuals interact within groups, how they construct language and how language transfers meaning. A theory of the social construction of human behavior, therefore, is likely to be extremely complex and so here we introduce only some of the key assumptions.

Every individual's subjective reality, which exists inside them, in social constructionism is clearly considered to be unique. Individuals have experienced different times and spaces, have drawn different information from these social contexts and have interpreted that information in different ways. An individual's unique past experiences (or stock of experience), therefore, will have an impact on their values, beliefs and motivations. It will also mean that how individuals assess social situations, how they choose to draw information from these social situations and how they interpret and store this information will have an impact on their future behavior. In other words, the influences behind an individual's internal values, beliefs and knowledge lead to 'limitations' on the number of possible choices in any given situation. The sheer complexity of the influences, the number of possible behavioral strategies that they lead to and the fact that these are unique for each individual effectively result in social constructionism of an assumption of '*non-determinant*' behavior (Chell, 1997, 2008; Hampson, 1982).

Such non-determinism has an impact on an individual's capacity to interpret the objective world, as well as their social environment. Understanding of the external environment is dependent on the typificatory schemes used by social groups. These typifications will only transfer habitual knowledge that has become accepted within the group. The behavioral strategies and choices open to an individual, therefore, may be dependent on the residual knowledge of the communities of which they are a part. In other words, one cannot act to make profit if no concept of profit exists within the residual knowledge of the community within which one lives (unless the concept is gained from a different community). Even if a concept exists an individual's past experience may influence their 'ranking' of the 'pursuit of profit' as a potential behavioral strategy and influence their choice. Thus, what an individual perceives as the potential outcomes of certain behaviors will have weight in their choice of behavior. There are, therefore, some identifiable assumptions within the social construction of human behavior.

i) An individual's past experiences may influence the strategies of behavior they believe are open to them.

ii) An individual's 'knowledge' or information about the external social environment may depend on the methods they use to accumulate and interpret external stimuli.

iii) Individuals may have many but not an unlimited number of possible behavioral strategies in any given situation.

iv) The influences on an individual's choice of behavior may be unique to each individual and the social context in which behavior occurs.

v) An individual's habitual knowledge may be dependent on the communities of which he/she is a member and this may restrict the behavioral strategies and choices available.

vi) Individuals have access to many behavioral strategies known within the community of which they are apart

vii) The community's 'culture' (i.e. how certain behaviors are rewarded or discouraged) may have an impact on how an individual considers the value of possible choices.

viii) The individual's perception of outcomes may enter into their choice of behavior.

Social reality is constructed by groups during interaction and is passed across generations by the use of a community's language. The coordinates for life within a social group, particularly expectations about appropriate and inappropriate behaviors in social constructionism, reside in language (Chell, 1997, 2008). Language and the stories used by a community communicate the community's expectations about accepted behaviors. These expectations are also fairly complex because most individuals interact with many communities and many levels of community. As a result, individuals may choose to adapt their behaviors and choices in different communities dependent on those community's expectations (Biddle & Edwin, 1966) or rebel against a community's expectations because they are aware (or can imagine) other approaches. It is also evident that individuals can choose to pursue behaviors deemed unacceptable in their community even when not influenced by expectations from somewhere else.

In social constructionism, an individual's remoteness or closeness in time and space to social reality also impacts on their choice of sustained behavior (Fischer et al., 1997; West & Meyer, 1997). Closeness or remoteness can impact on the objectives that an individual deems as achievable and desirable as they have more awareness of behaviors that need to be employed to gain their desired outcomes (Shackle, 1955). This awareness may be dependent on the individual's ability to accumulate and interpret information from their social environment, their ability to imagine new outcomes and the availability of information in their social environment (Shackle, 1955). For example, in the modern world an individual's opportunities are likely to be wider than in the past because improved communication technologies make more people aware of a greater number of possible objectives of sustained behavior. Such awareness can lead to greater choice. Choice of outcomes is further increased by an individual's ability to imagine new outcomes (Shackle, 1979). Imagination and intuition are important in the process because individuals can put together their unique internal 'knowledge' in new ways and externalize these thoughts to others. In doing so, new 'knowledge' can be created because of the uniqueness of each person's subjective reality, the mental processes being exercised on this 'knowledge' and the ability to share this 'knowledge' with others. A number of further principles guiding the social construction of behavior can, therefore, be illustrated.

i) The expectations of a community often reside in its language, metaphors and stories.

ii) Individuals experience many communities and levels of community and, as a result, may experience conflicting expectations that lead to many possible behavioral strategies. As a consequence individuals can choose from many potential options in any social context.

iii) Knowing about a behavioral strategy also allows an individual to rebel against and choose not to follow an expected community norm.

iv) An individual's awareness of the prior outcomes from options pursued by others may influence their confidence of their success if they pursue the same option.

v) An increase in the availability of information from other communities increases an individual's awareness of options and their perception of outcomes.

vi) Imagination allows individuals the ability to identify 'new' potential objectives for sustained behavior that fall outside those currently available to their immediate social group (Shackle, 1979).

vii) Individual thought processes, the uniqueness of each individual's subjective reality and the ability to externalize this 'knowledge' via language contribute to a community's ability to produce entirely 'new' options for behavior never before considered by the community of which the individual is a part.

The principles underlying the social construction of human behavior present a complex situation of non-deterministic behavior. In this view, behavior is essentially about choice, although at the same time this is not an assumption of 'free will', where an individual has no restrictions placed on what they can choose. In social constructionism, individuals can make choices about their actions but these choices are bounded by certain restrictions. Choice of a particular action is dependent on an individual's awareness that such an action is possible. It is restricted by the weight an individual gives to a particular course of action, which is informed by perceptions of its appropriateness derived by community acceptance. Choice is also restricted by an individual's ability to interpret their social environment; their specific social context at the time of the decision; the culture of the groups they interact with; their own cognitive skills; the habitual knowledge available in the communities in which they live and their capacity to imagine new choice options beyond those available in their immediate social context. These restrictions may limit an individual's awareness of possible objectives for behavior and restrict their knowledge of behavioral strategies and as such behavior is deemed to be socially constructed. Even with these restrictions, however, there are many behavioral strategies open to an individual in any social context. The individual may choose a desired outcome for behavior and choose a strategy of behavior that they believe will achieve the outcome they desire. As a consequence, therefore, an understanding about the nature of choice becomes essential when explaining 'entrepreneurial' behavior (Shackle, 1979) and so next we will explore social constructionist approaches in entrepreneurship.

Social constructionism in entrepreneurship research

The use of social constructionism to understand entrepreneurship is not new (Chell, 2008). Many researchers have applied it to differing aspects of the entrepreneurship research, including personality (Chell, 1997,2008), entrepreneurial opportunity (Fletcher, 2006), identity (Downing, 2005) and evolutionary theory (Aldrich & Martinez, 2010).

When Sir Francis Bacon (1561–1626) claimed that "*A wise man will make more opportunities than he can find,*" he probably did not anticipate that twenty-first century entrepreneurship scholars would still be struggling over the question: Are opportunities created or discovered by entrepreneurs? Indeed, a heated controversy opposes the entrepreneurship community between those who advocate that entrepreneurial opportunities exist in an objective manner, waiting to be discovered, and those, conversely, who posit that opportunities cannot exist independent to individuals who create them. This is not a vain debate given the centrality of the concept of opportunity in entrepreneurship research (Dimov, 2011; Shane & Venkataraman, 2000; Venkataraman, Sarasvathy, Dew, & Forster, 2012). Short, Ketchen, Shook, and Ireland (2010, p. 40) even claim that "*Without an opportunity, there is no entrepreneurship*" (see also Busenitz et al., 2003). In this part of the chapter, therefore, we review the main elements at the core of the opportunity discovery versus opportunity creation debate and focus on the main assumptions underpinning the objectivist-discovery and constructionist-creation views, and identify some important implications of these positions.

The debate: origins

For Kirzner (1971, 1973), opportunities exist in the market, and the role of the entrepreneur is to discover them. For Shackle (1979), opportunities are 'imagined,' that is, opportunities are constructed in the entrepreneur's imagination, they are created, and thus cannot exist independent of the entrepreneur. Given entrepreneurship theories' strong roots in economics, these two thoughts are a logical extension of competing views over uncertainty, a central concept in economics. White (1976, p. 91) summarized this issue as follows:

> *Uncertainty, like numerous other terms in economics, can be understood in two senses, one 'subjective' and the other 'objective'. The first designates an attitude or state of mind on the part of the decision-maker, while the second signifies the indeterminateness or unpredictability of future states of human affairs.*

More than four decades later, the entrepreneurship community is still strongly divided between discovery theorists who, following Kirzner, view opportunities as objective phenomena (Carsson, 1982; Shane & Venkataraman, 2000), and creation theorists who, akin to Shackle, view opportunities as subjective and intersubjective, or the product of a process of social construction (Alvarez & Barney, 2007, 2010; Baker & Nelson, 2005; Fletcher, 2006; Wood & McKinley, 2010). The debate is thus primarily ontological, based on a disagreement over the very nature of opportunities. The objectivist position holds that opportunities exist in the "real" world (Suddaby, Bruton, & Xi, 2015). The subjectivist view links the existence of opportunities to the entrepreneurs' perception or imagination of a possible or envisioned future (Venkataraman et al., 2012; Wood & McKinley, 2010).

Opportunity research thus covers the full spectrum of ontological and epistemological domains ranging from the positivist-realist to the subjectivist-constructivist positions (Dimov, 2011). As such, opportunity research builds on a multitude of – often competing – assumptions, informed by numerous philosophical roots. Recent conversations have taken place that seek to better bring to the fore those assumptions and their implications on predictions about entrepreneurial opportunities and effectiveness (Alvarez & Barney, 2007; Dimov, 2011; Fletcher, 2006; Sarasvathy, Dew, Velamuri, & Venkataraman, 2003; Venkataraman et al., 2012). This thread of conversation has served not only to draw our attention to the multitude of scientific roots informing entrepreneurship research in general, and entrepreneurial opportunities research in particular, but also to better identify and account for the assumptions they build upon. As Lindgren and Packendorff (2009, p. 25) further noted, these have the notable result to "*exclude and include different research questions and phenomena.*" This effort is critical to developing a more comprehensive research stream. More specifically, it has led to the acknowledgment that the variety of predictions over opportunity formation and emergence is a product of the different assumptions discovery and creation theories build upon (Alvarez & Barney, 2010, 2013; Dimov, 2011; Saras-vathy et al., 2003; Shane, 2012; Suddaby et al., 2015; Venkataraman et al., 2012). For instance, when Alvarez and Barney (2007) compare the objectivist-discovery view to the evolutionary realist-creation perspective, they identify three major assumptive tensions: the nature of opportunities, the nature of entrepreneurs, and the nature of decision-making. The authors further describe how these different assumptions impact predictions about the effectiveness of seven major entrepre-neurial actions – leadership, decision making, human resource practices, strategy, finance, marketing, and sustaining competitive advantages (Alvarez & Barney, 2007, p. 136). On a similar vein, Wood and McKinley (2010) show that when opportunity research builds on a social constructivist-creation vs. an objectivist-discovery perspective, consensus building stands as a central factor in the forma-tion and exploitation of opportunities. There is agreement, though, that while discovery and creation theory are strikingly different, they do converge in their efforts to explain the same dependent variable, namely the actions entrepreneurs take and the results of these actions on opportunity formation and exploitation (Alvarez & Barney, 2007). Next, we explain how a social constructionist-creation perspective diverges from the objectivist-discovery position, and the implications of these different views on three main opportunity research domains – the rela-tionship between entrepreneurs and their environment, the nature of opportuni-ties, and the actions of entrepreneurs and researchers.

Opportunity discovery vs. creation: assumptions and implications

Positivism assumes realist ontology of a world 'out there' which exists indepen-dent of those who observe it. Objects have inherent meanings which are there to be discovered. Under this view, reality is external, objective and independent of social actors. Conversely, constructionism views reality as subjective, socially constructed, multiple and changing. Of note and as previously highlighted, con-structionism does not deny the existence of a reality 'out there'; it does, however, question the existence of social reality independent of actors. Indeed, the meaning given to reality, under the constructionist view, is argued to be subjectively and inter-subjectively constructed. The ontological claim of reality as 'truth' is thus challenged as reality is viewed, instead, as multiple because constructed by actors according to their own worldviews. Reality is also changing as it is shaped by the constant interactions of actors with their environment. We identify and discuss three main domains where these different views about reality become reified, and result in strikingly different predictions.

Entrepreneurs and their environment

Discovery theory is strongly rooted in a deterministic view whereby individuals and environments exist independently of each other (Fletcher, 2006; Lindgren & Packendorff, 2009). The external environment is not only distinct from, but more importantly, more agentic than the entrepreneur (Suddaby et al., 2015; Wood & McKinley, 2010). Under this view, opportunities sit in the environment, and the only agentic process attributed to entrepreneurs is their ability to discover and exploit opportunities (Shane & Venkataraman, 2000). Conversely, the main tenet of – and insight from – social constructionism is that the environment and the entrepreneur are inter- and co-dependent. Following Berger and Luckmann's (1967) and Giddens' (1984) theories, entrepreneurs shape and are shaped by their environment, and as such, their co-evolution and co-existence is the result of these iterative relationships (Alvarez & Barney, 2007; Fletcher, 2006; Gaglio & Katz, 2001; Gartner, Carter, & Hills, 2003). The environment, under this view, is less concrete and inflexible and more amenable to being reconstructed (Fletcher, 2006; Suddaby et al., 2015). Importantly, the boundary between entrepreneurs and their environment is less distinct and the degree of agency between entrepreneurs and environment is more evenly distributed than under the discovery view (Suddaby et al., 2015). This perspective is thus particularly useful to illuminate our understanding of how entrepreneurs create opportunities.

These different assumptions about the relationship between entrepreneurs and their environment have sweeping implications not only on the direction of the relation between entrepreneurs and opportunities, but also, by extension, on the task of the researcher – a point we will later elaborate upon. Indeed, if opportunities wait to be discovered, the relationship of interest is that which brings the entrepreneur to the opportunity, a unilateral relationship described by Weick (1979) as "*bringing agency to opportunities.*" This is because the entrepreneur, under this view, is "*a detector to an external phenomenon that would exist whether or not the entrepreneur was present to record it*" (Wood & McKinley, 2010, p. 79). Under the constructionist assumption that the relationship between entrepreneurs and their environment is not only bilateral, but more importantly iterative, the direction of interest goes both from the entrepreneur to the environment and from the environment to the entrepreneur. The latter is best defined by Wood and McKinley (2010, p. 79), who view the entrepreneur as "*an influence agent, seeking to generalize an idea about an opportunity by creating consensus about its viability.*" When the directional arrow goes from the entrepreneur to the environment, it is generally to stress how entrepreneurs are conditioned by their institutionalized beliefs (Dimov, 2007).

The origins of opportunity

Disagreement over the very nature of the relationship between entrepreneurs and their environment results in another tension over the origin of opportunities. In discovery theory, opportunities are exogenous, originating from markets imperfections (Alvarez & Barney, 2007; Fletcher, 2006; Foss & Klein, 2017; Kirzner, 1973; Suddaby et al., 2015). Because agency is placed on the environment, it is only from changes in the environment that opportunities will emerge, notably changes in technology, consumer preferences, and, more generally, in the political, social, or economic context within which markets exist.

This view is strongly challenged by social constructionists, as changes in the environment are posited as acted and influenced by individuals and groups themselves (Berger & Luckmann, 1967; Giddens, 1984). Furthermore, because entrepreneurs and environment are co-evolving, claims about the exogenous nature of opportunities are strongly questioned. If, as posited by creation theory, opportunities do not exist without the entrepreneur (Wood & McKinley, 2010), opportunities are thus endogenous; they are the product of entrepreneurs' interpretations of their environment, as well as of negotiations between entrepreneurs and their environment as they seek to enact their imagined opportunities (Baker & Nelson, 2005; Bhide, 1999; Fletcher, 2006; Sarasvathy, 2001). In sum, entrepreneurs, under this view, *"do not wait for exogenous shocks to form opportunities and then provide agency to those opportunities, they act"* (Alvarez & Barney, 2007, p. 17). For instance, Hargadon and Douglas (2001) chronicle the ways Edison socially constructed the conditions for consumer acceptance of the electric light bulb.

What entrepreneurs and researchers do in discovery vs. creation theory

In discovery theory, because opportunities exist out there, waiting to be discovered, the main task of the entrepreneur is to discover and exploit them (Alvarez & Barney, 2007; Shane & Venkataraman, 2000). Under this view, then, variance lies in individuals who can be separated into two groups: the entrepreneurs, that is, those who are capable of discovering and exploiting opportunities, and the non-entrepreneurs, that is, those who cannot. This distinction between entrepreneurs and non-entrepreneurs has led to the emergence of the concept of alertness developed by Kirzner (1973) to stress that the role of entrepreneurs lies in their alertness to unnoticed opportunities (see also Yu, 2001, p. 48). Research in the discovery view is thus focused on variance, primarily concerned with uncovering systematic differences between entrepreneurs and non-entrepreneurs (Alvarez & Barney, 2007), notably factors such as individual traits, including degrees of alertness, or differential access to opportunities (Wood & McKinley, 2010). The trait approach (Cole, 1969; McClelland, 1961) has thus dominated entrepreneurship research seeking to solve the question "Who is an entrepreneur?" (Gartner, 1989; McKenzie, Ugbah & Smothers, 2007) and as has been highlighted previously falls into the traps common to trait-based personality theory (Pittaway & Tunstall, 2016).

In creation theory, the task of the entrepreneur is less deterministic and passive as the entrepreneur is portrayed as engaged in an iterative relationship with his/her environment (Alvarez & Barney, 2007; Fletcher, 2006). The iterative nature of this relationship stems from the social constructionist notion that agency is as much on the side of the environment as it is on the side of the entrepreneur (Fletcher, 2006; Suddaby et al., 2015). Under this view, then, the entrepreneur acts and re-acts: as the entrepreneur seeks to enact his/her imagined opportunity, s/he relies on the environment's responses to his/her actions (Alvarez & Barney, 2007) to move the opportunity from the status of imagined to the status of "real", that is, objectified and external (Berger & Luckmann, 1967; Fletcher, 2006; Sarasvathy, 2004; Wood & McKinley, 2010).

Research in the creation view is thus concerned with the becomingness of the opportunity, that is, the process through which the imagined opportunity becomes objectified. Process, instead of variance, is privileged in opportunity creation research. The researcher will ask process questions (Lindgren & Packendorff, 2009), such as "How do things go on?" (Fletcher, 2006), "How does action by entrepreneurs create opportunities?" or "How can entrepreneurs use incremental, iterative, and inductive processes to make decisions?" (Alvarez & Barney, 2007, p. 22). Importantly, a focus on processes draws researchers' attention to the relationship between entrepreneurs and their environment. Given that this relationship is viewed as iterative, research in the creation view can be summarized in three main streams. First, studies may investigate institutionalized belief systems and how those systems influence the development of opportunities (Dimov, 2007). Kostova (1997), for instance, examines several countries' institutional profiles to show how institutions in these countries constrain or enable entrepreneurship and shape entrepreneurial orientation. This top-down perspective is complemented by a bottom-up view whereby individuals act upon their environment to enact their imagined opportunities. In this second stream, researchers will seek to uncover the "*corridors*" individuals construct "*from their personal experiences to stable economic and sociological institutions*" (Sarasvathy, 2004, p. 289), i.e., the actions entrepreneurs develop to link their ideas to existing social structures. Finally, studies in the third stream take a more holistic perspective and are interested in understanding how entrepreneurs and their environment co-evolve. These studies are typically found in the structuration tradition. For instance, Sarason, Dean and Dillard (2006) and Chiasson and Saunders (2005) use Giddens' (1984) structuration theory to show how opportunities are the result of an ecology of interactions and negotiations between entrepreneurs and their institutional environment.

These differences in research emphasis can thus be summarized as either variance or process research, with the notable implication that the preferred methodological approach and level of analysis will vary accordingly. Indeed, an emphasis on variance – between entrepreneurs and non-entrepreneurs – in the discovery view, generally calls for quantitative analyses, and tends to focus on the micro-level of the entrepreneur. Conversely, interest on process – through which the imagined opportunity becomes objectified – in the creation view, calls for longitudinal, qualitative methods, and is more generally focused on the higher levels of analysis.

Conclusion

After more than four decades of debating over whether opportunities are discovered or created, various scholars lament that this debate is likely irreconcilable. Dimov (2011, p. 75), for instance, note that the idea that opportunities exist out there, waiting to be discovered, is "*very intuitive and hard to disprove.*" Alvarez and Barney (2007, p. 12) go a step further, arguing that neither discovery nor creation can be empirically demonstrated as, "*it will always be possible to inter- pret the formation of a particular opportunity as either a discovery or creation process.*" Gaglio and Winter (2009), though, do not agree with these positions, arguing instead that social constructionism has the potential to reconcile the ten- sions inherent to this debate. For instance, Garud and Giuliani (2013), in the tradi- tion of social constructionism, take a narrative approach to stress the possibility that discovery and creation exist simultaneously. The authors note that their occurrence, however, is characterized by different degrees of agency, and will be conditioned by distinct social and temporal settings. Sarasvathy (2001) made a similar observation that different contextual conditions will determine the pre- dominance of either opportunity discovery or opportunity creation. The author later refined this position (Sarasvathy et al., 2003) and identified three types of opportunities which will emerge as a result of uncertainties over the existence or non-existence of sources of supply and demand. When both supply and demand exist, the authors argue, opportunity recognition will arise. When only one side exists, the resulting type of opportunity is discovery. Finally, opportunity creation emerges when neither supply nor demand exist in an obvious manner. While Sarasvathy's work (Sarasvathy, 2001, 2004; Sarasvathy et al., 2003) does not specifically build on a social constructionist perspective, it does indicate a new pathway for opportunity research.

In social constructionism, the discovery perspective of entrepreneurial oppor- tunity sits firmly in the *objectification* part of its epistemology (Berger & Luck- mann, 1967). Objectifications (concepts) are embedded in language, which are learnt through human interaction and are used by individuals to make sense of everyday reality. These objects describe both 'materiality' (the natural world) and 'embodiment' (the social world). Verbal communication and symbols in language allow for the ordering and structuring of this 'external' reality. While these objec- tifications have a relativity in social constructionism, based on how they are his- torically constructed, they do 'exist' in the sense of forming a common-sense reality for members of a community. It is also notable that individuals can con- struct unique forms of awareness of common-sense reality by having access to multiple communities, by accessing information others have not found and through their personal ability to internalize and interpret these external objects. In this sense every individual has a unique alertness to objectifications of the material and social world based on their prior personal history. The discovery perspective in entrepreneurship focuses almost exclusively on this aspect of social reality. Here knowledge resides in information, information processing and cognitive aptitude. Entrepreneurs can learn strategies to gain better access than others to these objec- tifications, they can find new information by joining 'new-to-them' communities, they can transfer knowhow from one community to another, they can put together existing objects in new ways and they can find opportunities by listening to others. Even in a social constructionist philosophy, it is clear that this type of discovery- based entrepreneurship can still occur. Entrepreneurs must make choices, follow decision paths and engage in actions within an undetermined reality bounded by their perceptions and information and they must make changes as new information and awareness is acquired as they makes choices and follow action pathways. Only in a social constructionist stance, these opportunities do not 'exist' as concrete reality; they exist only in the sense of being shared perceptions and objects within a particular social community. In order to understand how these objects are being interpreted and acted upon by entrepreneurs, researchers are left to consider the role of language, linguistics and heuristics. This is because language is the repository of the typifications on which entrepreneurial insights (alertness) are based and heuristics are important to understand how individuals make sense and form new knowledge from these insights when they choose to act (Weick, 1969, 1995). One cannot escape the fact though that this remains an iterative process of '*sensemaking*' but one based on understanding the *existing social reality* and developing opportunities that seem to exist within the *status quo*.

The creation perspective in entrepreneurship, on the other hand, appears to be firmly linked to the *signification* part of social constructionism's epistemology. Here individuals use signs, symbols and language to externalize their subjective state. They bring forth new ideas, imaginative flights from the norm, rebellious counter-reactions and visions of the future. Language remains an important medium but a different type of process is occurring. Imagination, visions of 'what could be', intuitive leaps from current reality can be brought forth from the mind and shared with others. Stories, narratives, metaphors and analogies can be used to persuade others the future envisioned reality is worth creating. Through talk, resources can be mobilized and action to create the envisaged future can occur. Here understanding the '**sensecreating**' process seems more important and it seems clear that such opportunities are focused on *the disruption of the status quo*. It, therefore, seems evident that social constructionism can play a part in understanding both discovery and creation approaches to entrepreneurial opportunity but that these are indeed two different forms of entrepreneurship.

Note

1 In the modern world, this uniqueness is rarely absolute but differs in degree depending on a human group's closeness or remoteness to another human group.

References

Aldrich, H. E., & Martinez, M. A. (2010). Entrepreneurship as social construction: A multilevel evolutionary approach. In Z. J. Acs & D. B. Audretsch, *Handbook of entrepreneurship research* (pp. 387–427). New York: Springer.

Alvarez, S. A., & Barney, J. B. (2007). Discovery and creation: Alternative theories of entrepreneurship action. *Strategic Entrepreneurship Journal, 1*(1–2), 11–26.

Alvarez, S. A., & Barney, J. B. (2010). Entrepreneurship and epistemology: The philosophical underpinnings of the study of entrepreneurial opportunities. *Academy of Management Annals, 4*, 557–583.

Alvarez, S. A., & Barney, J. B. (2013). Epistemology, opportunities, and entrepreneurship: Comments on Venkataraman et al. (2012) and Shane (2012). *Academy of Management Review, 38*(1), 154–166.

Baker, T., & Nelson, R. (2005). Creating something from nothing: Resource construction through entrepreneurial bricolage. *Administrative Science Quarterly, 50*, 329–366.

Berger, P. L., & Luckmann, T. (1967). *The social construction of reality: A treatise in the sociology of knowledge.* Garden City, NY: Anchor Books Doubleday.

Bhide, A. (1999). *How entrepreneurs craft strategies that work.* Boston, MA: Harvard Business School Press.

Biddle, B. J., & Edwin, J. T. (1966). *Role theory: Concepts and research.* New York: Wiley.

Bird, B. J. (1988). Implementing entrepreneurial ideas: The case of intention. *Academy of Management Review, 13*(3), 442–453.

Bird, B. J. (1992). The operation of intentions in time: The emergence of the new venture. *Entrepreneurship Theory and Practice, 17*(1), 11–20.

Bird, B. J., & West, G. P. (1997). Time and entrepreneurship. *Entrepreneurship Theory and Practice, 22*(2), 5–10.

Blumer, H. (1969). *Symbolic interactionism: Perspectives and method.* Englewood Cliffs, NJ: Prentice Hall.

Bougon, M. G., Weick, K. E., & Binkhorst, D. (1977). Cognition in organizations: An analysis of the Utrecht Jazz Orchestra. *Administrative Science Quarterly, 22*, 606–639.

Burrell, G., & Morgan, G. (1979). *Sociological paradigms and organizational analysis.* London: Heinemann.

Busenitz, L. W., West, G. P., Shepherd, D., Nelson, T., Chandler, G. N., & Zacharakis, A. (2003). Entrepreneurship research in emergence. *Journal of Management, 29*, 285–308.

Butler, R. (1995). Time in organizations: Its experience, explanations, and effects. *Organization Studies, 16*(6), 925–950.

Bygrave, W. D. (1989). The entrepreneurship paradigm (I): A philosophical look at its research methodologies. *Entrepreneurship Theory and Practice, 14*(1), 7–26.

Carland, J. W., Hoy, F., & Carland, J. A. (1988). Who is an entrepreneur? is a question worth asking. *American Journal of Small Business, 3*(Spring), 33–39.

Carsson, M. (1982). *The entrepreneur: An economic theory.* Aldershot: Edward Elgar.

Chell, E. (1997). The social construction of the entrepreneurial personality. Paper presented at the *British Academy of Management Conference*, September, London.

Chell, E. (2008). *The entrepreneurial personality: A social construction.* London and New York, NY: Routledge.

Chell, E., & Pittaway, L. (1998). The social construction of entrepreneurship. *Institute of Small Business Affairs Conference: Celebrating the small business: 21 years of small business research*, 18–20 November, Durham University, 647–664.

Chell, E., & Rhodes, H. (1999). Exploring vertical relationships in SMES: A social constructionist approach. Paper submitted to the *British Academy of Management Conference*, 1–3 September, Manchester Metropolitan University.

Chiasson, M., & Saunders, C. (2005). Reconciling diverse approaches to opportunity research using structuration theory. *Journal of Business Venturing, 20*, 747–767.

Clark, P. A. (1985). A review of theories of time and structure for organizational sociology. *Research in the Sociology of Organizations, 4*, 35–79.

Cole, A. H. (1969). Definition of entrepreneurship. In J. L. Komives (Ed.), *Karl A. Bostrom seminar in the study of enterprise* (pp. 10–22). Milwaukee: Center for Venture Management.

Dimov, D. (2007). From opportunity insight to opportunity intention: The importance of person-situation learning match. *Entrepreneurship Theory & Practice, 31*(4), 561–583.

Dimov, D. (2011). Grappling with the unbearable elusiveness of entrepreneurial opportunities. *Entrepreneurship Theory & Practice, 35*(1), 57–81.

Downing, S. (2005). The social construction of entrepreneurship: Narrative and dramatic processes in the coproduction of organizations and identities. *Entrepreneurship Theory and Practice, 29*(2), 185–204.

Fischer, E., Reuber, A., Hababou, M., Johnson, W., & Lee, S. (1997). The role of socially constructed temporal perspectives in the emergence of rapid-growth firms. *Entrepreneurship Theory and Practice, 22*(2), 13–30.

Fletcher, D. E. (2006). Entrepreneurial processes and the social construction of opportunity. *Entrepreneurship & Regional Development, 18*, 421–440.

Foss, N., & Klein, P. (2017). Entrepreneurial discovery or creation? In search of the middle ground. *Academy of Management Review, 42*(4), 733–736.

Gaglio, C. M., & Katz, J. A. (2001). The psychological basis of opportunity identification: Entrepreneurial alertness. *Small Business Economics, 16*(2), 95–111.

Gaglio, C. M., & Winter, S. (2009). Entrepreneurial alertness and opportunity identification: Where are we now? In A. L. Carsrud, & M. Brännback (Eds.), *International Studies in Entrepreneurship* (Vol. 24, pp. 305–325). Dordrecht: Springer.

Garfinkel, H. (1967). *Studies in ethnomethodology.* Englewood Cliffs, NJ: Prentice Hall.

Gartner, W. B. (1989). 'Who is an entrepreneur?' Is the wrong question. *Entrepreneurship Theory & Practice, 13*(4), 47–68.

Gartner, W. B., Carter, N. M., & Hills, G. E. (2003). The language of opportunity. In C. Steyaert & D. Kjorth (Eds.), *New movements in entrepreneurship* (pp. 103–104). Cheltenham, UK: Edward Elgar.

Garud, R., & Giuliani, A. P. (2013). A narrative perspective on entrepreneurial opportunities. *Academy of Management Review, 38*(1), 157–160.

Gibb, A. A. (1996). Entrepreneurship and small business management: Can we afford to neglect them in the twenty-first century business school? *British Journal of Management, 7*(4), 309–321.

Giddens, A. (1976). *New rules of sociological method.* London: Hutchinson.

Giddens, A. (1984). *The constitution of society: Outline of the theory of structuration.* Berkeley, CA: University of California Press.

Grant, P., & Perren, L. (2002). Small business and entrepreneurial research: Meta-theories, paradigms and prejudices. *International Small Business Journal, 20*(2), 185–211.

Hampson, S. E. (1982). *The construction of personality.* London: Routledge and Keegan Paul.

Hargadon, A. B., & Douglas, Y. (2001). When innovations meet institutions: Edison and the design of the electric light bulb. *Administrative Science Quarterly, 46*, 476–501.

Isabella, L. A. (1990). Evolving interpretations as change unfolds: How managers construe key organizational events. *Academy of Management Journal, 33*, 7–41.

Kilby, P. (1971). *Entrepreneurship and economic development.* New York: Free Press.

Kirzner, I. M. (1971). Entrepreneurship and the market approach to development. In F. A. Hayek, H. Hazzlitt, L. R. Read, G. Velasco, & F. A. Harper (Eds.), *Toward liberty: Essays in honor of Ludwig von Mises on the occasion of his 90th birthday* (pp. 194–208). Menlo Park: Institute for Humane Studies.

Kirzner, I. M. (1973). *Competition and entrepreneurship.* Chicago, IL: The University of Chicago Press.

Kostova, T. (1997). Country institutional profile: Concept and measurement. *Proceedings in the Academy of Management,* 180–184.

Lindgren, M., & Packendorff, J. (2009). Social constructionism and entrepreneurship: Basic assumptions and consequences for theory and research. *International Journal of Entrepreneurial Behaviour & Research*, *15*(1), 25–47.

Martin, J., & Sugarman, J. (1996). Bridging social constructionism and cognitive constructivism: A psychology of human possibility and constraint. *The Journal of Mind and Behaviour*, *17*(4), 291–320.

McClelland, D. (1961). *The achieving society*. Princeton, NJ: Van Nostrand.

McKenzie, B., Ugbah, S. D., & Smothers, N. (2007). 'Who is an entrepreneur?' Is it still the wrong question? *Academy of Entrepreneurship Journal*, *13*(1), 23–43.

Nightingale, D. J., & Cromby, J. (1999). *Social constructionist psychology: A critical analysis of theory and practice*. Buckingham: Open University Press.

Parker, I. (1998). *Social constructionism, discourse and realism*. London: Sage.

Pfeffer, J. (1993). Barriers to the advance of organization science: Paradigm development as a dependent variable. *Academy of Management Review*, *18*, 599–620.

Pittaway, L. (2005). Philosophies in entrepreneurship: A focus on economic theories. *International Journal of Entrepreneurial Behaviour and Research*, *11*(3), 201–221.

Pittaway, L., & Tunstall, R. (2016). Is there still a Heffalump in the room? In H. Landström, A. Parhankangas, A. Fayolle, & P. Riot (Eds.), *Challenging Entrepreneurship Research* (pp. 173–209). London and New York, NY: Routledge.

Sarason, Y., Dean, T., & Dillard, J. (2006). Entrepreneurship as the nexus of individual and opportunity: A structuration view. *Journal of Business Venturing*, *21*, 286–305.

Sarasvathy, S. D. (2001). Causation and effectuation: Toward a theoretical shift from economic inevitability to entrepreneurial contingency. *Academy of Management Review*, *26*(2), 243–263.

Sarasvathy, S. D. (2004). Constructing corridors to economic primitives: Entrepreneurial opportunities as demand-side artifacts. In J. Butler (Ed.), *Opportunity identification and entrepreneurial behavior* (pp. 291–321). Greenwich, CT: Information Age Publishing.

Sarasvathy, S. D., Dew, N., Velamuri, S. R., & Venkataraman, S. (2003). Three views of entrepreneurial opportunity. In Z. J. Acs & D. B. Audretsch (Eds.), *Handbook of entrepreneurship research: An interdisciplinary survey and introduction* (pp. 141–160). Dordrecht: Kluwer Law International.

Schutz, A. (1967). *The phenomenology of the social world*. Evanston, IL: Northwestern University Press.

Shackle, G. L. S. (1955). *Uncertainty in economics*. Cambridge: Cambridge University Press.

Shackle, G. L. S. (1979). *Imagination and the nature of choice*. Edinburgh, UK: Edinburgh University Press.

Shane, S. (2012). Reflections on the 2010 AMR decade award: Delivering on the promise of entrepreneurship as a field of research. *Academy of Management Review*, *37*, 10–20.

Shane, S., & Venkataraman, S. (2000). The promise of entrepreneurship as a field of research. *Academy of Management Review*, *25*(1), 217–226.

Short, J. C., Ketchen, D. J., Shook, C. L., & Ireland, R. D. (2010). The concept of 'opportunity' in entrepreneurship research: Past accomplishments and future challenges. *Journal of Management*, *36*(1), 40–65.

Stainton-Rogers, W., & Stainton-Rogers, R. (1999). That's all very well but what use is it? In D. J. Nightingale & J. Cromby (Eds.), *Social constructionist psychology: A critical analysis of theory and practice* (pp. 190–204). Buckingham: Open University Press.

Suddaby, R., Bruton, G. D., & Xi, S. X. (2015). Entrepreneurship through a qualitative lens: Insights on the construction and/or discovery of entrepreneurial opportunity. *Journal of Business Venturing*, *30*(1), 1–10.

Venkataraman, S., Sarasvathy, S. D., Dew, N., & Forster, W. R. (2012). Reflections on the 2010 AMR Decade Award: Whither the promise? Moving forward with entrepreneurship as a science of the artificial. *Academy of Management Review, 37*, 21–33.

Weick, K. E. (1969). *The social psychology of organizing*. Reading, MA: Addison-Wesley.

Weick, K. E. (1979). *The social psychology of organizing*. New York: McGraw-Hill.

Weick, K. E. (1995). *Sensemaking in organizations*. Thousand Oaks, CA: Sage Publications Inc.

West, G. P., & Meyer, G. D. (1997). Temporal dimensions of opportunistic change in technology-based ventures. *Entrepreneurship Theory and Practice, 22*(2), 31–52.

White, L. H. (1990 [1976]). Entrepreneurship, imagination and the question of equilibration. In S. Littlechild (Ed.), *Austrian economics* (Vol. III, pp. 87–105). Brookfield: Edward Elgar.

Wood, M. S., & McKinley, W. (2010). The production of entrepreneurial opportunity: A constructivist perspective. *Strategic Entrepreneurship Journal, 4*, 66–84.

Yu, T. F. (2001). Entrepreneurial alertness and discovery. *The Review of Austrian Economics, 14*(1), 47–63.

5 Serious realist philosophy and applied entrepreneurship

Lee Martin and Nick Wilson

Introduction

In 2005, Luke Pittaway undertook a review of 'philosophies in entrepreneurship', which, amongst other things, acknowledged that researchers in entrepreneurship had 'recently begun to recognise that ideology, or the political basis of ideas, meta-theory and other "taken for granted" assumptions (axioms) have an influence on knowledge construction' (Pittaway, 2005, p. 202). Drawing on Burrell and Morgan's (1979) distinction between subjective and objective, and interpretive and functionalist paradigms, he went on to i) emphasise the predominance of functionalist and objective approaches in economic approaches towards entrepreneurship; whilst ii) indicating that there was a 'tolerance for alternative views and approaches' (Pittaway, 2005, p. 215; see also Grant & Perren, 2002). Over a decade later, it seems that there has indeed been an increasing interest in 'alternative philosophical approaches', including a growth of interest in alternative realist approaches to entrepreneurship (see, for example, Mole & Mole, 2010; Sarason, Dean, & Dillard, 2006; Sarason, Dillard, & Dean 2010; Alvarez & Barney, 2013; Ramoglou, 2013; Alvarez, Barney, McBride, & Wuebker, 2014; Wilson & Martin, 2015; Martin & Wilson, 2016; Ramoglou & Tsang, 2016).

However, as Pittaway was at pains to emphasise, disagreement within and across paradigms exposes a considerable level of confusion as to just what 'realist' actually means in the context of entrepreneurship theory (see the debate between Alvarez et al. (2014) and Ramoglou (2013), in particular). The distinction between a positivist (functionalist, objectivist) realism, which assumes an empirical realist ontology, and a critical realist approach (which is the basis for our research), founded on a transcendental realist ontology, is central. Leaving aside such confusions for now, we suggest that a striking feature that unifies all the realist positions put forward so far is that they have yet to 'cross the chasm' and be taken up by entrepreneurs in practice. It is this focus on *applied* entrepreneurship theory that motivates the unfolding arguments of this chapter. In particular, we look at the case for 'serious'[1] realist philosophy, i.e., demonstrating theory/practice consistency, to help us be better prepared, or more 'ready' to pursue entrepreneurial opportunities, knowing more clearly what they are, what sorts of conditions are involved in their actualisation, and what sorts of projects they involve.

The human capacity for acting in the face of uncertainty, risk, complexity and ambiguity (Gibb, 2005; Knight, 1921; McKelvie, Haynie, & Gustavsson, 2011; Mises, 1949) is a necessary characteristic of entrepreneurial action. As Casson and Wadeson (2007) have pointed out, the hypothesising of the opportunity after the event is usually of little analytical interest for the entrepreneur. Rather, what the entrepreneur wants to know is just how ready they are to exploit a given entrepreneurial opportunity, which they believe to exist. This is not just a reflexive question of 'do I have what it takes?' but would include an assessment of whether the prevailing conditions that distinguish market, technological, demographic, political and other exogenous characteristics of the environment, are conducive to the opportunity's exploitation. Such questions of 'opportunity readiness' are of the upmost importance to entrepreneurs but have so far served as naive questions for research; making predictions of entrepreneurial action is contradictory to an ontology of uncertainty in the social world. It is against this backdrop that we suggest there is a role for serious realist philosophy to help meet the needs of entrepreneurs.

For example, in the field of applied psychology, the need for a complete explanation of a set of events is not as necessary as the ability to reduce uncertainty for practitioners making decisions. Personality theory can be used to reduce uncertainty (of future employee success) in recruitment decisions by between 5% and 20%. In this context, even a small reduction in the rate of error brings significant financial reward. So, whilst understanding the nature of opportunities is important, it is also important to ask whether philosophically informed applied entrepreneurship theory can offer help to entrepreneurs, without the standards required for 'complete explanations'. Likewise, identifying applied theoretical concepts that work in practice could play a role for wider theoretical development. If, through applying critical realist philosophy, it can be demonstrated that there are aspects of an opportunity that *can* be identified and known in advance, then this also holds the promise of enhancing practice.

Such applied theoretical development necessarily presupposes that the possibility of an opportunity resulting in entrepreneurship (i.e. an entrepreneurial opportunity) exists only in situations where certain conditions are met. To demonstrate that this is the case, we draw upon previous work within the field of human development theory (Wilson & Martin, 2015) and use critical realism to outline six conditions that can be used in applied settings to assess whether any entrepreneurial opportunity is likely to be realised. Through doing this, a re-focusing of attention on the processes within the 'entrepreneurial project' (a hitherto under-theorised concept), as the primary means by which an opportunity is exploited, is identified as a crucial focus for applied theory development.

Serious philosophy and applied entrepreneurship theory

Paradoxically, we cannot conceptualise entrepreneurship without holding some theory of what it is in the first place. This poses particular challenges for those interested in providing an explanatory account of what entrepreneurship is, how it is best understood, and how it is (or should be) practiced. There are inevitable consequences of entrepreneurship being discussed from a wide variety of different theoretical perspectives or vantage points (Lawson, 1997). Teachers, practitioners, policy-makers and investors all hold different 'theories' about entrepreneurship. Understanding is therefore necessarily related to personal or professional goals and objectives. There are, of course, a wide range of different views about exactly what entrepreneurship is, and this raises some awkward issues. For some, entrepreneurship is associated with the creation of new organisations (Gartner, 1985, 1988, 2001; Kats & Gartner, 1988); others maintain that entrepreneurship can best be understood in terms of opportunity identification and exploitation (Shane & Venkataraman, 2000; Shane, 2003; Eckhardt & Shane, 2003; Klein, 2008). For others still, entrepreneurship is about risk-taking (Knight, 1921), market processes (Kirzner, 1973), or market creation (Schoonhoven & Romanelli, 2001). These viewpoints bring the question of entrepreneurship's existence centre stage but with serious practical consequences. For unless we ask this question with the intention of finding an answer that identifies what form this 'existence' takes, applied theory is likely to remain trapped by the relativism that characterises much of the debate in the field.

Critical realist scholars have emphasised the importance of conceptualising the object of study (Sayer, 1992; Danermark, Ekström, Jakobsen, & Karlsson, 2002). Indeed, Danermark et al. state that 'conceptualisation stands out as the most central social scientific activity' (p. 41). As theorists, we must offer assistance to decisions over 'the spontaneous appearance of ordered social and organizational structures and processes from a seemingly random assortment of pre-existing conditions that are governed by a set of rules and principles' (Phan, 2004, p. 618). For a new product or service to be successfully introduced, we must ask what are the necessary activities and behaviours of specific individuals, under certain external conditions and, depending on where one sits on the objective-subjective continuum between Kirznerian and Schumpeterian stances, how can an entrepreneur 'identify', 'discover', 'create', 'enact', 'effectuate' and 'realise' entrepreneurial opportunities?

Thus far, scholarly interest in entrepreneurial opportunities has polarised into a discussion of entrepreneurial individuals on the one hand, and opportunities on the other (see Shane, 2003). By focusing on applied entrepreneurship we can re-focus attention on the conditions through which an opportunity is exploited. This means recognising opportunities are for something, as well as someone. Consider an individual who has the 'opportunity' to win a gold medal at the Olympics. The opportunity would be for the 'gold medal', and for this particular individual, the opportunity would be realised only if certain conditions were met. For example, the athlete's times for a particular event were at a level where they can reasonably expect to compete at the games. In practice, a coach can make a relatively simple assessment of whether this opportunity exists for a particular athlete by assessing their current performance, their rate of training improvement and the time remaining before the games begin. If enabling conditions are met, it can be claimed there is still an opportunity for this particular athlete. This does not mean the opportunity has been exploited. The training and event still need to happen but an erstwhile assessment of the opportunity could be made before the athlete began their training programme through analysing the conditions surrounding the opportunity.

Whether an individual will in fact go on to win a gold medal, regardless of the existence of the opportunity, will depend upon a host of further conditions – there is no deterministic outcome. Even when the individual athlete has met all the conditions that one might think of as necessary to win the race (e.g. being the fastest runner on paper, drawn to run in their preferred lane, mentally and physically in peak form etc.), there is still no guarantee that the opportunity will be realised, but, and importantly for entrepreneurial practice, the assessment of conditions can reduce the uncertainty and enable the athlete to fail early, should performance not reach expected standards. In developing applied theory for entrepreneurship, the starting conditions, for a similar pre-start opportunity assessment, also need to be identified for practicing entrepreneurs (even if this means ignoring debates over what an opportunity might be).

This is consistent with an activity-based model of economics, which distinguishes between the set of possible activities and, within this, a subset of feasible activities. However, whereas activity-based models determine what is feasible primarily in relation to the state of technology at the time (see Casson & Wadeson, 2007, p. 289; Koopmans, 1951), feasibility in the context of entrepreneurship can be determined by a broader set of conditions. These conditions are both exogenous (i.e. not dependent on any particular individual for their existence), and endogenous (i.e. dependent upon the characteristics and/or actions of the individuals involved). Whilst our starting point will embrace the widest set of 'possible' opportunities, we can make an important distinction between conditions for all types of opportunities and those that hold as conditions necessary for an entrepreneurial outcome. The decision to exploit an entrepreneurial opportunity can be informed through recourse to a similar logic to the athlete and their coach and through asking: What is the minimum set of conditions I need to assess in order to decide whether to act on an entrepreneurial project? Identifying these starting conditions can be used to begin development of applied entrepreneurship theory.

The entrepreneurial project

Serious realist philosophy can help identify the nature of entrepreneurial enterprise, or, in Shane's (2003) terms, the 'individual-opportunity nexus' (see Mole & Mole, 2010 in debate with Sarason et al., 2006, 2010), through utilising realist conceptual abstraction. In this case, critical realist social theory and Archer's (2003) ideas on agential projects have something distinctive to say about the mediating role of human projects in both social reproduction and transformation of social structures. Archer identified three fundamental conditions for structural and cultural factors to exercise their powers of constraint and enablement (i.e. for these factors to actually impinge upon those involved). The first of these conditions is that there must be a 'project' of some kind. Archer (2003, p. 6) outlines the agential project as 'an end that is desired, however tentatively or nebulously, and also some notion, however imprecise, of the course of action through which to accomplish it.' As a first run past, therefore, we might conceptualise the *entrepreneurial project* as comprising an agential project understood within the specific domain of entrepreneurship.

Second, there must be a relationship (congruent or incongruent) between the prevailing cultural and structural conditions and the project. In other words, 'whether or not constraints and enablements are exercised as causal powers is contingent upon agency embracing the kinds of projects upon which they can impact' (Archer, 2003, p. 7). Understanding what sort of project might be impacted by market conditions, demographic changes, technological breakthroughs, and so on is, of course, a major focus of interest for the entrepreneurship field as much as for entrepreneurs themselves. Third, there must be reflexive choice on behalf of those individuals involved. As Archer notes (2003, p. 7) 'the influences of constraints and enablements will only be tendential because of human reflexive abilities to withstand them and strategically to circumvent them'. Thus, even where market conditions, demographic changes, technological breakthroughs etc. appear not to offer 'opportunities', we still encounter entrepreneurial projects that seem to defy the odds.

The agential project (which may build on the idea of an individual or an entrepreneurial team)[2] is therefore constantly being reproduced and/or transformed through the actions of those involved. In its early stages it may well comprise an end (or ends) that remain loosely articulated, as tacit rather than explicit knowledge (Nonaka & Takeuchi, 1995). This is consistent with the logic of effectuation, which draws attention to this nature of unfolding and 'unspecified ends' (see Sarasvathy, 2001). As the project develops, it can take on an explicit form, it is codified (e.g. in the form of a business plan or strategy), and it can assume 'a life of its own.' Archer's focus on the 'end that is desired' embraces a continuum from a fuzzy perception of unclear outcomes, including those more associated with feelings and stances towards risk-taking (e.g. 'taking a leap into the dark'), to clear plans for new products and services, new ventures and profitable opportunities. The aspiring young athlete's dream of Olympic gold constitutes the formation of an agential project. As we have seen, however, there is an important distinction between keeping the dream alive and undertaking the sort of project where realising this opportunity becomes possible.

Agential projects in general have some key features, related to structural and cultural conditions (especially those relevant to entrepreneurship). In seeking to better understand the entrepreneurial project, as opposed to projects in general, we can also draw on the project management literature, which since the mid 1990s has developed links with concepts from related disciplinary interests including strategic management, transaction cost economics and innovation theories (Frederiksen & Davies, 2008, p. 489). There are many different definitions of the 'project' (see Artto & Wikstrom, 2005; Engwall, 1998) but some generally agreed features include: a focus on non-routine, complex tasks; the pursuit of pre-defined goals within a precise budget (Lundin & Soderholm, 1995); the establishment of temporary organisational forms; and encounters with both internal (operational) and external (environmental) uncertainty (Frederiksen & Davies, 2008, p. 492; Kreiner, 1995).

Within the field of entrepreneurship studies, interest in projects has been largely confined to the study of corporate entrepreneurship (see Kuratko, Ireland, Covin, & Hornsby, 2005; Shepherd & Kuratko, 2009), where firms use projects to 'identify and test opportunities' (Frederiksen & Davies, 2008, p. 492). The organisational form of the project is considered optimal for exploring any direction that moves away from a firm's current technology and market (Von Hippel, 1977, p. 164). Entrepreneurial (Frederiksen & Davies, 2008) projects are therefore generally regarded as things that firms do, rather than being considered as integral to an understanding of the actions of entrepreneurs themselves. Casson and Wadeson's (2007) work on the economic theory of the entrepreneur is a notable exception to this. They treat the opportunity as a 'potentially profitable but hitherto unexploited project' and state that an opportunity is 'essentially a project that would prove beneficial, if it were exploited' (Casson & Wadeson, 2007, p. 285). Their approach categorises two types of mistake that the entrepreneur can make in pursuing a project, namely 'missing a profitable opportunity and exploiting an unprofitable opportunity' (Casson & Wadeson, 2007, p. 287). The authors define 'good' projects as those that give rise to 'true opportunities' (i.e. profitable projects), whilst 'bad' projects are those that give rise to 'false opportunities' (i.e. unprofitable projects).

An alternative position would maintain that *all* entrepreneurial opportunities (by definition) have the potential to produce profits – this is, in part, what such opportunities are for, after all. The 'false opportunity' would therefore be a non-opportunity in the context of entrepreneurship (see Ramoglou & Tsang, 2016) for an alternative conception of the 'non-opportunity'). But this begs the question for applied theory, what must be in place for an entrepreneur to consider whether an entrepreneurial opportunity is true or false and likewise, worth exploiting? Answering this question, given current conflicting explanations of entrepreneurial opportunities, is not straightforward but it is in such conflicting theoretical domains that, ironically, philosophy (as one of the most abstract humanities disciplines) can have direct benefits for applied theory. Through the use of philosophical abstraction, i.e. dialectical reasoning from generally agreed upon premises, the conditions necessary for exploitation can be identified for use in applied theory. Once identified, this can form the basis of an applied assessment tool for any particular opportunity. Achieving this requires a process of abstraction (from current theory) to make explicit the premises that all agree are involved in opportunity development (over and above its potential to produce profits). The end result should be the conditions all theorists agree upon as necessary for an entrepreneurial project to be possible. In other words, the basis for an applied theory of opportunity readiness.

Applied opportunity evaluation

Despite the different vantage points taken by theorists, there is considerable overlap in how theory treats the implicit conditions necessary for the realisation of an entrepreneurial opportunity (see Eckhardt & Shane, 2003; Shane & Venkataraman,

2000; Venkataraman, 1997). We suggest, along similar lines to Davidsson (2003), that differences in perspective largely betray areas of emphasis and interest, rather than constituting widely different ontological beliefs about entrepreneurship per se. Those emphasising *exogenous* conditions have highlighted market conditions, resource re-combination, innovation and value creation and appropriation, amongst others.[3] Those emphasising the *endogenous* conditions have highlighted features associated with the individual entrepreneur as being important, including their prior knowledge, creativity, risk-taking, motivation and propensity for action. Despite the general agreement as to what entrepreneurship entails, theory has not yet gone as far as to suggest that entrepreneurial opportunities require *specific* conditions to be in place in order to exist. However, doing so can provide the basis from which evaluations of opportunities, before they are acted upon, can be made.

Given the diversity of approaches, theoretical positions and empirical contexts, discussion of anything in terms of just a handful of conditions is prone to the accusation of being reductionist; this is not our intention here. There is also a need to avoid conflationary theorising – whether reducing entrepreneurship to discussion of the individual alone, or reifying the opportunity in some way. However, in common with scientific enquiry within applied settings, there is value in using philosophical abstraction (see Lawson, 1997) in order to be able to put forward, as a first step, some generalisable and universal features of the object of study. In this vein and following previous work exploring human flourishing within the context of entrepreneurship (Wilson & Martin, 2015), we propose that it *is* possible to identify a set of conditions that could prove useful when entrepreneurs evaluate potential entrepreneurial opportunities and we draw on that human development approach to explore those conditions here.

Though different schools of thought have chosen to focus on distinctive ends (e.g. Schumpeter (1934) on resource recombination and innovation; Kirzner (1973) on market process and opportunity alertness; Gartner (1988) on new venture/organisation creation), there is a broad consensus that entrepreneurship involves the production of innovative new products, services and, in some cases, processes (the development of new organisations *per se*, being a contingent outcome). *Innovation* is therefore a complex systemic-level emergent property and post-hoc outcome of realising the entrepreneurial opportunity. The question for entrepreneurs is what conditions need to be in place to make such innovation possible. To the extent that entrepreneurship gives rise to innovation outcomes, then successful entrepreneurship requires the *recombination of resources* (see Foss & Ishikawa, 2006; Holmquist, 2003; Lachmann, 1956; Nelson & Winter, 1982; Schumpeter, 1934; Wilson & Martin, 2015). Success also requires value production (being able to produce and appropriate more value than was expended in the course of the new product or service's production).[4] Finally, success also requires the ability to *exchange goods or services* in a market (Wilson & Martin, 2015).

Recombining resources, exchanging goods and appropriating value are universally agreed features of entrepreneurial behaviour and are directly associated with the existence of an opportunity. This gives applied theory three general conditions that can be assessed at the outset of an entrepreneurial project, influencing decisions to proceed. Either an entrepreneur can continue to work towards developing the necessary conditions to begin exploiting the opportunity (networking for access to resources, attempting to find cheaper resources, developing exchange networks and partnerships), or they might choose to seek another opportunity. In entrepreneurship, a fantastic idea for a potentially novel product is not an opportunity unless there is also the possibility for accessing or combining the required resources, exchanging the product (on the market) and making a profit. A key challenge is to establish the link between these abstract conditions and the possibility they can be met (or overcome – for example in the case of seeking to trade in a society with a restricted market structure). Attention can also be cast on the many structural and cultural conditions which enable and constrain the production of innovation outcomes, including issues such as path dependency, technological trajectory, national systems of innovation, lock-in and so forth (see Tidd & Bessant, 2009 for overview).

For the social realist, social phenomena are explained in terms of the interrelationship between existing social structures and the mediating role of human agency. As Archer (2003) emphasises, individuals are reflexive human beings who act strategically (i.e. make decisions to act or not to act based on their prior knowledge, intentions, creativity, and so forth). Therefore, applied entrepreneurship theory also needs to set out evaluative conditions that are *endogenous* to the entrepreneur (i.e. relating to the particular individuals involved). Wilson and Martin (2015) identified three such conditions that can also prove useful to applied theories of entrepreneurship. Novel and useful ideas are deemed the 'lifeblood of entrepreneurship' (Ward, 2004, p. 174) and *creativity* has been described as the 'soul of entrepreneurship' (Morris & Kuratko, 2002, p. 104) because it is required to spot the patterns and trends that define the opportunity. According to Sternberg and Lubart (1999), entrepreneurship is a form of creativity and can be labelled as business or entrepreneurial creativity because often new businesses are original and useful (Lee, Florida, & Acs, 2004; see also Stokes & Wilson, 2010). Alvarez and Barney (2007), also argue that opportunities are neither discovered nor created but 'imagined'. Subsequently, to the extent that entrepreneurship gives rise to innovation outcomes of some kind, this ability to be creative is a ubiquitous requirement of entrepreneurship and therefore an important evaluation criteria for potential entrepreneurs.

A second condition relates to what Archer (2003) identifies as human *reflexivity*. This is regarded as an important condition for the development of projects per se and so an assessment of individual reflexivity will also be important for decisions to pursue an entrepreneurial project. The ability to take informed strategic choices, make decisions and apply judgment based on access to information is a feature of the entrepreneurship field that has received much attention (see Busenits, 1999; Casson, 1982; Knight, 1921; Mises, 1949; Tang, Kacmar, & Busenits, 2012; Wadeson, 2006). Prior knowledge and recognising differential and asymmetric access to information is also a key condition worthy of assessing prior to subsequent entrepreneurial activity (Corbett, 2007; Kirzner, 1973; Schumpeter, 1934; Ucbasaran, Westhead, & Wright, 2009; Vaghely & Julien, 2010). Indeed, a key assessment of opportunity readiness related to reflexivity might include whether or not the entrepreneurial team have the requisite power and legitimacy (see Stinchcombe, 1965 on the 'liability of newness') to take appropriate decisions within a given context.

A third condition Wilson and Martin (2015) identified is *performativity*. As McMullen and Shepherd observe 'Entrepreneurship requires action' (2006, p. 132), hence the focus in entrepreneurship education on 'learning by doing.' A key issue of opportunity readiness relating to this condition is whether or not the individuals concerned have the necessary ability to practice within the context they work. Medical science teaches us there is a difference between understanding what needs to be done (in surgery, for example) and having the performative skills to do so. This condition requires an assessment of the practical skills, behaviours and attributes of those involved within the particular context in question, as well as the countervailing conditions that prevent these human capacities from being realised.

Opportunity readiness and the entrepreneurial project

Having identified conditions that can be used to explore the readiness of any particular opportunity for exploitation (albeit, we acknowledge, at a relatively high level of abstraction), we can now explore what this means for understanding the entrepreneurial project in practice. Prior to (and during), any entrepreneurial project being undertaken, the entrepreneur (or any other stakeholder with access to relevant knowledge), can make an assessment over whether the six conditions outlined are fulfilled. To explain why this is significant, we can refer to the relationship between the entrepreneurial project and the entrepreneurial opportunity, as graphically presented in Figure 5.1. This suggests that entrepreneurial

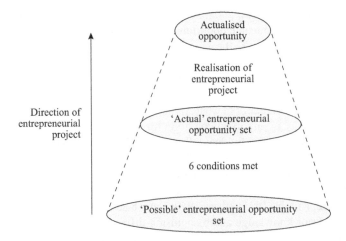

Figure 5.1 The relationship between entrepreneurial project and entrepreneurial opportunity

opportunities that have these conditions met are a sub-set of a wider (and unknowable) set of 'possible' opportunities taken up by individuals. In cases where the six conditions outlined have been met, the decision to proceed with developing an opportunity can be made, as the chances of it being realised would be increased. The aim of the entrepreneurial project is thus to realise *these* opportunities.

Returning to the athlete whose 'desired end' is Olympic gold, we can distinguish between their 'possible' agential project, which involves the dream, belief, and some level of active training, and the 'actual' project to realise the opportunity. As we have seen, this is not just about bringing the goal of wining at the Olympics to a conscious level, but also depends on certain conditions being met (such as being entered for the games). In the context of entrepreneurship, Dimov has referred to this whole process of 'shaping, discussion, and interpretation' as 'opportunity development' (Dimov, 2007, p. 714; see also Ramoglou & Tsang, 2016 on the 'propensity' mode of existence of entrepreneurial opportunities). Applied entrepreneurship theory can build on these ideas to suggest that the opportunity development process will involve decision making that progresses from possible – to actual – to realised opportunities.[5] This means applied theory would also need to identify whether there are in fact distinctive and analytically separable stages of entrepreneurial practice (beginning with investigative or exploratory and moving through to confirmatory and developmental activities). In addition, given the overall similarities here with stage-models of the creative process, and with creative problem solving (CPS) models in particular (see Puccio, Murdock, & Mance, 2007), development of applied theory may find such stage based models of entrepreneurship useful for applied settings.

Applied theory tends to offer the practitioner a set of actions, drawn from theory, that should increase the chances of successful outcomes. In this case, the assessment of antecedent conditions might involve asking questions of the type 'am I in a position to be able to . . . (e.g. recombine resources; proceed with market exchange; appropriate value)'? or 'do I (or my team) have the necessary . . . (e.g. creativity; reflexivity; intentionality; performativity) to develop this entrepreneurial project successfully?' A lack of a coherent body of applied entrepreneurship theory is perhaps a surprising absence within entrepreneurship theory, as is the current lack of empirical work exploring the most beneficial diagnostic approaches to opportunity development.

Taking the possibility of recombining resources as an example, there is broad scope for assessing all sorts of aspects related to accessing and managing resources (information, human, social and financial, equipment, social networks etc.). The 'serious' practical contribution applied entrepreneurship theory can make should enable, in some way, a reduction in the complexity facing the would-be entrepreneur. In practice, nascent and experienced entrepreneurs often begin what they believe to be an entrepreneurial endeavour based on an idea about a possible opportunity (i.e. in the widest pool of opportunities in Figure 5.1). Applied theory should be able to guide them, in the course of enacting the endeavour, to make decisions as to whether this is more or less likely to be a mistaken activity. In Casson and Wadeson's terms, do they have a 'bad' entrepreneurial project? Those involved in developing entrepreneurial projects can be encouraged to focus on a limited set of key issues that will help them evaluate action, or stop early in the case where the conditions for such an opportunity do not (or cannot) exist.

Whilst entrepreneurial projects can start out as no more than hunches, there is value for theorists and philosophers to change focus from developing and perfecting pure theory, to assisting in the development of applied theory. The rigorous assessment of the conditions involved in embarking on an entrepreneurial project is not only useful to entrepreneurs but can help guide theory development through identifying theory/practice inconsistencies. What we have offered here is a very modest first step towards such an applied theory of opportunity readiness, achieved through philosophical abstraction. Over and above an assessment of these generalised conditions for the realisation of an entrepreneurial opportunity, there would need to be a more detailed domain-level assessment that can provide support for any specific entrepreneurial project undertaken. In principle, this would involve analysis of how each of the conditions outlined might be further understood and elaborated upon within the context of particular industry, national and regional, political and economic, technological and socio-cultural contexts. In turn, this would also provide new learning and understanding that could inform theory, benefitting entrepreneurs more generally.

Summary and conclusions

'Serious' realist philosophy has the potential to inform applied entrepreneurship. In this chapter we have introduced an argument that upholds this assertion, with particular regard to the philosophy of critical realism. Thus far, critical realism (and other forms of realist theory) has tended to be discussed somewhat removed from the pragmatic interests of 'real' entrepreneurs. But this does not have to be so. Indeed, our argument is that critical realism is a serious philosophical approach that can come to the aid of the entrepreneur, in this case, through providing the background structure for informed decisions concerning developing entrepreneurial projects and the implications for the type of entrepreneurial project required to bring about entrepreneurship. We argue, an actual entrepreneurial opportunity is only worth pursuing in a situation where there is the possibility of the following conditions being in place: the possibility of (market) exchange, recombining resources, appropriating value; developing creative potential, appropriate reflexivity and sufficient performative skills. Whilst acknowledging these conditions remain at a relatively high level of abstraction, they nonetheless offer a means of facing the complexity that inevitably faces the entrepreneur, through providing the basis for an assessment of opportunity readiness.

In the course of the chapter, we have also introduced the entrepreneurial project as the 'nexus' where entrepreneurial opportunities are realised. Though the relevance of entrepreneurial projects has been implicit in much of the literature, especially that focusing on opportunity development (Dimov, 2007) and entrepreneurial action (McMullen & Shepherd, 2006), explicitly recognising the project's role as the nexus between opportunities in potential (or in 'propensity' – see Ramoglou & Tsang,

2016) and those that are fully exploited means project management techniques can begin to inform applied entrepreneurship theory. Whilst applied theory cannot be epistemologically certain, it is possible to say something meaningful and with foresight about decisions concerning the development of entrepreneurial opportunities. Developing such an *ex ante* opportunity readiness assessment tool, to promote better entrepreneurial project outcomes, is therefore an important goal. Likewise, such a tool can simultaneously inform philosophical development. Serious philosophy has to pass the theory-practice test, if our practice is inconsistent with theory, then identifying such contradictions directly informs theoretical development.

In drawing on realist philosophy to expose the promise of opportunity readiness, we hope to encourage future progress towards two related outcomes, each of which will require further research. First, a greater awareness and understanding of the entrepreneurial opportunity as the potential for entrepreneurship, requiring (market) exchange, recombination of resources, value appropriation, creativity, reflexivity and performativity. This heralds a timely re-appraisal of the somewhat paradoxical situation whereby entrepreneurial opportunities are regarded as central to entrepreneurship and yet are easily side-stepped and viewed as being of little more than metaphoric or heuristic value. The polarisation of arguments about the objectivist versus subjectivist nature of the entrepreneurial opportunity might also represent less of a hurdle for applied theory development.

Second, we have demonstrated the potential for serious realist philosophy in the domain of entrepreneurship; in this case, putting understanding of opportunity readiness to applied use. This brings applied entrepreneurship theory in line with other social sciences, whereby practical relevance determines the value of applied theory. Whilst the purpose of both philosophy and science should always be an earnest attempt at arriving at sustainable explanations of the (social) world, this need not be done at the expense of applied theoretical development. Keeping this firmly in mind, and recalling critical realism's commitment to emancipatory concerns, we conclude by highlighting that if the conditions necessary for an opportunity to be exploited can be identified, it becomes possible to assess who does *not* have access to the benefits of entrepreneurship, as well as those that do. Identifying who lacks opportunity ought to be something we get serious about, and critical realist philosophy can guide us in just this respect.

Notes

1 'Seriousness is a term of art deriving from the German idealist philosopher G.W.F. Hegel. It involves the idea of the unity of theory and practice, of being able to walk one's talk, of not saying one thing and doing something completely different' (Bhaskar, 2016, p. 2).
2 All ideas are cognitive and therefore have their origins in individuals. However, we also want to recognise the importance of the iterative and social nature of idea generation (creativity) such that it is not often clear (including to those involved), whose idea is actually being taken forward.
3 Some of these features are written into the definition of the opportunity itself. Most existing definitions of opportunities (reflecting their heritage in economic theories), contain the final outcome of their actualisation – understood in terms of profitability, innovation, the creation of future goods and services etc.

4 This conceptualisation of 'value' does not denote solely the economic value created by the for-profit business. Entrepreneurship may be associated with other forms of value e.g. political, educational, cultural, aesthetic, providing this is within the context of (market) exchange.

5 Dimov's (2007, p. 719) 'potential', 'nascent', and 'emerged' entrepreneurs can usefully be mapped directly on to this progression.

References

Alvarez, S. A., & Barney, J. B. (2007). Discovery and creation: Alternative theories of entrepreneurial action. *Strategic Entrepreneurship Journal, 1*(1–2), 33–48.

Alvarez, S. A., & Barney, J. B. (2013). Epistemology, opportunities, and entrepreneurship: Comments on Venkataraman et al. (2012) and Shane (2012). *Academy of Management Review, 38*, 154–157.

Alvarez, S., Barney, J. B., McBride, R., & Wuebker, R. (2014, April). Realism in the study of entrepreneurship. *Academy of Management Review, 39*(2), 227–231.

Archer, M. S. (2003). *Structure, agency and the internal conversation.* Cambridge: Cambridge University Press.

Artto, K. A., & Wikstrom, K. (2005). What is project business? *International Journal of Project Management, 23*(5), 343–353.

Bhaskar, R. (2016). *Enlightened common sense: The philosophy of critical realism.* Abingdon: Routledge.

Burrell, G., & Morgan, G. (1979). *Sociological paradigms and organizational analysis.* London: Heinemann.

Busenits, L. W. (1999). *Entrepreneurial behaviour.* Glenview, IL: Scott, Foresman & Co.

Casson, M. (1982). *The entrepreneur: An economic theory.* London: Martin Robertson.

Casson, M., & Wadeson, N. (2007). The discovery of opportunities: Extending the economic theory of the entrepreneur. *Small Business Economics, 28*, 285–300.

Corbett, A. C. (2007). Learning asymmetries and the discovery of entrepreneurial opportunities. *Journal of Business Venturing, 22*, 97–118.

Danermark, B., Ekström, M., Jakobsen, L., & Karlsson, J. (2002). *Explaining society: Critical realism in the social sciences.* London: Routledge.

Davidsson, P. (2003). The domain of entrepreneurship research: Some suggestions. In J. Kats & S. Shepherd (Eds.), *Advances in entrepreneurship, firm emergence and growth* (pp. 15–372). Oxford: Elsevier/JAI Press, Chapter 6.

Dimov, D. (2007, September). Beyond the single-person, single insight attribution in understanding entrepreneurial opportunities. *Entrepreneurship Theory and Practice, 31*(5), 713–731.

Eckhardt, J. T., & Shane, S. A. (2003). Opportunities and entrepreneurship. *Journal of Management, 29*(3), 333–349.

Engwall, M. (1998). The ambiguous project concept(s). In R. A. Lundin & C. Midler (Eds.), *Projects as arenas for renewal and learning processes* (pp. 5–36). Boston, MA: Kluwer Academic Publishers.

Foss, N. J., & Ishikawa, I. (2006, April). Towards a dynamic resource-based view: Insights from Austrian capital and entrepreneurship theory. *Centre for Strategic Management and Globalisation*, Working Paper 6.

Frederiksen, L., & Davies, A. (2008). Vanguards and ventures: Projects as vehicles for corporate entrepreneurship. *International Journal of Project Management, 26*, 487–496.

Gartner, W. B. (1985). A framework for describing and classifying the phenomenon of new venture creation. *Academy of Management Review, 10*(4), 696–706.

Gartner, W. B. (1988). 'Who is an entrepreneur' is the wrong question. *American Small Business Journal* (Spring), *12*(4), 11–31.

Gartner, W. B. (2001). Is there an elephant in entrepreneurship? Blind assumptions in theory development. *Entrepreneurship Theory and Practice, 25*(Summer), 27–39.

Grant, P., & Perren, L. (2002). Small business and entrepreneurial research: Meta-theories, paradigms and prejudices. *International Small Business Journal, 20*(2), 185–211.

Holmquist, C. (2003). Is the medium really the message? Moving perspective from the entrepreneurial actor to the entrepreneurial action. In C. Steyaert & D. Hjorth (Eds.), *New movements in entrepreneurship*. Cheltenham: Edward Elgar, Chapter 5, 73–85.

Kats, J., & Gartner, W. B. (1988). Properties of emerging organisations. *Academy of Management Review, 13*(3), 429–441.

Kirzner, I. (1973). *Competition and entrepreneurship*. Chicago: University of Chicago Press.

Klein, P. G. (2008). Opportunity discovery, entrepreneurial action, and economic organisation. *Strategic Entrepreneurship Journal, 2*, 175–190.

Knight, F. (1921). *Risk, uncertainty and profit*. Boston: Houghton Mifflin.

Koopmans, T. C. (1951). *Activity analysis of production and allocation*. New York: Wiley.

Kreiner, K. (1995). In search of relevance: Project management in drifting environments. *Scandinavian Journal of Management, 11*(4), 335–346.

Kuratko, D. F., Ireland, R. D., Covin, J. G., & Hornsby, J. S. (2005). A model of middle-level managers' entrepreneurial behavior. *Entrepreneurship Theory and Practice, 29*(6), 699–716.

Lachmann, L. M. (1956). *Capital and its structure*. 1977 re-issue. Kansas City: Sheed Andrews and McNeel.

Lawson, T. (1997). *Economics and reality*. London: Routledge.

Lee, S. Y., Florida, R., & Acs, S. J. (2004). Creativity and entrepreneurship: A regional analysis of new firm formation. *Regional Studies, 38*(8), 879–891.

Lundin, R., & Soderholm, A. (1995). A theory of the temporary organisation. *Scandinavian Journal of Management, 11*(4), 437–455.

Martin, L., & Wilson, N. (2016). Opportunity, discovery and creativity: A critical realist perspective. *International Small Business Journal, 34*(3), 261–275.

McKelvie, A., Haynie, J. M., & Gustavsson, V. (2011). Unpacking the uncertainty construct: Implications for entrepreneurial action. *Journal of Business Venturing, 26*(3), 273–292.

McMullen, J. S., & Shepherd, D. A. (2006). Entrepreneurial action and the role of uncertainty in the theory of the entrepreneur. *Academy of Management Review, 31*(1), 132–152.

Mises, L. V. (1949). *Human action: A treatise on economics* (4th revised ed.). San Francisco: Fox & Wikes.

Mole, K. F., & Mole, M. (2010). Entrepreneurship as the structuration of individual and opportunity: A response using a critical realist perspective. Comment on Sarason, Dean and Dillard. *Journal of Business Venturing, 25*, 230–237.

Morris, M. H., & Kuratko, D. F. (2002). *Corporate entrepreneurship*. Mason, OH: South Western College Publishers.

Nelson, R., & Winter, S. (1982). *An evolutionary theory of economic change*. Cambridge, MA: The Belknap Press.

Nonaka, I., & Takeuchi, H. (1995). *The knowledge-creating company: How Japanese companies create the dynamics of innovation*. USA, New York: Oxford University Press.

Phan, P. H. (2004). Entrepreneurship theory: Possibilities and future directions. *Journal of Business Venturing, 19*, 617–620.

Pittaway, L. (2005). Philosophies in entrepreneurship: A focus on economic theories. *International Journal of Entrepreneurial Behavior & Research, 11*(3), 201–221.

Puccio, G. J., Murdock, M. C., & Mance, M. (2007). *Creative leadership: Skills that drive change*. Thousand Oaks, CA: Sage Publications Inc.

Ramoglou, S. (2013). On the misuse of realism in the study of entrepreneurship. *Academy of Management Review, 38*, 463–465.

Ramoglou, S., & Tsang, E. W. K. (2016). A realist perspective of entrepreneurship: Opportunities as propensities. *Academy of Management Review, 41*(3), 410–434.

Sarason, Y., Dean, T., & Dillard, J. F. (2006). Entrepreneurship as the nexus of individual and opportunity: A structuration view. *Journal of Business Venturing, 21*, 286–305.

Sarason, Y., Dillard, J. F., & Dean, T. (2010). How can we know the dancer from the dance? Reply to 'Entrepreneurship as the structuration of individual and opportunity: A response using a critical realist perspective'. *Journal of Business Venturing, 25*, 238–243.

Sarasvathy, S. D. (2001). Causation and effectuation: Toward a theoretical shift from economic inevitability to entrepreneurial contingency. *Academy of Management Review, 26*(2), 243–263.

Sayer, A. (1992). *Method in social science: A realist approach*. London: Routledge.

Schoonhoven, C. B., & Romanelli, E. (Eds.). (2001). *The entrepreneurship dynamic*. Stanford: Stanford University Press.

Schumpeter, J. A. (1934). *The theory of economic development: An inquiry into profits, capital, credit, interest and the business cycle*. Translated by R. Opie. Cambridge, MA: Harvard University Press.

Shane, S. (2003). *A general theory of entrepreneurship: The individual-opportunity nexus*. Cheltenham: Edward Elgar.

Shane, S., & Venkataraman, S. (2000). The promise of entrepreneurship as a field of research. *Academy of Management Review, 25*(1), 217–226.

Shepherd, D. A., & Kuratko, D. F. (2009). The death of an innovative project: How grief recovery enhances learning. *Business Horizons, 52*, 451–458.

Sternberg, R. J., & Lubart, T. I. (1999 reprinted 2007). The concept of creativity: Prospects and paradigms. In R. J. Sternberg (Ed.), *Handbook of creativity* (pp. 3–15). Cambridge: Cambridge University Press, Chapter 1.

Stinchcombe, A. L. (1965). Social structure and organisations. In J. G. March (Ed.), *Handbook of organisations* (pp. 142–193). Chicago: Rand McNally.

Stokes, D., & Wilson, N. (2010). *Small business management & entrepreneurship*. Andover: Cengage.

Tang, J., Kacmar, K. M., & Busenits, L. (2012). Entrepreneurial alertness in the pursuit of new opportunities. *Journal of Business Venturing, 27*(1), 77–94.

Tidd, J., & Bessant, J. (2009). *Managing innovation: Integrating technological, market and organisational change* (4th ed.). London: Wiley.

Ucbasaran, D., Westhead, P., & Wright, M. (2009). The extent and nature of opportunity identification by experienced entrepreneurs. *Journal of Business Venturing, 24*, 99–115.

Vaghely, I. P., & Julien, P. (2010). Are opportunities recognised or constructed? An information perspective on entrepreneurial opportunity identification. *Journal of Business Venturing, 25*(1), 73–86.

Venkataraman, S. (1997). The distinctive domain of entrepreneurship research: An editor's perspective. In J. Kats & R. Brockhaus (Eds.), *Advances in entrepreneurship, firm emergence, and growth* (pp. 119–138). Greenwich, CT: JAI Press.

Von Hippel, E. (1977). Successful and failing internal corporate ventures: An empirical analysis. *Industrial Marketing Management, 6*(3), 163–174.

Wadeson, N. S. (2006). Cognitive aspects of entrepreneurship: Decision-making and attitudes to risk. In M. Casson, B. Yeung, A. Basu, & N. Wadeson (Eds.), *The Oxford handbook of entrepreneurship* (pp. 91–114). Oxford: Oxford University Press.

Ward, T. B. (2004). Cognition, creativity, and entrepreneurship. *Journal of Business Venturing, 19*, 173–188.

Wilson, N., & Martin, L. (2015). Entrepreneurial opportunities for all? Entrepreneurial capability and the capabilities approach. *The International Journal of Entrepreneurship and Innovation, 16*(3), 159–170.

6 Critical realism as a supporting philosophy for entrepreneurship and small business studies

John Kitching

Introduction

Philosophy of science issues are under-appreciated in entrepreneurship and small business (ESB) research (Kenworthy & McMullen, 2014). Occasional calls are made for researchers to provide a stronger philosophical footing for studies but few heed them (Grant & Perren, 2002). The inference might easily be drawn that philosophical standpoints are arbitrary or of little consequence in ESB studies. Yet ESB researchers – like all other social investigators – necessarily make assumptions about the nature of the world they study (ontology) and how it can be known (epistemology) (Bhaskar, 1979; Fleetwood, 2005); the sum total of these presuppositions constitutes a philosophy of science (Porpora, 2015). This chapter seeks to increase appreciation of ontological issues to show how a better understanding of them can contribute to ESB studies. Ontological reflection can support ESB research, encouraging researchers to propose clear conceptions of the social objects[1] they believe exist and their properties. Critical realism is therefore intended as a philosophy *for*, as well as *of*, ESB research as it directs attention to what needs to be included in a powerful explanation of entrepreneurial action and, in particular, to the conditions that make such action possible.

Three aims motivate the chapter. First, to demonstrate that ontological presuppositions cannot be avoided in ESB research. Such commitments are inevitable in all research and are important for the kinds of explanation that can be made (Archer, 1995; Fleetwood, 2005). To be clear, therefore, researchers ought to be as explicit about these commitments as possible. Second, to argue for a particular standpoint, critical realism, and, to show why I believe it is superior to currently available alternatives (Bhaskar, 1978, 1979; Collier, 1994; Lawson, 1997; Sayer, 2000; Groff, 2004). Critical realism focuses on ontological questions, with what exists; such issues are logically prior to the epistemological question of what we can know. Third, to show that, in practice, ESB researchers often make assumptions close to those of critical realism, whatever their declared commitments. Fleetwood and Ackroyd (2004) have made a similar point in relation to the organisation and management literature. Where ESB researchers implicitly make ontological assumptions similar to those of critical realism, studies might be improved by applying critical realist thinking systematically in making conceptual, methodological and analytical choices.

The chapter is organised as follows. Section 2 elaborates why researchers inevitably make ontological commitments, either intentionally or inadvertently, in their studies. Section 3 traces the origins and development of critical realism through immanent critiques of the main philosophical alternatives – positivism, social constructionism and pragmatism. Section 4 sets out the main features of critical realist social ontology, drawing principally on the early work of Bhaskar. To illustrate the benefits, section 5 brings a critical realist-inspired framework to bear on one particular topic, entrepreneurial identity, where most studies have adopted a constructionist approach. Section 6 concludes.

The necessity for ontological commitments in entrepreneurship and small business research

Every researcher makes ontological assumptions in their theoretical and empirical work (Bhaskar, 1978; Archer, 1995; Fleetwood, 2005). Ontological assumptions refer to the kinds of social objects that exist and might be studied, or to generic features of the world. ESB researchers assume the existence of entrepreneurs, businesses, products, opportunities and markets, for instance. Where researchers refer to these objects in their analyses, they take them to be real (Archer, 1995); to argue otherwise is to commit a theory/practice contradiction. Moreover, ESB researchers frequently make causal claims – that X influences, produces or impacts Y. They thereby assume that objects – firms and markets, for instance – stand in a causal relation to one another. Such claims presuppose that causality is a feature of the social world (Groff, 2016). Researchers may state ontological commitments explicitly or, more commonly, adopt them implicitly in their research practice. Ontological presuppositions are therefore non-optional (Fleetwood, 2005); failure to be explicit about them only leads to their unacknowledged reintroduction into data collection, analysis and explanation. Such assumptions necessarily influence research practice, shaping conceptions of the social objects alleged to exist and the methods used to study and analyse them.

Bhaskar (1978) distinguishes between philosophical and scientific (regional or domain-specific) ontologies. Scientific ontologies are those presupposed by theories in a particular field positing the existence of particular entities. Philosophical ontologies specify generic features of reality with which scientific ontologies must be consistent; critical realism is a philosophical ontology. It does not posit the existence of particular entities as a scientific theory would, so it does not say anything about specific objects such as new ventures, business practices or market relations. The value of critical realism lies in supporting robust, though fallible, *causal explanations* of ESB objects such as venture creation, product development or business performance by providing strong accounts of agency, causality, social structure and emergent properties. Critical realism cannot adjudicate between rival theories that are consistent with its ontological assumptions; these are substantive matters for ESB researchers to debate.

Arguably, all ESB researchers are committed to what might be termed a minimal ontological realism, the claim that the social world exists and is what it is largely independently of any particular observer (Searle, 2010). Such a 'thin' realism, however, may be of little help to researchers because it permits approaches that have arguably had a damaging effect such as positivism (Sayer, 2004), about which I say more in section 3. 'Thicker' versions of realism may be of more help to researchers because they set a higher bar for theory to meet. Not every realist philosophy can meet these more demanding standards with regards to issues such as causality, for instance. Critical realism supplies a thicker set of ontological commitments to support research and theorising (e.g. Bhaskar, 1979; Archer, 1995; Elder-Vass, 2010), licensing a range of theories that are consistent with them, while judging those that are inconsistent with such assumptions to be either false or incomplete (Bhaskar, 1978).

Critics of critical realism claim that Bhaskar makes ontologically foundationalist – i.e. infallible – claims that the world *must* possess particular characteristics if science is to be possible (Pleasants, 1999; Cruickshank, 2004). While Bhaskar's comments on this issue have been seen as ambiguous, he has insisted that his approach was the only theory of science then consistent with the scientific data (Bhaskar, 1978). But, as others have noted, this cannot guarantee that another future ontological theory will not do better (Chalmers, 1988). Critical realists can accept that all knowledge claims, including ontological ones, are in principle fallible and revisable.

Following Bhaskar, therefore, I contend, first, that ontology cannot be avoided, and, second, that critical realism offers the best approach – but do not claim that no better ontological argument will ever be developed (Bhaskar, 1978; Lawson, 1997). The argument against critical realism that ontology should not regulate, and thereby limit, the conduct of social inquiry (Kemp, 2005) or form of explanation (Tsilipakos, 2015) needs to be balanced against Bhaskar's (2016, p. 209) view that critical realism is 'maximally inclusive' and open to the discovery of new entities and layers of reality. Critical realism permits a wider range of social objects as potentially significant for scientific explanation than rival philosophical positions.

Immanent critiques of alternative philosophical standpoints

From a realist perspective, philosophy is wrong to start with the problem of epistemology, with how we know things. What we can know depends on what there is to know, that is, on the nature of reality (Potter & López, 2001). This is the problem of ontology. Epistemological questions presuppose answers to ontological ones. Hence Bhaskar's (1978, 1979) interest in the ontological question: what must the world be like for science to be possible? The word *possible* is necessary here to make it clear that scientific explanations depend on the activities of researchers in the respective fields to produce them. Philosophy cannot provide such explanations; rather, it underlabours for the sciences, striving for conceptual clarity and specifying the conditions the sciences presuppose (Bhaskar, 1978).

Bhaskar (1978, 1979) developed critical realism out of immanent critiques of prior philosophical positions, notably positivism and hermeneutics. Immanent critique takes a particular argument and demonstrates theory/practice inconsistencies within it or shows how adopting the argument generates problems that are insoluble in its own terms (Hartwig, 2007). Bhaskar (2016) distinguishes his approach to the natural sciences, which he terms transcendental realism, from that of the human sciences, which he terms critical naturalism. The term 'critical realism' originated in the elision of these two separate approaches. Positivism and hermeneutics are now discussed in turn.

Positivism claims that scientific laws are grounded in exceptionless empirical regularities – 'whenever X, then Y' – which, in turn, presuppose an ontology of constant conjunctions of events. Theoretical claims are confirmed or falsified by their empirical instantiation (Bhaskar, 1978). To critique positivism in the natural sciences, Bhaskar takes experimentation as his starting point because it is widely regarded by scientists as a successful knowledge-generating practice. His analysis shows brilliantly that experiments presuppose an ontological distinction between scientific laws and patterns of events. For Bhaskar, laws are simply the ways that entities act, not their empirical manifestations in regular (or irregular) sequences. Through experimental activity, scientists produce experimental events but not the causal powers/mechanisms that such events enable them to identify. Only by assuming the real ontological independence of powers from the events they generate can we assume they endure and continue acting outside the experimentally closed conditions that allow scientists to identify them. Positivism, presupposing an ontology of invariant events, cannot explain what governs events in open systems where exceptionless regularities do not obtain. To be consistent, positivists would have to say that scientific laws apply only in the laboratory where the regularities occur or that events outside the laboratory are not governed by laws!

Bhaskar (1978) refers to event-based ontologies like positivism as guilty of actualism, that observable events exhaust the real. Actualism restricts science to that which can be observed. Positivism has no place for 'unobservables' as possible objects of scientific investigation. What cannot be perceived cannot be known and is therefore inadmissible to science (Fleetwood, 1996). This rules out reference to businesses, markets, institutions and discourses, none of which can be observed. Realist explanations, conversely, permit a causal criterion for reality as well as an experiential one. Theory can posit entities which cannot be observed directly and whose existence can only be inferred from the *effects* they cause (Sayer, 1992; Danermark, Ekstrom, Jakobsen, & Karlsson, 2001). Critical realism rejects positivism as a philosophy of both the natural and the human sciences on the grounds that *exceptionless* regularities presuppose closed systems, that is, social objects and their contexts of operation remain invariant over time. But both the natural and social worlds are open systems involving the interaction of multiple entities that generate novel events that we (sometimes) experience.

In the human sciences, a long tradition of research has pointed to their important differences from the natural sciences, specifically that researchers study meaningful action and seek interpretive understanding rather than causal explanation (Winch, 1958). The meaning of action is argued to be constructed through interaction between people (Gergen, 2009). Constructionist accounts typically emphasise the role of language or discourse in the constitution of social reality. Four points might be made by critical realists in relation to such arguments. First, construction is a misleading metaphor and often confuses ontological and epistemological talk (Porpora, 2015). It confuses in two ways by evading the question of the relationship between social constructions and their referents (Sayer, 1997): first, it elides the material construction of a practice or event with the naming, categorising, interpreting or construal of it and, second, it conflates agents' and researchers' interpretations/construals. Hacking (2002) poses the question, 'the social construction of what?' to capture these ambiguities: just what is being constructed when constructionists make knowledge claims?

Second, social life is inherently conceptual (meaningful) but it is not exhausted by the conceptuality it depends upon (Bhaskar, 2016). Meanings are real (Maxwell, 2012) – they exist independently of the researcher studying them – but are not all there is. Although semiosis (meaning-making) is an aspect of any social practice, no practice is reducible to semiosis alone (Fairclough, Jessop, & Sayer, 2002). Meaning-making necessarily occurs in a social context of structured relations that pre-date meaning-making (Fairclough et al., 2002). Material relations of resource inequality, autonomy and dependence enable and constrain activities, even where agents consciously draw on cultural rules to act (Porpora, 1993). Moreover, making sense of events, even recent ones, is inevitably a historical act, that is, an act taking place at a particular time; agents give meaning to a world that pre-dates, and therefore exists (or existed) apart from, their interpretations/construals.

Third, people are not only meaning-endowing creatures attributing meanings to relations, events, human-made artefacts and nature; they are also causal agents capable of intervening in, and transforming, the social and natural worlds (Bhaskar, 1979; Archer, 1995). Persons are proactive emergent bio-psycho-social realities, conscious, reflexive, embodied, self-transcending centres of subjective experience and durable identity (Smith, 2010). Bhaskar (2016, p. 88) notes how conceptuality is both causally conditioned by, and causally efficacious on, the material, extra-conceptual, extra-discursive, extra-linguistic dimensions of human life. Not just any meanings will do; to argue otherwise is to insist that agents' descriptions/construals can never be mistaken. Agents' accounts are limited by the existence of unacknowledged conditions, unintended consequences, tacit skills and unconscious motivations, and therefore corrigible (Bhaskar, 1998). Researchers need to investigate the extra-semiotic conditions that make semiosis possible and secure its efficacy. We cannot, in most cases, change reality merely by redescribing it (Bhaskar, 1991).

Fourth, agents may construe practices, events and relations in certain ways – but it is always possible to conceptualise these social objects in different ways for different purposes. Multiple descriptions may be 'practically adequate' (Sayer, 1992). For example, individuals going to work every day might construe their activity as earning a livelihood. A third party observer might, in contrast, describe it as reproducing a market economy and that this is the case whether the individuals involved are aware of, or intend, this. So we do not have to rely solely on agents' own construals to provide an adequate description. Critical realists are comfortable with 'moderate' forms of constructionism that acknowledge the epistemic relativity of meanings and the socio-historical variability of knowledge claims, while denying 'radical' constructionist claims that that the reality of social processes is exhausted by agents' culturally shaped descriptions (or constructions) of them (Elder-Vass, 2012).

A newer entrant to philosophical debates in the ESB field is pragmatism (Sarasvathy, 2008; Berglund & Wennberg, 2016). Pragmatists try to stand clear of ontology (Powell, 2003), avoiding ontological questions as being impossible to settle (e.g. Rorty, 1982; Baert, 2005). Talking about ontology is treated simply as a language game played by a particular breed of philosopher (Kivinen & Piiroinen, 2004). Pragmatists prefer to emphasise the usefulness of ideas and beliefs as guides to action. Against this kind of thinking, two points might be made. First, as argued in section 2, ontological claims cannot be avoided. There is no way to think or talk about social reality without committing oneself, metaphysically; it is a myth to believe otherwise (Groff, 2016). Pragmatists, like everyone else, make ontological assumptions and represent the world through their descriptions. Terms like 'ontology', 'breed of philosopher', 'language game' and 'usefulness' must be intended to refer to something in order to be meaningful and thereby useful. Otherwise, entirely different words might be used and be expected to be equally useful. Second, one might ask: what is it about a particular belief that makes it a useful guide to action? To engage in a practice successfully, one might argue that one's beliefs must not be inconsistent with the way the world actually is, although one cannot take the further step and assume that one's beliefs mirror the world. Pragmatists are therefore caught in theory/practice inconsistencies where they assume their analyses do not assume certain ontological features or represent the world in particular ways.

To end this section, it is important to distinguish philosophical accounts of social science from researchers' *actual* practices. It is often thought that quantitative research is underpinned by positivism, and qualitative approaches are supported by some form of interpretivism/constructionism. I cannot recall, however, a single instance of a quantitative ESB researcher making an explicit argument for positivism to support their work. Rather, the approach has become entirely conventional, with authors perceiving no need to argue why *probabilistic* empirical regularities – exceptionless ones hardly ever occur, if at all – constitute good grounds for knowledge claims. Probabilistic associations do not, however, satisfy the standard for positivist knowledge claims because there are unexplained exceptions. It seems more plausible to argue instead that, in the absence of invariant event regularities, quantitative researchers work, implicitly, with a different set of ontological assumptions.

Similarly, constructionist approaches often refer to non-experiential entities in their analyses. Alvarez and Barney (2007), for instance, in their constructionist approach to opportunity creation, make reference to market imperfections but these appear to be treated as real independently of anyone perceiving them or construing their existence. Gergen (2009, p. 161) reports that realist talk is essential to carry out life in a particular tradition but that we cannot describe the world as it really is. Such claims assume the existence of different traditions of life, but to be consistent a constructionist would have to limit reference to people's *perceptions/constructions* of traditions of life. Many constructionists thereby assume, unwittingly, the existence of non-experiential objects independent of agents' constructions of them.

In both cases, researchers refer to a wider range of objects in explanations than is strictly permitted by either a positivist or a constructionist ontology. This suggests that quantitative and qualitative research practices might be better conceptualised within a more encompassing ontology, one allowing experiences and events but also the powers that generate them. Such powers should include purposive human agents and the relations that influence action. A robust social ontology should allow for both agents and social relations without depending on event regularities for their identification or restricting what exists to what the agents involved in particular practices say exists.

Critical realism: an ontological framework for the sciences?

Critical realism is intended, ambitiously, to provide an overall philosophical framework for the natural and human sciences (Bhaskar & Hartwig, 2010; Bhaskar, 2016). In contrast to both positivism and constructionism, critical realism prioritises ontology rather than epistemology, and within ontology, shifts the emphasis from events and experiences to the generative powers that produce events and experiences (Bhaskar, 1978, 1979). An adequate philosophy of science must be able to sustain both a transitive dimension and an intransitive dimension (Bhaskar, 1978). The transitive dimension refers to the existing knowledge that researchers use to generate new knowledge. No-one starts with a blank page; all start with preunderstanding, derived either from prior practical activity or scientific learning (Alvesson & Sköldberg, 2009). The intransitive dimension refers to the real entities that exist and act independently of the conditions that allow observers epistemic access to them. The world can only be known under particular descriptions, in terms of available conceptual resources (Bhaskar, 1978; Sayer, 2000) but our knowledge is always *of* or *about* something that exists (or existed) apart from the observation.

Realism does not entail claims that we can achieve foundational, infallible knowledge. On the contrary, realism and fallibilism presuppose one another (Sayer, 1992). To be a fallibilist about knowledge, it is necessary to be a realist about things (Bhaskar, 1978). Beliefs cannot be fallible unless there is something independent of the believing of them that would make them true or false (Collier, 2003).[2] It is the evident fallibility of our knowledge – the experience of getting things wrong – that justifies us in believing that the world exists regardless of what we happen to think about it (Sayer, 2000). Contrary to the constructionists, agents' definitions of the situation are fallible. If the world is *necessarily* just as agents say, they could never be wrong.

Critical realism is a philosophical ontology that offers an answer to the question 'what must the world be like for science to be possible?' The centrepiece of critical realism is the transcendental deduction of the stratified, open nature of the world arising from analysis of the experimental activity of scientists. Bhaskar's (1978) ontological stratification between the three domains of the real, the actual and the empirical is central to critical realist thinking:

- the real – the powers (or mechanisms) that generate events, including the capacity (liability) to undergo certain kinds of change;
- the actual – the events that occur; and
- the empirical – experience.

This 'deep', or stratified, ontology can be distinguished from the 'flat', actualist ontologies of positivism and constructionism that centre on experience and events but ignore powers, mechanisms and capacities. Causation is simply the activation of powers to produce effects, although the existence of a power does not guarantee the occurrence of particular events. A few examples should suffice to illustrate the difference between powers and events. Barcelona footballer, Lionel Messi, possesses the power to play even when he's at home asleep in bed! Businesses retain the power to produce goods and services, even when they are closed for the weekend and not actually producing anything. Markets possess the power to transform the terms upon which businesses conduct trade and to eliminate some from competition, even as new firms enter the marketplace and incumbent firms persist with existing practices.

These three ontological domains of the real, the actual and the empirical are commonly out of phase (Bhaskar, 1978). The existence of a power does not determine events or entail that someone experiences those events. Powers may be possessed unexercised, exercised and actualised in a variety of events, and events may go unobserved. Contrary to positivism, event regularities are therefore neither sufficient nor necessary to identify a power. Given that society is an open system with multiple powers operating simultaneously, invariant event regularities are unlikely to occur. Powers, when exercised, often counteract the effects of one another. Ontologically speaking, powers must therefore be distinct from the pattern of events they generate, and from our observation of events. This moves us towards a science concerned with possibilities not actualities – there is more to reality than what actually happens. The task of the sciences is therefore to penetrate deeper levels of reality, showing how new powers emerge from the interaction of existing ones, making novel events and experiences possible.

Turning to the human sciences, Bhaskar (1979) starts from the widely held belief that what makes them different is intentional agency, the capacity for human beings to act on reasons.[3] Critical realists, along with constructionist thinkers, accept the meaningful character of social life but make stronger arguments in relation to the intransitivity of reasons, their capacity to be causally efficacious, and the fallibility of the beliefs upon which reasons depend. Social life is not, however, exhausted by intentional agency. Critical realism incorporates meaningful activity within wider causal explanations of the reproduction and transformation of social practices and settings. The social world is also constituted by the relations between agents whose interaction produces events that nobody specifically willed. Society is the unintended outcome of agents' intentional actions (Archer, 1995).

This brings us to the controversial issue of structure and agency. Societies are irreducible to people; from birth, individuals are enmeshed in a framework of social-structural relations that influence, but do not determine, what they can do (Archer, 1995). The social context is a necessary condition for any intentional act (Bhaskar, 1979). The pre-existence of social forms, such as businesses and markets, establishes their *autonomy* as possible objects of scientific investigation and their *causal power* establishes their reality (Bhaskar, 1979). Entrepreneurs establishing a company presuppose a legal system setting out rights and obligations; hiring employees presupposes a labour market; paying suppliers in 30 days presupposes a business norm regarding settling invoices; and cutting prices to increase sales presupposes a commodity market populated by rival producers and prospective buyers, themselves both motivated to act by their own socially structured positions.

The structure/agency approach seeks to avoid the twin problems of structural determinism (where large-scale social forces such as class, gender or nation determine events) and voluntarism (where events can be explained solely by reference to agent motivations). Much ESB research veers towards voluntarism, assuming that imaginative, creative and daring entrepreneurs can re-make the world at will while paying insufficient attention to the social context that enables, as well as constrains, resource acquisition and mobilisation (e.g. Sarasvathy, 2008; Chiles, Vultee, Gupta, Greening, & Tuggle, 2010). Archer (2000a) refers to this kind of voluntarist approach as a 'stop-the-world-while-we-get-off-and-change-it' condition, as if agents can simply choose to interpret their social relations differently independently of the influence of unequal resource distributions and agents' vested interests in retaining, or changing, society. Social relations necessarily involve the exercise of power to reproduce or transform the social context, whether or not agents notice or conceptualise this (Porpora, 2015).

The pre-existence of social forms entails a transformational model of social activity, a relational conception of the subject matter of social science in which society is both the ever-present condition (material cause) and the continually reproduced outcome of human agency (Bhaskar, 1979). Social structures such as organisations and markets are relationally emergent products of human interaction that generate the material circumstances, positions and relations within which agents must act and which motivate them to act in certain ways (Bhaskar, 1979; Porpora, 1989; Sayer, 1992; Lawson, 1997). Social structures are constituted by relationships between internally related positions,[4] possessing the power to influence the exercise of agency by those occupying particular positions. For example, the activities of entrepreneurs, as suppliers of goods and services, are influenced by relations with rival producers, consumers and suppliers. All action is positionally conditioned; agents' activities are conditioned by their inherited structural and cultural context (Archer, 1995). Martinez Dy, Marlow, and Martin (2017), for example, note how individual positioning within intersecting class, gender and race hierarchies influences the social privileges and material resources available to invest in digital ventures and thereby constrain entrepreneurial potential.

We can separate, analytically, cycles of structural and cultural conditioning, agential interaction and structural and cultural elaboration (Archer, 1995). Agential interaction, drawing on prior structural and cultural conditioning, gives rise intentionally and unselfconsciously (Sayer, 2009; Akram, 2013) to structural and cultural emergent properties (Archer, 1995). Entrepreneurs forming new ventures, for instance, contribute to the modest or substantial transformation of a market economy whether or not they intend or understand this.

Emergent properties turn back to confront human actors with circumstances which are not fully of their own making. Changing market contexts causally shape the exercise of future agency; they enable and limit what entrepreneurs are able to do next. Such circumstances exist and exert autonomous effects, largely through the actions of important close and distant stakeholders, regardless of how entrepreneurs themselves perceive such circumstances. For example, an entrepreneur might experience a fall in demand for her firm's product but be unaware whether this is due to the introduction of a direct competitor product, shifting consumer tastes, rising or falling disposable consumer incomes, or changing transport costs for overseas exporters. Constructionist accounts cannot simply wish such conditions away by encouraging agents to redescribe them (Gergen, 2009).

Critics of critical realism argue that it is mistaken to grant social structures causal powers (Varela & Harré, 1996; King, 1999; Manicas, 2006) or to accord them emergent properties (Le Boutillier, 2013). For these critics, to ascribe causal powers to social structure is to mislocate them. Only people possess causal powers, it is argued; people coordinate their activities through their conversational practices. Structures, it is argued, are virtually real because they cannot exist independently of human activity; people's changing practices are the only social reality. But critical realists might argue that while people are the only efficient causes of action in the social world, in that social events can only happen through their activities, social structures are sources of material causality (Lewis, 2000). So, although social structures can generate effects only through people exercising their agential powers, structures nevertheless shape *how* individuals exercise their agency (Mutch, 2004). Without reference to the structural and cultural context, explanations of entrepreneurial action are inevitably unanchored in real social settings characterised by unequal resource distributions, diverse vested interests and good or bad reasons for action that enable and constrain what entrepreneurs can do (Archer, 1995).

The open, emergent nature of the social world encourages researchers to focus on explanation not prediction (Sayer, 1992). Although, retrospectively, we can often give well-grounded explanations of past events, prospectively we are very rarely, if ever, able to do so because we do not know which of the myriad of possible sets of circumstances will actually materialise (Bhaskar, 1986). Causal explanation requires description of explanatory powers, narratives of the contingent conjunctures of powers and adjudication between rival explanations (Porpora, 2015). Critical realists contend that the social world can be studied in the *same sense* if not the same way as the natural world, in terms of an ontology of powers, events and experience (Bhaskar, 1978). But because the objects of the natural and human sciences are very different, methods of data collection and analysis also differ (Bhaskar, 1979; Sayer, 1992).

Why critical realism matters to entrepreneurship and small business research: revisiting entrepreneurial identity

This section briefly discusses studies of entrepreneurial identity, a stream of research dominated by constructionist approaches that define identity in terms of narrative or discourse. The purpose of the discussion is threefold: first, to propose an alternative critical realist-informed conception of entrepreneurial identity as a personal causal power rather than as a narrative performance; second, to show how such a framework can encompass and explain the findings of narrative-based studies while also directing research attention to the conditions that make successful narrative performances possible; and, third, to demonstrate how constructionist accounts inevitably presuppose a stratified ontology of powers, events and experience *despite* an actualist focus on practice.

Constructionist works in the entrepreneurial identity literature focus on self-narration (e.g. Down & Reveley, 2004; Essers & Benschop, 2007), often performed by appropriating elements of wider discourses of enterprise to tell particular stories about themselves (Cohen & Musson, 2000; Watson, 2009; Anderson & Warren, 2011).[5] Hence entrepreneurial identities are described as situated, fluid and multiple (Hytti, 2005) to the extent that entrepreneurs perform, or construct, different identities in dialogical interaction with diverse stakeholders including financiers, customers, suppliers, family and community members. To the extent entrepreneurs succeed in accomplishing a desirable and credible identity with important stakeholders, this enables entrepreneurs to access resources and markets (Lounsbury & Glynn, 2001).

An alternative conception of entrepreneurial identity might define it as a personal causal power, one that motivates and enables action, rather than as a narrative performance (Kašperová & Kitching, 2014). Drawing on Archer (2000b), this conception distinguishes personal identity as the set of concerns that makes each of us a unique person, and social identity as the public roles in which we can invest ourselves and commit to (Archer, 2000b; Marks & O'Mahoney, 2015). Being an entrepreneur, or being a particular kind of entrepreneur, is one such social identity. If we conceptualise entrepreneurs as agents with particular properties and powers, pursuing particular projects to further their concerns, then the capacity to enact particular narrative performances is one of their powers. Such performances, however, are quite distinct from the *concern* to establish oneself as a credible, legitimate entrepreneur. Such concerns make diverse narrative performances possible but do not dictate that identity powers are exercised, or how they are exercised, or that, if exercised, that they will necessarily produce the desired effects.

There are a number of problems with the constructionist conception of entrepreneurial identity from a critical realist standpoint. First, accounts that reduce identity to narrative performance presuppose an actualist ontology. Entrepreneurs' identities are constituted solely by narrative practices as they are performed and endure only for the duration of the performance. Consequently, practitioners do not have identities when they are not performing narratively. Such approaches ignore, or do not theorise adequately, the conditions of possibility of particular instances of narrative performance and thereby risk reducing the analysis of entrepreneurial identity to descriptions of discursive practices. Accounts of identity are incomplete without reference to a non-discursive reality (O'Mahoney, 2012). Accomplishing a successful social identity such as being an entrepreneur requires interaction with important stakeholders but is not reducible to self-narration.

Second, accounts that reduce identity to narrative performance accord a limited explanatory role to the conditions enabling such practices. These conditions include entrepreneurs themselves as embodied agents with particular properties and powers (Kašperová & Kitching, 2014), and relations with important stakeholders. Entrepreneurs perform identity work in specific social contexts that influence outcomes. Identity work might not succeed; the influence of narrative practices should be demonstrated not assumed (Alvesson & Kärreman, 2011). Prospective entrepreneurs may fail in their efforts to present themselves as credible and legitimate to stakeholders with the consequence they are unable to obtain finance from investors, win orders from customers, secure inputs from suppliers or receive emotional support from family and community. Entrepreneurs from disadvantaged groups, in particular, may confront severe constraints in convincing important stakeholders they are worthy of support. Conceptualising identity as self-narration can divert attention from the circumstances that might constrain individuals from accomplishing a successful entrepreneurial identity, even where discrimination and prejudice are recognised to be important features of the wider political context (Tedmanson & Essers, 2016). Critical realists would argue that identity work practices, and their effects, must be explained with reference to entrepreneurs' positioning within particular social relations. The well-financed, well-educated and well-connected might be better able to accomplish a credible, legitimate entrepreneurial identity in dialogue with stakeholders than others.

Third, constructionist accounts must presuppose an entrepreneurial agent, one whose positioning in relation to various social hierarchies – class, gender, ethnicity, dis/ability – is likely to influence interaction with stakeholders, as well as a wider social context, one that may be characterised by discrimination and prejudice (Essers & Benschop, 2007). Entrepreneurial identity work does not therefore reduce to how entrepreneurs present themselves narratively in micro-level interactions with university researchers or even with business stakeholders. Entrepreneurs cannot control all of the signals they give off. Stakeholders endow entrepreneurs' appearance and action with meaning, consciously and inadvertently; these meanings are likely to vary with the relative social positioning of the entrepreneur and the interacting stakeholder. Focusing research on the stories entrepreneurs tell about themselves may be insufficient to explain what particular entrepreneurs do, or are able to do, with regard to accessing resources and markets. This task requires attention to wider dimensions of context, reaching beyond a constructionist focus on narrative. Explaining identity work, and its effects, requires an ontology that goes beyond experience, one that treats causation as a feature of the social world and acknowledges a distinction between causal powers, events and entrepreneurs' experiences. This points towards a more encompassing ontological framework than one reliant solely on agents' narrative constructions.

Conclusion

Entrepreneurship/small business researchers cannot avoid making ontological commitments in their empirical and theoretical work. Few, however, make such commitments explicit and these have to be inferred from how researchers conceptualise and analyse the objects they study. ESB researchers conventionally assume the existence of entities such as firms, resources, products and markets – as well as causal relations between entrepreneurs and their stakeholders. This does not mean that such entities do, in fact, exist – but these constitute the ingredients of the analysis.

I have proposed critical realism as a superior ontology to the major current alternatives of positivism, constructionism and pragmatism which either implicitly acknowledge the existence of entities they formally deny, or place no limits on what can be said. Critical realism is inclusive and open to the discovery of new entities, or layers of social reality, in facilitating (fallible) explanations of ESB objects such as new venture creation and various forms of market activity. Critical realism is therefore a philosophy *for*, as well as of, ESB research as it directs attention to the conditions of possibility of particular business practices. Adopting such an ontology permits explanation that goes beyond positivism's emphasis on empirical regularities and constructionism's emphasis on agents' descriptions. Explanation of ESB objects does not depend on the identification of empirical regularities; nor do agents' descriptions exhaust social reality.

Notes

1 Social objects are the product of human interaction, for example, practices, organisations, markets, social norms, institutions and discourses. Material entities arising from interaction such as cars, computers and chairs are excluded from the definition. Social objects are not necessarily born of purposeful design, nor do they exist fully autonomously from the people whose activities produce them or possess invariant properties through time.
2 This issue is separate from the epistemological question of how we *know* what is true or false. Given a commitment to fallibility, we can never know for certain whether a claim is true or not. But, by that same token, it is possible to make true claims without knowing it.
3 A strict positivist would have to rule out reasons (and intentions, beliefs, emotions or other conscious states) as inadmissible to science because they are unobservable.
4 Positions are internally related when their existence and causal powers necessarily depend on relations with others. Examples include employer and employee.
5 Interestingly, accounts that refer to enterprise discourses presuppose their causal powers to influence contemporary agents' self-narration practices. Such arguments appear more consistent with critical realism than the micro-level interactionist studies that focus on narrative performance. This section focuses on arguments that tie identity to agents' self-narration practices.

References

Akram, S. (2013). Fully unconscious and prone to habit: The characteristics of agency in the structure and agency dialectic. *Journal for the Theory of Social Behaviour, 43*(1), 45–65.

Alvarez, S., & Barney, J. (2007). Discovery and creation: Alternative theories of entrepreneurial action. *Strategic Entrepreneurship Journal, 1*(1–2), 11–26.

Alvesson, M., & Kärreman, D. (2011). Decolonializing discourse: Critical reflections on organizational discourse analysis. *Human Relations, 64*(9), 1121–1146.

Alvesson, M., & Sköldberg, K. (2009). *Reflexive methodology: New vistas for qualitative research* (2nd ed.). London: Sage.

Anderson, A., & Warren, L. (2011). The entrepreneur as hero and jester: Enacting the entrepreneurial discourse. *International Small Business Journal, 29*(6), 589–609.

Archer, M. (1995). *Realist social theory: The morphogenetic approach*. Cambridge: Cambridge University Press.

Archer, M. (2000a). For structure: Its reality, properties and powers: A reply to Anthony King. *Sociological Review, 48*(3), 464–472.

Archer, M. (2000b). *Being human: The problem of agency*. Cambridge: Cambridge University Press.

Baert, P. (2005). *Philosophy of the social sciences*. Cambridge: Polity.

Berglund, H., & Wennberg, K. (2016). Pragmatic entrepreneurs and institutionalized scholars? On the path-dependent nature of entrepreneurship scholarship. In H. Landström, A. Parhankangas, A. Fayolle, & P. Riot (Eds.), *Challenging entrepreneurship research* (pp. 37–52). London: Routledge.

Bhaskar, R. (1978). *A realist theory of science* (2nd ed.). Hassocks: Harvester.

Bhaskar, R. (1979). *The possibility of naturalism*. Brighton: Harvester Wheatsheaf.

Bhaskar, R. (1986). *Scientific realism and human emancipation*. London: Verso.

Bhaskar, R. (1991). *Philosophy and the idea of freedom*. Oxford: Blackwell.

Bhaskar, R. (1998). General introduction. In M. Archer, R. Bhaskar, A. Collier, T. Lawson, & A. Norrie (Eds.), *Critical realism: Essential readings* (pp. ix–xxiv). London: Routledge.

Bhaskar, R. (2016). *Enlightened common sense: The philosophy of critical realism*. London: Routledge.

Bhaskar, R., & Hartwig, M. (2010). *The formation of critical realism: A personal perspective*. London: Routledge.

Chalmers, A. (1988). Is Bhaskar's realism realistic? *Radical Philosophy, 49*(Summer), 18–23.

Chiles, T., Vultee, D., Gupta, V., Greening, D., & Tuggle, C. (2010). The philosophical foundations of a radical Austrian approach to entrepreneurship. *Journal of Management Inquiry, 19*(2), 138–164.

Cohen, L., & Musson, G. (2000). Entrepreneurial identities: Reflections from two case studies. *Organization, 7*(1), 31–48.

Collier, A. (1994). *Critical realism: An introduction to Roy Bhaskar's philosophy*. London: Verso.

Collier, A. (2003). *In defence of objectivity and other essays*. London: Routledge.

Cruickshank, J. (2004). A tale of two ontologies: An immanent critique of critical realism. *Sociological Review, 52*(4), 567–585.

Danermark, B., Ekstrom, M., Jakobsen, L., & Karlsson, J. (2001). *Explaining society: Critical realism in the social sciences*. London: Routledge.

Down, S., & Reveley, J. (2004). Generational encounters and the social formation of entrepreneurial identity: 'Young Guns' and 'Old Farts'. *Organization, 11*(2), 233–250.

Elder-Vass, D. (2010). *The causal power of social structures: Emergence, structure & agency*. Cambridge: Cambridge University Press.

Elder-Vass, D. (2012). *The reality of social construction*. Cambridge: Cambridge University Press.

Essers, C., & Benschop, Y. (2007). Enterprising identities: Female entrepreneurs of Moroccan or Turkish origin in the Netherlands. *Organization Studies, 28*(1), 49–69.

Fairclough, N., Jessop, B., & Sayer, A. (2002). Critical realism and semiosis. *Journal of Critical Realism, 5*(1), 2–10.

Fleetwood, S. (1996). Order without equilibrium: A critical realist interpretation of Hayek's notion of spontaneous order. *Cambridge Journal of Economics, 20*(6), 729–747.

Fleetwood, S. (2005). The ontology of organisation and management studies: A critical realist approach. *Organization, 12*(2), 197–222.

Fleetwood, S., & Ackroyd, S. (Eds.). (2004). *Critical realist applications in organisation and management studies*. London: Routledge.

Gergen, K. (2009). *An invitation to social construction* (2nd ed.). London: Sage.

Grant, P., & Perren, L. (2002). Small business and entrepreneurial research: Metatheories, paradigms and prejudices. *International Small Business Journal, 20*(2), 185–211.

Groff, R. (2004). *Critical realism, post-positivism and the possibility of knowledge*. London: Routledge.

Groff, R. (2016). On the myth of metaphysical neutrality: Cheryl Frank memorial prize lecture 2015. *Journal of Critical Realism, 15*(4), 409–418.

Hacking, I. (2002). *The social construction of what?* Cambridge, MA: Harvard University Press.

Hartwig, M. (2007). *Dictionary of critical realism*. London: Routledge.

Hytti, U. (2005). New meanings for entrepreneurs: From risk-taking heroes to safe-seeking professionals. *Journal of Organizational Change Management, 18*(6), 594–611.

Kašperová, E., & Kitching, J. (2014). Embodying entrepreneurial identity. *International Journal of Entrepreneurial Behavior and Research, 20*(5), 438–452.

Kemp, S. (2005). Critical realism and the limits of philosophy. *European Journal of Social Theory, 8*(2), 171–191.

Kenworthy, T. P., & McMullen, W. E. (2014). From philosophy of science to theory testing: Generating practical knowledge in entrepreneurship. In A. Carsrud & M. Brännback (Eds.), *Handbook of research methods and applications in entrepreneurship and small business* (pp. 20–55). Cheltenham: Edward Elgar.

King, A. (1999). Against structure: A critique of morphogenetic social theory. *Sociological Review, 47*(2), 199–227.

Kivinen, O., & Piiroinen, T. (2004). The relevance of ontological commitments in social sciences: Realist and pragmatist viewpoints. *Journal for the Theory of Social Behaviour, 34*(3), 231–248.

Lawson, T. (1997). *Economics and reality*. London: Routledge.

Le Boutillier, S. (2013). Emergence and reduction. *Journal for the Theory of Social Behaviour, 43*(2), 205–225.

Lewis, P. (2000). Realism, causality and the problem of social structure. *Journal for the Theory of Social Behaviour, 30*(3), 249–268.

Lounsbury, M., & Glynn, M. A. (2001). Cultural entrepreneurship: Stories, legitimacy, and the acquisition of resources. *Strategic Management Journal, 22*(6–7), 545–564.

Manicas, P. (2006). *A realist philosophy of social science*. Cambridge: Cambridge University Press.

Marks, A., & O'Mahoney, J. (2015). Researching identity: A critical realist approach. In P. Edwards, J. O'Mahoney, & S. Vincent (Eds.), *Studying organizations using critical realism* (pp. 66–85). Oxford: Oxford University Press.

Martinez Dy, A., Marlow, S., & Martin, L. (2017). A web of opportunity or the same old story? Women digital entrepreneurs and intersectionality theory. *Human Relations, 70*(3), 286–311.

Maxwell, J. (2012). *A realist approach for qualitative research.* London: Sage.

Mutch, A. (2004). Constraints on the internal conversation: Margaret Archer and the structural shaping of thought. *Journal for the Theory of Social Behaviour, 34*(4), 429–445.

O'Mahoney, J. (2012). Embracing essentialism: A realist critique of resistance to discursive power. *Organization, 19*(6), 723–741.

Pleasants, N. (1999). *Wittgenstein and the idea of a critical social theory: A critique of Giddens, Habermas and Bhaskar.* London: Routledge.

Porpora, D. (1989). Four concepts of social structure. *Journal for the Theory of Social Behaviour, 19*(2), 195–211.

Porpora, D. (1993). Cultural rules and material relations. *Sociological Theory, 11*(2), 212–229.

Porpora, D. (2015). *Reconstructing sociology: The critical realist approach.* Cambridge: Cambridge University Press.

Potter, G., & López, J. (2001). General introduction: After postmodernism: The millennium. In G. Potter & J. López (Eds.), *After postmodernism: An introduction to critical realism* (pp. 3–16). London: Athlone Press.

Powell, T. (2003). Strategy without ontology. *Strategic Management Journal, 24*(3), 285–291.

Rorty, R. (1982). *Consequences of pragmatism.* Brighton: Harvester.

Sarasvathy, S. (2008). *Effectuation: Elements of entrepreneurial expertise.* Cheltenham: Edward Elgar.

Sayer, A. (1992). *Method in social science* (2nd ed.). London: Routledge.

Sayer, A. (1997). Essentialism, social constructionism and beyond. *Sociological Review, 45*(3), 453–487.

Sayer, A. (2000). *Realism and social science.* London: Sage.

Sayer, A. (2004). Realisms through thick and thin. *Environment and Planning A, 36*(10), 1777–1789.

Sayer, A. (2009). Reflexivity and the habitus. In M. Archer (Ed.), *Conversations about reflexivity* (pp. 108–122). London: Routledge.

Searle, J. (2010). *Making the social world.* Oxford: Oxford University Press.

Smith, C. (2010). *What is a person? Rethinking humanity, social life, and the moral good from the person up.* Chicago: University of Chicago Press.

Tedmanson, D., & Essers, C. (2016). Challenging constructions of entrepreneurial identities. In H. Landström, A. Parhankangas, A. Fayolle, & P. Riot (Eds.), *Challenging entrepreneurship research* (pp. 210–233). London: Routledge.

Tsilipakos, L. (2015). Realist social theory and its losing battle with concepts. *Philosophy of the Social Sciences, 45*(1), 26–52.

Varela, C., & Harré, R. (1996). Conflicting varieties of realism: Causal powers and the problems of social structure. *Journal for the Theory of Social Behaviour, 26*(3), 313–325.

Watson, T. (2009). Entrepreneurial action, identity work and the use of multiple discursive resources: The case of rapidly changing family business. *International Small Business Journal, 27*(3), 251–274.

Winch, P. (1958). *The idea of a social science and its relation to philosophy.* London: Routledge & Kegan Paul.

7 The other reading

Reflections of postcolonial deconstruction for critical entrepreneurship studies

Anna-Liisa Kaasila-Pakanen
and Vesa Puhakka

Introduction

Critically oriented entrepreneurship studies have proliferated in recent years, yielding different and inspiring implications for entrepreneurial as well as academic subjectivity, practice, and questions of power and politics within the field. In accordance with this development, we set out in this chapter to analyze the role of postcolonial deconstruction for entrepreneurship research through considering our own position as researchers in a recent study on micro-entrepreneuring within the context of development aid. On this basis, we wish to explicate the intertwining of theorizing, empirical research, and relations of power. Such an explication illustrates the use and importance of postcolonial deconstruction for entrepreneurship studies. Writing merely on postcolonial deconstruction as a location for theorizing entrepreneurship would separate us as researchers from the epistemic context of the phenomenon, thus losing the key feature of understanding postcolonial deconstruction – contextualization. As postcolonial deconstruction can happen only in relation to the specific context, understanding it also needs to happen through it. Therefore, we engage in a postcolonial deconstructive theorizing of entrepreneurship in relation to a previous empirical analysis of project materials from a Ugandan non-governmental organization offering entrepreneurship and enterprise skills training for disadvantaged rural women. In the previous study, we analyzed project materials stemming from a wider development project and, through a deconstructive approach, we illustrated the dynamic ambiguity of micro-entrepreneuring with its immanent emancipatory and oppressive potential, and the effects of imperialist subject-constitution and epistemic violence for the project participants (Kaasila-Pakanen & Puhakka, 2016). However, in this chapter, our intention is to showcase the special aptitude of postcolonial deconstructive thinking in connection with entrepreneurship and appeal to other scholars to engage with the possibilities and emphases it offers for expanding the philosophical, theoretical and methodological domains of the field.

Through the offered analysis, we join the endeavor of many critical entrepreneurship scholars to re-imagine the predominant conceptualizations of entrepreneurship phenomena and widen its realm (e.g. Steyaert, 1997; Ogbor, 2000; Ahl, 2002, 2004, 2006; Armstrong, 2005; Jennings, Perren, & Carter, 2005; Pio, 2005;

Steyaert & Hjorth, 2006; Essers & Benschop, 2007, 2009; Calás, Smircich, & Bourne, 2009; Weiskopf & Steyaert, 2009; Jones & Spicer, 2009; Özkazanç-Pan, 2009, 2014, 2015; Goss, Jones, Betta, & Latham, 2011; Steyaert, 2011; Verduijn & Essers, 2013; Muntean & Özkazanc-Pan, 2015, 2016; Özkazanc-Pan & Muntean, 2016; see more in Tedmanson, Verduijn, Essers, & Gartner, 2012 and Verduijn, Dey, Tedmanson, & Essers, 2014). While a postcolonial perspective offers other ways of seeing this world – a world made up of historical power relations that contribute to material and conceptual representations of different groups of people – it also offers other ways for theorizing entrepreneurship, which only a very few scholars have taken advantage of (Özkazanç-Pan, 2009, 2014; Özkazanc-Pan & Muntean, 2016; Banerjee & Tedmanson, 2010; Essers & Tedmanson, 2014). In our exploration, we go beyond disciplinary boundaries and challenge the traditional conceptualizations of entrepreneurship studies and the ways we do entrepreneurship research.

Emerging from the nexus of critical entrepreneurship studies and Spivak's (1981a, 1985, 1987a, 1987b, 1988) and Derrida's (1976, 1981, 1991) insights into postcolonial deconstruction, we outline a critical perspective to the phenomena of micro-enterprising as a social change process and to the specific relation between ourselves as writers and the research text we produce. We argue that, through our theoretical positionality, we are deeply intertwined in the power relations of knowledge production, and that without open acknowledgment of our complicity in this process, the research we do may end up perpetuating unreflectively produced assumptions and inequalities between different groups of people within entrepreneurship discourse. In this chapter, we also point out that deconstruction is not only a dismantling method or mode of reading and analyzing a text (Derrida, 1981), but it can be seen as reconstructive and productive in the way it expands the limits of an established field of conversation, such as entrepreneurship.

Questions of knowledge production and subjectivity are key to any postcolonial inquiry (Loomba, 1998), but to build on Spivak's contributions (e.g. 1981a, 1985, 1987a, 1987b, 1988) requires contemplating the responsibility and institutional place of an academic to bring out the ways we became entangled in imperial practices and universal categories of Anglo-American academic knowledge. As known, postcolonial perspectives are not only relevant for developing unique criticisms of complex discourses of modernity, capitalism, colonialism, and Eurocentrism, among others, but also for acting as a constant reminder of the way these critiques need to be performed from a theoretical position that seeks disengagement from Eurocentric epistemologies, categories, modes of enunciation, and protocols of knowledge production (Prasad, 2012, p. 16). In accordance with broader postcolonial thought, we aim to utilize the ambivalence of colonial discourse, casting its ambiguity also on the relation between the investigator and theoretical "method" used (Young, 1990), and through deconstructionist critique, to show how representations of Others are inscribed in both the texts we read and the texts we write.

Based on Derrida's (1976) interpretation on language, the sign marks a place of difference and the structure of the sign is determined by the trace of the Other, which in this case refers to deferral of meaning and the unstable nature of language. For this, we cannot but trace the path along which the meaning, research, and subsequent knowledge has been constructed through the chain of signifiers in our study. Thus, this text is organized as follows: We start with a discussion of postcolonialism and deconstruction from the point of view of this study's objectives. Second, we outline our reading of the entrepreneurial stories of Ugandan women from this perspective and then reflect on the crossroads of postcolonial deconstruction and critical entrepreneurship studies. This is followed by a consideration of the philosophical implications of postcolonial deconstruction for critical entrepreneurship research. Last, we explain how this study will advance our understanding of critical entrepreneurship research.

Building a framework for the study

As the geography of entrepreneurship is always geopolitical (Steyaert & Katz, 2004), we chose a postcolonial starting point for the analysis of the project reports. This enabled us to view the texts through lenses sensitive to the perpetuation of unequal economic and cultural relations and in doing so, enabled us to place the discussion of micro-entrepreneuring in a broader geographic and historic context (Ashcroft, Griffiths, & Tiffin, 2003). By approaching the universalizing discourse of entrepreneurship (e.g. Essers & Tedmanson, 2014) from a postcolonial perspective and addressing its potential for creating social change, we constructed a framework that allowed us to interrogate the desired entrepreneurial self as hegemonic construction under the mantle of modernity and development. In the marginalized, neocolonial context where our empirical material is derived from, the main features of the dominant entrepreneurship discourse did not make sense (Imas, Wilson, & Weston, 2012), as the daily experiences of the entrepreneurs of the study could barely be expressed through the traditional vocabulary of entrepreneurship research based on theories from economics and individualist psychology (Steyaert, 2005). For this, a wider theoretical, ethical, and political space needed to be created. In the Derridean sense, a non-space was required through which we could genuinely reflect upon our position and influence as writers and enquire about entrepreneurship. The rest of this section discusses how we found this space to be intrinsic within texts through postcolonial deconstruction.

Postcolonialism

Post(-)colonial studies or, as a more uniting title for this field of research, postcolonialism, could be described as a broad set of heterogeneous theoretical positions attentive to the perpetuation of colonial relations of power and suppressions, with a special focus on questions of subjectivity, knowledge, and production of cultural representations (Loomba, 1998; Prasad, 2003). In addressing all aspects of the colonial process from the beginning of colonial contact, postcolonial viewpoints make an ethico-political commitment to recognizing (neo-)colonialism as both a physically and discursively violent action, and thus as indefensible (Ashcroft et al., 2003; Prasad, 2012). By focusing attention, for example, on the processes of discursive Othering and the construction of fictive binary oppositions (Said, 1978), on issues of colonial ambivalence, mimicry, and hybridity (Bhabha, 1994), and on imperialism and the voice of the gendered subaltern and different aspects of neo-colonialism in academy (Spivak, 1981a, 1985, 1987a, 1987b, 1988), postcolonial viewpoints aim to contest and dismantle the unquestioned superiority of categories of Western thought – to "provincialize Europe" (Chakrabarty, 1992, 2000; Prasad, 1997, 2003).

Space for postcolonial enquiries within entrepreneurship studies has recently started to emerge, with an emphasis on feminist postcolonial perspectives and questions of identity formation, processes of marginalization and othering, as well as resistance to hegemonic discourses of entrepreneurship (e.g. Özkazanc-Pan, 2014; Essers & Tedmanson, 2014). In continuation with this tradition, we focus on Spivak's contributions to theorizing entrepreneurship. In postcolonial scholarship Spivak's work has been fundamental in playing out the epistemic violence taking place in the "worlding" of the now-called Third World (Spivak, 1985) by Western discourses of knowledge, which are never disinterested from the interests of its producers (Spivak, 1988). Through her engagement in feminism, Marxism, and deconstruction, Spivak has embodied the material and textual relations between the North and South to postcolonial discussions, which often place significant emphasis on the cultural aspects of colonial and neocolonial discourses (e.g. Said, 1978; Bhabha, 1994). Throughout her essays (e.g. 1987a, 1987b, 1988), Spivak emphasizes the institutional place and responsibility of an academic and thus makes us inescapably intertwined in the power relations of knowledge production. Before exploring a closer framework of our postcolonial position, we briefly review the constructive ideas behind Derrida's (1976) quasi-concept of deconstruction.

Deconstruction

In *Letter to a Japanese Friend* (1991), Derrida has offered some schematic and preliminary reflections on the word "deconstruction", which he first used in *Of Grammatology* (1976) to translate and adapt his own view on the Heideggerian word Destruction or Abbau. For him, the word "deconstruction", like all other words, acquires its use value only from its inscription in a chain of possible substitutions, in what is often called a "context" (Derrida, 1991, p. 275). What he emphasizes is how things change from one "context" to another, and how the same word can be attached to very different connotations, inflections, and emotional or affective values depending on it (Derrida, 1991, p. 270). Having its roots in the structural linguistics of Ferdinand de Saussure and in an idea of language as a system of signs that are constituted of the signifier (sound image or sound of a word) and signified (the concept or the idea to which the word refers), deconstruction as a textual strategy is based on its ability to reveal the signified itself as yet another signifier (de Saussure, 1972; Derrida, 1991, 1976; Chia, 1994).

As broader poststructuralist analysis, deconstruction exemplifies how signification takes place through a constant deferral of meaning from one linguistic symbol to another and thus suggests that there is no stable foundation for meaning – what remains is the differences between meanings (Calás & Smircich, 1999, p. 653). Another pervasive idea of deconstruction is the logic of supplementarity, or, as Chia (1994, p. 785) has described it, the logic of the necessity of "otherness", which implies that the meanings always contain their opposites, their negations, and thus open a discussion free from the paralyzing effect of the *is/is not* binary of Western logocentrism. From this ambivalent base of deconstructive analysis rises the possibility for criticism, which we have used in our study. It needs to be noted though, especially if the technical and procedural significations of the words are stressed, that deconstruction is not an *analysis*, nor a *critique* or a *method* and we do not approach it as such (Derrida, 1991). Rather, we understand deconstruction as a textual event that follows from the indeterminacy of the meaning, an event that cannot have any distinct conceptual meaning without its immanent context that the words and sentences provide (Derrida, 1976, 1981, 1991). In a sense, there is no deconstruction without a specific text and there is always deconstruction in a specific text.

Empirical material

The reflections and empirical material to which this chapter refers to are drawn from a larger ongoing postcolonial study on entrepreneuring that the researcher (first author) is conducting. The empirical material of the study consists of project materials (official project reports, including activity reports, project guidelines, pictures, short interviews produced in the period 2014–2015) gathered from a Ugandan non-governmental organization funded by international development aid agencies. The goal of the project is to promote women's rights and empowerment, community participation, and local ownership by means of savings-led and group-based micro-financing, vocational skills development, income generation and enterprise skills development, market access support, business literacy, development of functional literacy and numeracy, strengthening of life and civic skills, and networking, which are being taught in the project. A broader ambition for the project is to increase the participation of women in northern Uganda in economic activities and to increase their access to productive resources by 2017.

Reading for difference and intervention: reflections from the crossroads of postcolonial deconstruction and critical entrepreneurship studies

Our approach to the study was informed by the viewpoint that sees deconstruction as a way to take critical distance from Western culture and thus offers the possibility to rethink Western values and goals, and to overstep the limits of tradition (Enwald, 2004). Despite the conceptual tensions of deconstructionist approaches to political thought and action, deconstruction does involve the ideas of decentralization and decolonialization of European thought (Young, 1990), for which we see it as being inherently prone to postcolonial reading. Inspired by the idea of the performativity of knowledge in enacting different realities (e.g. Law & Urry, 2004; Gibson-Graham, 2008; Steyaert, 2011), a deconstructive position offers us the ability to question oppositions and therefore enables us to deal with the paradoxalities of entrepreneurship that, for us, became manifested in its emancipatory and oppressive potential. Through our reading, it was apparent that the project material pointed us towards a double-edged sword when considering the effects brought about by micro-entrepreneuring. On one side, we could not ignore the text's positive affirmations of the very tangible results the project had yielded for the participants to improve their livelihoods. Yet, at the same time, the text led us to read stories of very different realities, where seemingly innocent and idealistic pro-poor actions seized the agency of the entrepreneurs and turned the project into colonial subject-constitution that maintains an unequal and neocolonial world order. In such a situation, engagement in postcolonial deconstruction provided us a space through which to understand worlds as multiply produced in diverse and contested social and material relations (Law & Urry, 2004, p. 397). Foremost, this space allowed us to see that these worlds and "truths" should therefore be understood as flux constructions, which we cannot avoid producing of ourselves (Spivak, 1987b, p. 246).

Performativity of text and knowledge plays out not only through the undoing, decomposing, and desedimenting elements of deconstruction, but through the reconstructed ensemble it offers – for which we claim it to be a positive operation (Derrida, 1991). In our reading of the project reports, we emphasized the act of reading in its transactional mode, as (the possibility for) action (Spivak, 1987a) and intervention (Steyaert, 2011; Dey & Steyaert, 2010, 2012). Steyaert (2011, p. 78) has encouraged entrepreneurship scholars to see methodologies as more than just tools, as interventions that take account of the ontological politics of method. According to Dey and Steyaert (2012, pp. 101–102), interventionist research suggests a rethinking of the conventional academic understandings of critical research; it becomes an event that speaks out against authority and creates reality in the name of another truth (see also Steyaert, 2011). As Derrida (1981) has insisted, deconstruction is not neutral, it intervenes. For this, our motif of deconstruction is deeply interventionist (see also Chia, 1994).

In following Spivak (1988), our aim was not to privilege our reading and the subsequent narrative created as the correct one – but rather, to provide a description of how certain understandings and narratives of the reality of entrepreneurship have became established as normative ones and with what possible social consequences. Our main task thus became to unravel the project material and make visible the assigning of subject-positions (Spivak, 1987b, p. 241) throughout the text. To show how language practices in a text can be associated with different experiences of power, and to highlight that when research on entrepreneurship closes its eyes to the political effects it creates and which it is itself a part (Dey & Steyaert, 2012, p. 93), it is pretending to an innocence that it can no longer claim (Law & Urry, 2004, p. 404). We assert that entrepreneurship scholars, as with any scholars, should take responsibility for the knowledge claims we make in and through our writing (Rhodes & Brown, 2005, p. 469).

For Spivak, the greatest gift of deconstruction is "to question the authority of the investigating subject without paralyzing him, persistently transforming conditions of impossibility into possibility" (Spivak, 1987a, p. 201). We interpret this to mean that while the authority and intention of the investigating subject fades along the lines of words and sentences (contexts) that the text produces (Derrida, 1976, 1981), an unlimited number of possibilities rises from within the text. As Chia (1994, p. 783) clarifies, due to the instability of meaning in a new context, the distinction between the text, context, and their boundary becomes impossible and leads to infinite contexts invading the text regardless of authorial intention. What is then the effect of this intertextuality? It relocates the focus away from the context to the contextualization of us, our research, and the multiple ways of knowing.

In Spivak's (1988) reading of Derrida and "Of grammatology as a positive science", the question of how to keep the ethnocentric Subject from establishing itself by selectively defining an Other is confronted. Therefore, we need to ask what now differentiates us – two white academics talking postcoloniality and interference – from the benevolent Western intellectual and the continuing construction of the gendered subaltern through the conducted study. Examining our own institutional place and our relationship to the strategies of power that we aim to highlight complicates our position as knowledge producers. Spivak's (1981b, p. 383) interest (and ours) in deconstruction is explained exactly by this leverage that deconstruction offers, with "its insistence that in disclosing complicities the critic-as-subject is herself complicit with the object of her critique".

Therefore, we must acknowledge that our criticism (i.e. the managerial nature of micro-entrepreneuring rising from the project reports) of a certain system (i.e. the research field of entrepreneurship) is constrained and dependent on the prevailing discourse of that system (Derrida, 1976). Present in all Spivak's contributions is her concern for postcolonial academics' obligation to take his or her complicity into account in the production of knowledge, which can only happen through acknowledging our theoretical positionality and "unlearning" our privilege (Spivak, 1988, 1985 in Young, 1990). Thus, engagement in postcolonial deconstruction guides us to make an ethical choice to include ourselves as investigators complicit in possibly – but not preferably – constituting both the phenomena we wish to offer an alternative to and new realities by decolonizing entrepreneurship studies. What we mean by this is that we cannot escape our complicity in constructing dominant social formations; in writing a text for the highly Western academic community, we cannot help but reproduce this privileged community further, and thus possibly silencing its others even further (Spivak, 1985; Calás et al., 2009).

Through the research process, we became aware of the modes of textuality through which we could approach the difference between us, as academics, and the representations of Others that, through the logic of supplementarity, are inscribed in both the texts we read and the texts we write. Through deconstruction and the subsequent escape from dichotomies, we came to distance ourselves from freezing the subaltern as the "object of investigation" and strived to break free of the process of inscribing the marginalized into their positions by elaborating on how this can take place even in actions that are intended by their performers (i.e. us as writers of this text or the project funders) to be benevolent. Thus, we became to emphasize that the work we produce needs, by necessity, to be situated in the historical and political landscape of the broader academia that has enabled and guided our writing (Spivak, 1988). Therefore, being deeply intertwined in the practices we aim to break free from is part of our theoretical position of postcolonial deconstruction.

We interpret Spivak's (1988) notion of "unlearning" privilege to rest on the difference that defines the concept of subaltern and respecting that difference in the writing process – an interpretation which is colored by the indeterminacy of meanings constructed through difference and deferral. The tensions and leverages offered by the difference in the social positions of our study do not derive merely from the subject-position of the subjects described in the project reports and us as the authors of this text, but they arise also from within. As a (Caucasian female) doctoral candidate and an established (Caucasian male) professor, we do react from different and multiple social locations, which influence our analysis and the way this research project is conducted (Essers, 2009). Although our privilege remains as "white academics" (see e.g. Banerjee & Tedmanson, 2010), within our surroundings we are differentially situated and cannot help but react from our own reference point, for which we believe it is equally important to emphasize the social as well the theoretical situatedness of the knowledge we produce (Essers, 2009). During the research process and aiming to "unlearn" our privilege, we realized that the privilege we have has become so mundane it is hard to recognize, not to mention unlearn. For example, feeling privileged for the fact that we are able conduct research in the first place (having funding, time, a stable state of society), writing for an international academic audience in a foreign language and academic style, or being able to travel to international conferences to communicate our research is often replaced by seeing them as aspects and requirements of academia, when in fact, these are privileges that only a few people have. In our approach of postcolonial deconstruction, the concern with privilege is not its mere existence, but its usage to theorize unprivileged groups on behalf of them without vigilance to their assigned subject-positions – in other words, appropriating and constructing the colonial subject as Other (Spivak, 1988, 1987b).

Reflecting on our subject-positions as researchers should not be understood as limited to our geographical or institutional locations, gender, or academic rankings. We do believe that research is a journey of the whole person, a journey in which emotions, emotional growth, and engagement play a role (Campbell, 2011; Gaggiotti & Case, 2014). Our curiosity for different ways of knowing has guided our engagement in the community of critical entrepreneurship scholars, an affiliation that has had concrete implications for choosing to do this type of study, and for the way we have experienced the process of constructing the study. We have aimed to challenge ourselves and let go of those systems of thought and writing that we feel most comfortable with and to relocate ourselves through the space created by postcolonial deconstruction to engage in forms of thought that would enable other possibilities to emerge. To be able to proceed with the research, and as a part of our theoretical positionality, we also had to bear the feelings of trying to unlearn our privilege and learning, and with the realization of and respect for the difference between us and the Others (of the text). For us, postcolonial decon-struction has offered another way of making sense of entrepreneurship discourse and it has revealed how broader societal processes of othering have also functioned within the processes of constructing knowledge of entrepreneurship and a univer-sal entrepreneurial self imposed on the project participants. In the following, we outline the philosophical implications of these reflections for critical entrepreneur-ship research.

Philosophical implications of postcolonial deconstruction for critical entrepreneurship research: responsibility and multiple ways of knowing

The critical tradition of entrepreneurship research that we build on has already assigned interest to a) a closer consideration of the meta-theoretical foundations of our research (e.g. Shane & Venkataraman, 2000; Busenitz et al., 2003; Fletcher, 2006; Calás et al., 2009; Gartner, 2013); and thus b) striving towards a more onto-logical understanding of methods (Steyaert, 2011) and the performativity of knowledge in general in the sense of understanding the role of our work in creating and performing the worlds we inhabit, as Gibson-Graham (2008) has elaborated; c) achieving a more complete picture of these worlds by being sensitive to the power(/knowledge) relations that create them (Calás et al., 2009; Hjorth, 2013); d) enhancing reflexive, historically and culturally contextualized and multidisci-plinary entrepreneurship research (e.g. Steyaert & Katz, 2004; Steyaert, 2005; Hjorth, 2013; Gartner, 2013; Down, 2013); which e) has directed the research interest towards the real life and everydayness of entrepreneurial processes (e.g. Steyaert, 2005); f) enlarging entrepreneurial spaces and guiding us to understand entrepreneurship as part of society and social, not only in terms of economics and business (e.g. Steyaert & Katz, 2004; Hjorth, Jones, & Gartner, 2008; Calás et al., 2009; Hjorth, 2013); and thereby g) offering alternatives to the mainstream's indi-vidual representations of the heroic (male) entrepreneur (e.g. Spilling, 2011; Campbell, 2011) and creating a theoretical space in which multiple "Other" entre-preneurial subjectivities and collectives can be considered (Ahl, 2004, 2006; Pio, 2005; Essers & Benschop, 2007, 2009; Özkazanç-Pan, 2009; Essers, Benschop, & Doorewaard, 2010; Verduijn & Essers, 2013).

The contributions of postcolonial deconstruction to the epistemological, onto-logical, and even metaphysical questions of the critical theory of entrepreneurship focus on language as performative, as constitutive of meaning. Derrida's (1976) interpretation of language as a trace-structure presents it as unstable, while ques-tioning the unity of a word, which points to the earlier-mentioned indeterminacy of meanings. In the previous section, we brought up how through a postcolonial deconstructive reading, the relation between a "theoretical method" of knowing and an author becomes equally "indeterminate", fragmented and ambivalent, and how authorial intention fades through the performative and contextual nature of the text and knowledge created. Postcolonial deconstructive theoretizations of entrepreneurship would therefore act outside and to subvert the logic of Western logocentrism and thus would claim the undecidability and impossibility of the dichotomous and hierarchical system of traditional Western thought (such as speech/writing, mind/body, theory/practice, West/non-West and so on), to find ways of knowing without explanatory models and stable conceptual definitiveness.

Along with its emphasis on polyphonic knowledge and ways of knowing, as a research approach postcolonial deconstruction implies constant self-vigilance for an author's (unknown) role in maintaining dominant social formations. From a postcolonial deconstructionist point of view, one would consider questions such as what entrepreneurship and entrepreneurship research is, what are the boundaries and taken-for-granted assumptions of entrepreneurship research, and what has been included and excluded from this research, as well as asking from which meta-theoretical positions have these processes of inclusion or exclusion taken place. Without looking for a univocal answer, one could for example question the relation of certain sub-categories of entrepreneurship, such as *ethnic* or *indigenous* entrepreneuring, to the processes of othering, speaking on behalf of Others, and in general, to enforcing an information retrieval approach in science (Spivak, 1988).

In sum, this study has shown how the concepts produced by humans do not fall easily into alleged categories, since concepts in reality are formed and exist in relation to other concepts in their contexts, making them inherently ambiguous. Consequently, the deeper, structured lineage of entrepreneurship's concepts potentially conflicts with emerging manifestations of it. Therefore, for the development of future entrepreneurship research, we argue the importance of analyzing the deeper processes of the production of entrepreneurship from the perspective of postcolonial deconstruction. This also leads us to underline the importance of taking into account an academic's responsibility and role in the power relations of knowledge production by acknowledging her theoretical positionality and striving to unlearn her privilege. Being always partial and preliminary as a textual strategy, postcolonial deconstruction shelters paradoxalities and inconsistencies within the text and thus offers a way out of the closure of knowledge.

Acknowledgments

We would like to thank the Eudaimonia Research Center (University of Oulu) and the Martti Ahtisaari Institute of Global Business and Economics for funding this research.

References

Ahl, H. (2002). The construction of the female entrepreneur as the other. In B. Czarniawska & H. Höpfl (Eds.), *Casting the other: The production and maintenance of inequalities in work organizations* (pp. 52–67). London: Routledge.

Ahl, H. (2004). *The scientific reproduction of gender inequality: A discourse analysis of research texts on women's entrepreneurship.* Copenhagen: CBS Press.

Ahl, H. (2006). Why research on women entrepreneurs needs new directions. *Entrepreneurship: Theory & Practice, 30*(5), 595–621.

Armstrong, P. (2005). *Critique of entrepreneurship.* Basingstoke: Palgrave.

Ashcroft, B., Griffiths, G., & Tiffin, H. (2003). *The post-colonial studies reader.* London: Routledge.

Banerjee, S. B., & Tedmanson, D. (2010). Grass burning under our feet: Indigenous enterprise development in a political economy of whiteness. *Management Learning, 41*(2), 147–165.

Bhabha, H. K. (1994). *The location of culture.* London: Routledge.

Busenitz, L., West, G., Shepherd, D., Nelson, T., Chandler, G., & Zacharakis, A. (2003). Entrepreneurship research in emergence: Past trends and future directions. *Journal of Management, 29,* 285–308.

Calás, M., & Smircich, L. (1999). Past postmodernism? Reflections and tentative directions. *Academy of Management Review, 24,* 649–671.

Calás, M., Smircich, L., & Bourne, K. (2009). Extending the boundaries: Reframing 'entrepreneurship as social change' through feminist perspectives. *Academy of Management Review, 34*(3), 552–569.

Campbell, K. (2011). Caring and daring entrepreneurship research. *Entrepreneurship & Regional Development, 23*(1–2), 37–47.

Chakrabarty, D. (1992). Postcoloniality and the artifice of history: Who speaks for 'Indian' pasts? *Representations, 37,* 1–26.

Chakrabarty, D. (2000). *Provincializing Europe.* Princeton: Princeton University Press.

Chia, R. (1994). The concept of decision: A deconstructive analysis. *Journal of Management Studies, 31*(6), 781–806.

Derrida, J. (1976). *Of grammatology.* Translated by G. Chakravorty Spivak. Baltimore and London: The Johns Hopkins University Press.

Derrida, J. (1981). *Positions.* Chicago: University of Chicago Press.

Derrida, J. (1991). Letter to a Japanese friend. In D. Wood & A. Benjamin (English trans.), *A Derrida reader: Between the blinds* (pp. 270–276). New York: Harwester Wheatsheaf.

de Saussure, F. (1972). Chapter two: Course in general linguistics. In C. Bally, A. Sechehaye, & A. Riedlinger (Eds.), *Course in general linguistics* (pp. 76–89). La Salle, IL: Open Court.

Dey, P., & Steyaert, C. (2010). The politics of narrating social entrepreneurship. *Journal of Enterprising Communities: People and Places in the Global Economy, 4*(1), 85–108.

Dey, P., & Steyaert, C. (2012). Social entrepreneurship: Critique and the radical enactment of the social. *Social Enterprise Journal, 8*(2), 90–107.

Down, S. (2013). The distinctiveness of the European tradition in entrepreneurship research. *Entrepreneurship & Regional Development, 25*(1–2), 1–4.

Enwald, M. (2004). *Displacements of deconstruction, academic dissertation, faculty of information sciences of the university of Tampere.* Tampere: Tampereen yliopistopaino Oy Juveniles Print.

Essers, C. (2009). Reflections on the narrative approach: Dilemmas of power, emotions and social location while constructing life-stories. *Organization, 16*(2), 163–181.

Essers, C., & Benschop, Y. (2007). Enterprising identities: Female entrepreneurs of Moroccan and Turkish origin in the Netherlands. *Organization Studies, 28,* 49–68.

Essers, C., & Benschop, Y. (2009). Muslim businesswomen doing boundary work: The negotiation of Islam, gender and ethnicity within entrepreneurial contexts. *Human Relations, 62*(3), 403–424.

Essers, C., Benschop, Y., & Doorewaard, H. (2010). Female ethnicity: Understanding Muslim immigrant businesswomen in the Netherlands. *Gender, Work and Organization, 17*(3), 320–339.

Essers, C., & Tedmanson, D. (2014). Upsetting 'Others' in the Netherlands: Narratives of Muslim Turkish migrant businesswomen at the crossroads of ethnicity, gender and religion. *Gender, Work and Organization, 21*(4), 353–367.

Fletcher, D. (2006). Entrepreneurial processes and the social construction of opportunity. *Entrepreneurship & Regional Development, 18*(5), 421–440.

Gaggiotti, H., & Case, P. (2014). Organizing through displacement, travel and movement. *Culture and Organization, 20*(3), 179–184.

Gartner, W. (2013). Creating a community of difference in entrepreneurship scholarship. *Entrepreneurship & Regional Development, 25*(1–2), 5–15.

Gibson-Graham, J. K. (2008). Diverse economies: Performative practices for 'other worlds'. *Progress in Human Geography, 32*(5), 613–632.

Goss, D., Jones, R., Betta, M., & Latham, J. (2011). Power as practice: A Micro-sociological analysis of the dynamics of emancipatory entrepreneurship. *Organization Studies, 32*(2), 211–229.

Hjorth, D. (2013). Public entrepreneurship: Desiring social change, creating sociality. *Entrepreneurship & Regional Development, 25*(1–2), 34–51.

Hjorth, D., Jones, C., & Gartner, W. (2008). Introduction for 'recreating/recontextualising entrepreneurship'. *Scandinavian Journal of Management, 24*, 81–84.

Imas, J., Wilson, N., & Weston, A. (2012). Barefoot entrepreneurs. *Organization, 19*, 563–585.

Jennings, P., Perren, L., & Carter, S. (2005). Introduction: Alternative perspectives on entrepreneurship research. *Entrepreneurship: Theory & Practice, 29*(2), 145–152.

Jones, C., & Spicer, A. (2009). *Unmasking the entrepreneur*. London: Edward Elgar.

Kaasila-Pakanen, A.-L., & Puhakka, V. (2016). Empowerment by oppression: Managing poverty by creation of an entrepreneurial self. Paper presented at the *European Group for Organizational Studies (EGOS)*, July 7–9, Naples.

Law, J., & Urry, J. (2004). Enacting the social. *Economy and Society, 33*(3), 390–410.

Loomba, A. (1998). *Colonialism/postcolonialism*. London: Routledge.

Muntean, S. C., & Özkazanc-Pan, B. (2015). A 'gender integrative conceptualization of entrepreneurship'. *New England Journal of Entrepreneurship, 18*(1), 27–40.

Muntean, S. C., & Özkazanc-Pan, B. (2016). Feminist perspectives on social entrepreneurship: Critique and new directions. *International Journal of Gender and Entrepreneurship, 8*(3), 221–241.

Ogbor, J. (2000). Mythicizing and reification in entrepreneurial discourse: Ideology-critique of entrepreneurial studies. *Journal of Management Studies, 37*(5), 605–635.

Özkazanç-Pan, B. (2009). *Globalization and identity formation: A postcolonial analysis of the international entrepreneur*. Amherst: Isenberg School of Management. University of Massachusetts-Amherst.

Özkazanc-Pan, B. (2014). Postcolonial feminist analysis of high-technology entrepreneuring. *International Journal of Entrepreneurial Behaviour and Research, 20*(2), 155–172.

Özkazanç-Pan, B. (2015). Secular and Islamic feminist entrepreneurship in Turkey. *International Journal of Gender and Entrepreneurship, 7*(1), 45–65.

Özkazanc-Pan, B., & Muntean, S. C. (2016). International high-technology entrepreneurs: Hybrid identities and entrepreneurial activities. *Journal for International Business and Entrepreneurship Development, 9*(1), 23–40.

Pio, E. (2005). Knotted strands: Working lives of Indian women migrants in New Zealand. *Human Relations, 58*(10), 1277–1300.

Prasad, A. (1997). Provincializing Europe: Towards a postcolonial reconstruction. *Culture and Organization, 3*, 91–117.

Prasad, A. (2003). The gaze of the other: Postcolonial theory and organizational analysis. In A. Prasad (Ed.), *Postcolonial theory and organizational analysis: A critical engagement* (pp. 3–43). New York: Palgrave Macmillan.

Prasad, A. (2012). Working against the grain: Beyond Eurocentrism in organization studies. In A. Prasad (Ed.), *Against the grain: Advances in postcolonial organization studies* (pp. 13–31). Copenhagen: Copenhagen Business School Press.

Rhodes, C., & Brown, A. (2005). Writing responsibly: Narrative fiction and organization studies. *Organization, 12*(4), 467–491.

Said, E. (1978). *Orientalism*. London: Routledge & Kegan Paul.

Shane, S., & Venkataraman, S. (2000). The promise of entrepreneurship as a field of research. *Academy of Management Review, 25*(1), 217–226.

Spilling, O. (2011). Mobilising the entrepreneurial potential in local community development. *Entrepreneurship & Regional Development, 23*(1–2), 23–35.

Spivak, G. (1981a). French feminism in an international frame. *Yale French Studies, 62*, 154–184.

Spivak, G. (1981b) "Draupadi" by Mahasveta Devi. *Critical Inquiry, 8*(2), 381–402.

Spivak, G. (1985). Three women's texts and a critique of imperialism. *Critical Inquiry, 12*(1), 243–261.

Spivak, G. (1987a). Subaltern studies: Deconstructing historiography. In G. Spivak (Ed.), *In other worlds: Essays in cultural politics* (pp. 197–221). New York: Methuen.

Spivak, G. (1987b). A literary representation of the Subaltern: A woman's text from the third world. In G. Spivak (Ed.), *In other worlds: Essays in cultural politics* (pp. 241–268). New York: Methuen.

Spivak, G. (1988). Can the subaltern speak? In C. Nelson & L. Grossberg (Eds.), *Marxism and the interpretation of culture* (pp. 271–313). Urbana: University of Illinois Press.

Steyaert, C. (1997). A qualitative methodology for process studies of entrepreneurship. *International Studies of Management & Organization, 27*(3), 13–33.

Steyaert, C. (2005). Entrepreneurship: In between what? On the 'frontier' as a discourse of entrepreneurship research. *International Journal of Entrepreneurship and Small Businesses, 2*, 2–16.

Steyaert, C. (2011). Entrepreneurship as in(ter)vention: Reconsidering the conceptual politics of method in entrepreneurship studies. *Entrepreneurship & Regional Development, 23*(1–2), 77–88.

Steyaert, C., & Hjorth, D. (Eds.). (2006). *Entrepreneurship as social change: A third movements in entrepreneurship book*. Cheltenham: Edward Elgar.

Steyaert, C., & Katz, J. (2004). Reclaiming the space of entrepreneurship in society: Geographical, discursive and social dimensions. *Entrepreneurship and Regional Development, 16*(3), 179–196.

Tedmanson, D., Verduijn, K., Essers, C., & Gartner, W. (2012). Critical perspectives in entrepreneurship research. *Organization, 19*, 531–541.

Verduijn, K., Dey, P., Tedmanson, D., & Essers, C. (2014). Emancipation and/or oppression? Conceptualizing dimensions of criticality in entrepreneurship studies. *International Journal of Entrepreneurial Behaviour and Research, 20*(2), 98–107.

Verduijn, K., & Essers, C. (2013). Questioning dominant entrepreneurship assumptions: The case of female ethnic minority entrepreneurs. *Entrepreneurship & Regional Development, 25*(7–8), 612–630.

Weiskopf, R., & Steyaert, C. (2009). Metamorphoses in entrepreneurship studies: Towards an affirmative politics of entrepreneuring. In D. Hjorth & C. Steyaert (Eds.), *The politics and aesthetics of entrepreneurship* (pp. 183–201). Cheltenham: Edward Elgar.

Young, R. (1990). *White mythologies: Writing history and the west.* London: Routledge.

8 Cruel optimism

The stories of entrepreneurial attachments

*Natasha Slutskaya, Oliver Mallett
and Janet Borgerson*

Introduction

Drawing on Berlant's concept of cruel optimism, the chapter explores entrepreneurial attachment to success ethics (a system of legitimation that prioritizes norms and actions consistent with institutionalized notions of success) (Berger & Luckmann, 1966) generated by a cluster of promises afforded by the enterprise culture. Based on five life stories of entrepreneurs who had first-hand experience of bankruptcy, this chapter aims at gaining a more nuanced understanding of why the uniformity and orthodoxy of identities around an entrepreneurial ideal persist and grow in the context of entrepreneurial failure. The chapter is motivated by an interest in the human consequences of bankruptcies and focuses on exploring how the appropriation and internalization of social norms propounded by the enterprise culture might fix life narratives in a way that hinders the very possibility of identities that are 'more sensitive to themselves' (Cohen, 1992, p. 178). Firstly, the chapter highlights the strength and endurance of the attachment to these principles even in the face of the totality of bankruptcy loss and extreme disruptions to the emancipatory dream. Secondly and relatedly, the chapter examines how failure may strengthen the optimistic nature of the entrepreneurial attachment to success ethics. We argue that continuous participation in enterprise culture is central to the construction of entrepreneurial subjectivity as it provides a sense of proximity (Ahmed, 2010) to the 'right' values – values that arguably contain the promise of success, status and future. To understand participants' attachment to extremely stressful, and often traumatic, entrepreneurial lives and their propensity to promulgate and reproduce the entrepreneurial ideal, we need to think about social norms related to the entrepreneurial ideal not only as aspirational but also as redeeming and reassuring about the present and future experience of social belonging that can be lived in affective transactions that take place alongside the more instrumental ones (Berlant, 2011).

Literature review

In their consideration of the complex relationship between subjectivities at work and discursive and normative powers that are implicated in the formation of working subjects, scholars in the field have highlighted subjects' stubborn adherence to the normative terms and conditions. Drawing on such authors as Butler, Lacan and Foucault, a growing number of studies have offered multiple interpretations of the ways in which subjects are susceptible to societal norms and therefore identify closely with externally prescribed notions of success, achievement, individualism, good life, ethical living and many others (see Driver, 2009; Ekman, 2013; Hoede-maekers, 2009; Kenny, 2010, 2012). All these studies are grounded in the premise that, despite the potentially constraining and limiting nature of normativity in relation to individual agency, the subject adheres to its terms as the integrity and possibilities of self-realization of human beings are understood to depend on approval being forthcoming from others. Rather than the more traditional reliance on individual self-interest as a shaping mechanism of human interactions, this literature recognizes the human need for recognition as a prevailing force in sub-ject formation. These scholars also highlight how falling outside the norm could be experienced as abjection and a source of sufferings (see Kenny, 2010) as rejec-tions and recognitions fashion reflections of itself; they offer confirmation of the self; they promise its endurance or, on the contrary, they threaten its esteem. Inexo-rably, subjects respond in affective and emotional ways by developing intense attachment to fantasmatic images about recognition by the other (Ekman, 2013). For example, Kenny (2010) talks about such passionate attachments as a way of understanding the workplace identification processes. She draws on Butlers' notion of the ek-static subject to advance the field's understanding of how an individual psyche is inscribed by 'societal' norms. Exploring examples of enactment of ethi-cal living in one of the development sector organizations, Kenny demonstrates how, despite its members' original endorsement of openness to 'difference', the reinforcement of normativity 'took place there through the exclusion of ethically unsound others, both within and outside of organization, accompanied by constitu-tion of selves as ethically sound' (Kenny, 2010, p. 8). Ekman (2013) further high-lights the dark side of identification in creative industries by demonstrating how hiding in the limitless concern about identity might hinder the possibility of more productive and responsible interactions at work. Although employees' engagement with a fantasmatic field with its intense desire for mutual recognition undoubtedly generates an extra competitive drive, it also, according to the study, produces a wide range of vulnerabilities and defences that obscure the workings of power relations in the organizational setting. Similarly, Bloom and Cederstrom (2009) explore the nature of fantasy in the age of market rationality. Drawing on an under-standing of fantasy as a key mechanism of stabilizing and destabilizing reality, the authors invite attention to its potentially regulatory power to order employees' emotional investments and attachments. For them, fantasy occupies the unique space between the subjective and the objective – a space that affectively grips humans within broader normative discourses. In the same way, in her analysis of organizational change, Driver (2009) illustrates how organizational story-telling can be seen as a way of both maintaining and disrupting fantasies of work, self and organization.

All these scholars have agreed that the key component of the logic of fantasy is the subject's attachments to fantasy – the greater the attachment the stronger the grip of normativity. Exploring the nature of attachment to something that has already been denied might generate further insights into individual adherence to often limiting and compromised conditions of possibility.

The internalization of enterprise culture

In the enterprise culture, as Marquand (1992) argues, economic expectations (what benefits the market) become normative expectations and get transformed into 'righteously' presented demands. In short, society rewards economic agents who live up to these expectations and punishes those who fail to fulfil their demands. What we get attached to is closely connected to notions of value and worth (Taylor, 1985) – the latter shaped by economic, cultural and historical classificatory sets of values (Skeggs, 2004). These economic tenets open up space for a new form of political ideology grounded in the notion of the 'enterprising self' (Rose, 1989) i.e. the self which is expected to be capable of both re-evaluating and changing its social, economic and moral positions according to the market (Heelas & Morris, 1992). Here, the process of internalization of enterprise discourse is seen to contribute to the creation of entrepreneurial identities in different spheres of contemporary life (Du Gay, 1996, 2003; Fournier, 1998; Nicholson & Anderson, 2005; Ogbor, 2000) – based on the 'liberating' capacities to surmount obstacles, be innovative and take risks (Skillen, 1992). In recent years, this 'innovative self' (Betta, Jones, & Latham, 2010) has come to represent a new emancipatory force (Rindova, Barry, & Ketchen, 2009) with diverse social change activities and practices (Calas, Smircich, & Bourne, 2009; Fournier & Grey, 2000; Hjorth, 2007; Steyaert, 2007; Steyaert & Katz, 2004). Hence, the notion of entrepreneurship has been reframed as a process of 'entrepreneuring' in order to emphasize the role of actions, entrepreneurial agency and choice in the entrepreneurial 'drive for autonomy, expression of personal values and making a difference in the world' (Goss, Jones, Betta, & Latham, 2011; Rindova et al., 2009, p. 478). Here, new innovative subjects (Betta et al., 2010) are expected to break free from authority and author their environments through declarations regarding their economic and social worth (Rindova et al., 2009). In this context, for the entrepreneurial drive to be sustainable, entrepreneurs' powers to succeed need to be emphasized (Goss, 2005) and supported by individual stories of success. Failure, if temporary, can be an important backdrop to the success story through accounts of challenge and of 'fighting back'. As Bouchikhi (1993) argues, enormous energy is expended in resisting failure. Therefore, 'success ethics' and the 'achievement principle' function as a set of instructions for what entrepreneurs must do to be worthy of their title where success may be rendered a 'compulsory condition' of establishing self-worth. In contemporary society, a 'successful' or 'achieved' self is granted a special status and rewarded with privileges and power. Therefore, success is desirable both for the status that one gains and for the sense of self-worth that accompanies it (Elkins, 1985). 'Success ethics' reinforce the significance of such traits and drives as asset accruing, work competition, risk taking as a potential source of *valued* social identity (Goffman, 1990).

If respect and recognition are to be conferred only on those who classify as achievers (Skeggs, 2004), insecurities about self can become a permanent feature of everyday experience (Collinson, 2003) especially as entrepreneurial aspiration is unlikely to be achieved in full. Further, a society where self-worth is conditional upon limiting, fleeting and mostly unattainable notions of 'success' sets off recurrent insecurities and anxieties about self and status (Berger & Luckmann, 1966). Bankruptcy is a particularly interesting case where the position of the failed subjects often cannot be redeemed because of the specific type of social stigma attached (Efrat, 2005). Historically, various shaming and demeaning practices, including publicly cutting the bankrupt's hair, branding the person's palm with the letter 'T' for 'thief', and publicly piercing the debtor's ear with a nail, were used in order to direct attention at social deviants (Mann, 2002). As Goffman (1990) argues, deviancy that emanates from characteristics understood as the individual's own fault attracts more reprobation. This is supported by Efrat (2005), who suggests that, historically, harsher treatment was meted out to those who were considered blameworthy and responsible for their deviant behaviour. This resonates with meanings attached to and manifestations of bankruptcy where stigma persists precisely because bankruptcy is still deemed the individual's fault – even though, as Austin, Stevenson, and Wei-Skillern (2006) claim, individuals possess very limited control over contextual factors such as the macro-economy, tax and regulatory structures and the sociopolitical environment. The taxonomies of difference between an 'achieved self' and a failed subject can become increasingly problematized by individuals' attachment to the notion of success, achievement and the concept of a worthy self. These normative demands and the ensuing struggles for recognition are likely to be condensed within the bankruptcy experience, the focus of this study, as individuals encounter the often profound effects of business failure. This chapter draws on Berlant's notion of cruel optimism and her notion of optimistic attachment to explores managing simultaneously incoherent narratives of in the context of bankruptcy failure and how success ethics and the achievement principle are implicated in this process. This has implications for the pursuit of symbolic security.

Berlant's cruel optimism

For Berlant (2011), optimism is a force 'that moves you out of yourself and into the world in order to bring you closer to the satisfying something that you cannot generate on your own but sense in the wake of . . . a way of life, a project, a concept, or scene' (Berlant, 2011, p. 1). Optimism is rendered cruel when something one strives and longs for becomes 'an obstacle to his/her flourishing' (Berlant, 2011, p. 1). Berlant highlights that not every instance of optimism is cruel; however, optimism grows cruel when the project that entices one's attachment becomes an impediment to the accomplishment of one's original goal. In her discussion of the affective structure of an attachment she draws attention to the sustaining need to return to the desirable – to the scene of fantasy. This return ignites a repeated sense of possibility even if the possibility is absent. Thus, cruel optimism, for

Berlant, designates a relation of attachment to compromised conditions of the possible whose realisation is discovered . . . to be impossible' (Berlant, 2007, p. 33), it also implies that the affective attachment to the 'right' project – where right stands for normatively defined 'right' – can potentially turn out for many to be a harmful life. As Berlant puts it, sustaining optimistic attachment 'wears out the subjects who nonetheless and at the same time, find the conditions of possibility within it' (Berlant, 2007, p. 35). Using Berlant's notion of cruel optimism we would like to think about why entrepreneurs 'choose to ride the wave of the system of attachment that they are used to', to unceasingly adhere to the same hopes, visions, aspirations and confidences that have been repeatedly failing them.

Methodology

This project set out to explore the nature of optimistic attachments through biographical narrative accounts. Life stories are directly concerned with the attachment to anonymous (in the sense of not always obvious or easily traceable) discursive codes (Culler, 1981) and the arrangement of these discursive codes into some meaningful and legitimate narrative accounts (Bauman, 2004; Giddens, 1991). Such accounts are fragile, because the biographical project of the subject is an enforced act of self-narration (Steedman, 2000) whereby identity is born out of the effort to bridge the gap between the 'ought' and the 'is' (Bauman, 2004, p. 20). At the same time, biographical narratives are persistent, because to 'consider oneself as oneself' (Locke cited in Rudd, 2007) requires consistency and continuity in terms of a subject's ability to think of him or herself as *persisting through time* (Rudd, 2007). In this context, a life narrative can be read as a subject's attempt to make oneself intelligible to oneself and others (Rudd, 2007) through his or her attachment to norms, systems of judgement and vocabularies granted to them – an attachment that shapes the subjects' views on such vital concepts as dignity, success and virtues and moulds their sense of self-worth (Rose, 1996).

Data collection

Our research site comprised small high street businesses located in Devon – an area that has the highest level of entrepreneurial activity nationwide (Department for Business, Innovation and Skills, 2011). This may reflect the fact that for a significant number of people self-employment remains the *only* route given the lack of job opportunities in the region. The number of small businesses going bankrupt in Devon and Cornwall has increased by more than 45% in the time of recession. Statistics compiled by the Ministry of Justice show almost 30 firms are going bankrupt in the region every day, with 2,618 firms in the South West filing for bankruptcy in the first three months of 2010–600 more than in the same period the year before (Ministry of Justice).

Similar to other studies of identity (Beech, Gilmore, Cochrane, & Greig, 2012; Garcia & Hardy, 2007; Humphreys & Brown, 2002; Mallett & Wapshott, 2012) this project set out to explore the identity implications of failure through narrative accounts.

A life story approach was adopted in order to overcome potential reticence in disclosure of the events and experiences of bankruptcy (Bertaux & Kohli, 1984). As Goffman (1963) points out, an individual often struggles to describe a situation that might challenge conceptions of him or herself. In the current context, the specific type of stigma and sensitivity attached to bankruptcy (Efrat, 2005) were likely to make engagement with the topic problematic and troublesome. Within a life story format participants are asked to explore, reconstruct and re-live experiences within their own frame of reference (Denzin, 1989). As Flyvbjerg (2006) argues, the closeness of life stories to real-life situations is not just important for understanding individual experience but also for the development of a nuanced view of reality.

Interviews were conducted in two stages. Firstly, only the most general questions were asked about individual lives (e.g. can you tell me about your childhood; can you tell me about your family) with follow up questions and prompts relating largely to these broad areas. In the second stage, and after some trust and rapport had been built, respondents were re-interviewed. Here, participants were asked more overt questions that captured the thematic sequence of the initial account (e.g. the events leading up to business failure and how these were interpreted and perceived by respondents as well as by family and peers). This encouraged recall of difficult experiences. Following Atkinson's (1998) suggestions, the second set of interviews were transcribed and a copy given to the participants to read and review with any corrections and amendments.

Interviews lasting between 90 and 180 minutes at each stage were conducted with five entrepreneurs who had firsthand, fairly recent (within the last five years), experience of bankruptcy. All entrepreneurs were male and had the experience of running the business for five or more years. According to Goodley (2004) and Merrill and West (2009) the small sample is justified on the grounds that life stories provide rich material and a great deal of detail regarding participants' lives (an average interview length in these studies was between 90 and 180 minutes). Merrill and West (2009) also demonstrated that it might be more productive to focus on smaller groups with 'particular and rich experience to share'. Clough, Goodley, Lawthom, and Moore (2004) advocate a sample of no more than six people when doing life story research, while Carolyn Steedman's life story (1986) project is based on two people.

Data analysis

In analysis, the interpretive approach was adopted (Denzin, 1989). Each case was explored separately and the same steps were followed. Firstly, general life course experiences were identified (childhood, education, employment) in order to separate narrative segments and useful categories within the interview story. This helped to highlight both general and unique features of respondents' lives – their values, attitudes and forms of socialization. Here, responses were treated as displays of perspectives and moral evaluations (Silverman, 2001). Secondly, following Denzin (1989) classificatory categories were then established: (1) structural

processes in the life course (i.e. parents' influence and expectations, type of education, societal expectations, etc.); (2) career/employment paths; (3) personal aspirations, evaluation of achievements and future intentions. Finally, once the individual
case analyses were finalized, comparisons between the cases were made. This
allowed researchers to identify and categorize narrative discontinuities and inconsistencies and to capture contradictions that may have otherwise been masked as
a result of individuals' searching for coherence in their life-story accounts. This
stage of the analysis focused on the detection of the external and internal logics of
the story (Bourdieu, 1984) – the logic of the social field where a life is played out
and the logic of the personal life (Denzin, 1989) in the attempt to uncover the larger
ideologies that structure the life stories and the complexities of the structuring
process. This was a highly iterative process as we reviewed and recapped (Garcia
& Hardy, 2007) potential connections and relationships between larger cultural
and social discourses and individual understandings. By exploring the functioning
of internal and external logics within the five narrative accounts, we were able to
show how attachment to norms, systems of judgement and vocabularies granted
to us can dictate the way practices and narratives of the self are organized and how
they persist in time (Rose, 1989). This is a result of commitment, despite the experience of failure, to a particular model of self.

Findings

Adherence to an enterprising self

Though mediated by personal experience, participants' attachment to the notion
of an 'enterprising self' revealed itself in life accounts based on traditional conceptualizations of an entrepreneurial ethos. This was demonstrated through the
reading of enterprise culture as 'inspiration' (Marquand, 1992) as well as through
the construction of self narratives that drew on early competitiveness and success
(being at the top of the class, winning at sports), self-reliance and ambition (wanting early career advancement), a dislike for institutional and bureaucratic environments, and an aspiration to lead.

> *Promotion was too slow. . . . and I was by then 23, 24 and the youngest, the*
> *next step up was to be an Area Manager and the youngest Area Manager at*
> *that time was over 40 and even if I'd accelerated the situation you know I*
> *knew I was going to do the same job for another ten years before I could get*
> *promoted . . . So that made me unsettled and thought about 'well perhaps I*
> *should be doing something else.*
>
> (P3)

> *The industry was changing; it started to become more controlled. I didn't like*
> *it quite so much, you know I had to start filling more forms in. . . . I suppose*
> *I didn't quite like the control so much. . . . I was asked to be doing more and*
> *more admin . . . The whole industry was changing and we had the Monopolies*

and Mergers Commission looking into the business and telling us how we had to operate . . . That was at the point when I decided to start working for myself.

(P3)

As these quotes illustrate, rejection of bureaucratic constraint, a need for self-determination and for a 'fast-track' career – the desire to regain control and to pursue preferred life-styles – were strong motivating factors symptomatic of valued capacities of self-ownership and self-management. These decisions were based on a strong self-belief in possession of entrepreneurial capabilities such as confidence, experience, previous success, willingness to work hard and to take risks:

I knew I could do this, I had a past record of being successful at doing that, I had no reason to think that I was going to be unsuccessful.

(P5)

What we needed to do was to grow so we'd have something to sell that was a lot more substantive and . . . that what we should do is to create something with real presence off which could springboard growth, that was the whole philosophy.

(P1)

Self-narratives, therefore, confirmed a strong attachment to traditional principles of the entrepreneurial self as self-steering, determined and risk taking. Attachment to success, common within entrepreneurialism, was a continuous theme even within subsequent accounts of business failure. Here, there was often an acknowledged reluctance to relinquish the potential of the business idea:

If you have a positive moment, it may only be a complimentary statement or a small boost in funds that won't really make much difference to your overall position, but it gives you a glimmer of hope. You aren't a failure, your original idea was a good one. It could still work.

(P3)

*The business idea was great and I think to be honest, to be absolutely honest the idea seemed great, yes, we could do this, could do that but it **went out of all proportions** for lots of different reasons which we don't have to go into.*

(P2)

Respondents' stories of failure accordingly contained an ongoing, contradictory adherence to the potential for success ("*you aren't a failure*"; "*the business idea was great*") as well as an avoidance of the reasons for failure (discussed further below). This attachment to the ethics of entrepreneurialism persisted despite the devastating consequences of its failure – the latter frequently evoked through references to the totality of loss and of descriptions of lives going 'out of control'.

I lost a lot of money, you know I'd spent a long time building up, as many people do, some funds and when I started the business I was able to fund it and I lost it all.

(P3)

It is a harrowing time when you are being chased by creditors and you don't have money to pay them and you are worried about every phone call . . . and you are worried about . . . you know crazy everyday things, crazy everyday things, you know are a pain, are a headache, the postman arriving you don't want that postman to turn up and you hope he doesn't have any letter for you.

(P3)

Stories of loss, the pressures of debt and isolation (as trade-fellows and other professionals "*turned their backs*") lie in contrast to accounts of earlier optimism and conviction in entrepreneurial ideals. Here, the desire for autonomy and for greater control clashed with the reality of 'struggle, stress, debt and failure' (Jones & Spicer, 2009, p. 1). In this respect, the wider the gap between an intention and an outcome, the more fragile narrative accounts can become (Bauman, 2004). Where the outcome is 'non-appealing', as Ahmed (2010) argues, the story becomes less shareable in terms of having less value. For the story to be recognized, shared and approved by others a subject needs to be able to tell a story in a manner that makes sense to others. This struggle for acceptance and approval may explain the high level of attachment, despite the experience of failure, to a normative model of self, based on achievement, productivity, and an ability to surmount obstacles. This can be seen in the ongoing, contradictory attachment to the soundness of the venture and the concentration of narrative around an entrepreneurial ideal.

The need for entrepreneurial belonging

Not only does attachment to what is of value dictate how practices and narratives of the self are organized, and what techniques of self-representation are chosen (Rose, 1989), but it also invites the repetition and re-iteration of signs of 'belonging' to the system of shared values. For the respondents, life stories functioned as an important tool empowering and naturalizing their participation in the enterprise discourse. The attachment to enterprise values reveals itself in complex acts of narration through what Taylor (1985) describes as remembering the 'right self'. The formation of the 'right self' was achieved by participants through the emphasis on memorializing significant individual achievements and awards, personal associations with success and fame through, for example, friendship with celebrities and public figures.

That was quite a good job, yes. It was a lot of money, money flew around, there was just so much money, so much money. Then we did (celebrity name) interviewing (celebrity name) at the Savoy, that was a job a half . . . Then I set up my own production company . . . I became a sort of eminence grise in business, because I won more awards in my time than anybody had even done.

(P3)

By selecting and repeating certain facts, participants reframed and re-edited their lives, intentionally or unintentionally factoring out what was undesirable or non-fitting, and revisiting and reliving the desirable. Participants' life stories were not always, however, concerned directly with the past. As Goffman (1990) argues, for the self-story to be successful, an individual must also construct a favourable future destiny. The experience of bankruptcy challenges and disrupts future potentialities in a way that one's abilities to exhibit belonging to the world of the future with its focus on dreams of ownership (including self-ownership) might be doubted. As an individual's hold on the present becomes shaky and fragile, the need to demonstrate one's grip on the future acquires a particular importance as a way of re-aligning oneself with what is of value (the dream). Despite the often catastrophic consequences of bankruptcy, all interviewees expressed the desire to continue their projects in the future, making plans for innovation and expansion. This is captured in the following account which documents, with passion and conviction, the future potential of a new entrepreneurial idea:

> *I am convinced the next step is buying a vineyard. It could be really worthwhile. In fact this is it might be a dream possibility, because if you are able to ensure the quality of the wine and then sell it to the end-consumer you can have a direct influence on the vineyard viability. For example if the average vineyard makes a profit of 40p per bottle and if you raise the retail price by 20p and pass this extra profit directly back to the vineyard you are effectively increasing the vineyard profit by 50%. So last year I decided to go to France and look at some that were up for sale. I enlisted the help of my friend who had left his father's wine business and bought a chateau of his own. He would be able to give me some advice. We visited a number of properties but all had faults, out-dated vinification equipment, poor position and too much value in the living accommodation were the most common problems. But I did find a property that was ideal. Perfectly positioned in* (French town). *I stood in the vineyard, basking in the autumn sunshine and gazing at the view towards the Gironde. It only had a simple two bed-roomed house and a small but well equipped winery. The vines were well looked after and in very good condition. I tasted the last vintage which was excellent. This was the one!! Unfortunately it was not for sale.*

This quote is particularly instructive as it reveals the contradictory nature of participants' aspirations and attachments. Despite the experience of failure, the respondent expresses conviction in a new (and seemingly promising) venture – suggestive of a continuing alignment with the entrepreneurial ideal. Juxtaposing the possible and the impossible, feasible and unfeasible, realistic and unrealistic he devotes attention to the pragmatics of the enterprise (e.g. the value of the living accommodation and the worth of the existing equipment) and expresses enthusiasm and passion (*'this was the one!!'*) for what might be seen as grandiose plans. The dream, however, has no foundation – captured in the pathos of the concluding statement: *'it was not for sale'*. This was a common theme in respondents' accounts as they outlined future plans or dreams. For example, a bankrupt but aspiring florist rejected the notion of an '*everyday sort of flower shop*' and presented plans to do '*big, big jobs for celebrities*', which would take him to '*the Caribbean and that kind of thing*' – a seemingly unrealistic goal in the light of his current financial circumstances and (small town) location.

In the context of the present study, where bankruptcy involves extreme financial constraints and where abilities to act are impaired by self-doubt, participants' often grandiose plans for the future may be expressive of aspirations to belong to and desire to participate in the enterprise culture and its emancipatory promise – even though these have previously failed them. Entrepreneurial identity can therefore be seen as a product of its normative dominance (Brown, 1995) – predicated on the reproduction of a very limited range of legitimized means of self-construction. What gets preserved in respondents' stories therefore is their desire to belong to and their qualification to participate in the entrepreneurial norm with its attribution of social, economic and moral value.

Conclusion

Drawing on five life stories, this chapter reveals the 'dark side' (Jones & Spicer, 2009) of entrepreneurship by focusing on the role of cruel optimism in self-production in the context of failure as a result of the pressure towards entrepreneurial success (in the forms of 'success ethics' (Berger & Luckmann, 1966) and the 'achievement principle' (Offe, 1976) and the demand for entrepreneurial identities to 'function smoothly'. We find, firstly, strong adherence to notions of an enterprising self through constructions of self-narratives that draw on a need for self-determination and on the possession of entrepreneurial skills. This adherence persists despite the experience of entrepreneurial failure and the totality of loss that bankruptcy entails – evidenced, partly, in a common reluctance to relinquish the original entrepreneurial ideal. Secondly and relatedly, by drawing on past successes and future possibility, respondents demonstrate a continuing desire to belong to and to participate in a normative entrepreneurial culture with its emancipatory potential and attribution of worth – even though this entrepreneurial ideal has failed them.

Our chapter makes the following contributions to the literature on entrepreneurship. *Firstly*, despite the experience of failure, there is a fixedness around a normative entrepreneurial identity through a strong attachment to an entrepreneurial ethos and a desire to be positioned within its domain. Our data shows the strength and endurance of the attachment to these principles even in the face of the totality of bankruptcy loss and extreme disruptions to the emancipatory dream.

Secondly, and relatedly, failure may exacerbate the optimistic attachment to the values reflected in the enterprise culture as individuals strive to relive their original aspirations. Anxiety produced by the unattainability of the success dream drives entrepreneurs to adopt a more 'rigid set of values' to establish the imagined proximity to what is desired, this proximity, simultaneously, evokes insecurity through the inability, via bankruptcy, to live up to its ideal. Through remembering and silences and through dedication to future potential, success can be seen as a compromised condition in the process of establishing belonging and self-worth in the face of an enterprise culture to which they claim membership, which has rejected and expelled them. The ethic of success therefore reflects not just success in itself, given the context of failure, but its seductive promise of belonging and proximity to identity affirming values.

Through our research, we have highlighted some of the problematic and contradictory aspects of optimistic attachments to entrepreneurial success in the context of failure. In particular we have demonstrated a fixedness around an entrepreneurial ideal based on normative conceptions of success and achievement. This has added to our understanding of the complexities of affective processes within entrepreneurialism – an understanding that may translate into other business and organizational contexts and so inform future research.

References

Ahmed, S. (2010). *The promise of happiness*. Durham: Duke University Press.

Atkinson, R. (1998). *The life story interview*. Thousand Oaks, CA: Sage Publications Inc.

Austin, J., Stevenson, H., & Wei-Skillern, J. (2006). Social and commercial entrepreneurship: same, different, or both? *Entrepreneurship Theory and Practice, 30*(1), 1–22.

Bauman, Z. (2004). *Wasted lives: Modernity and its outcasts*. Oxford: Polity.

Berger, P. L., & Luckmann, T. (1966). *The social construction of reality: A treatise in the sociology of knowledge*. Garden City, NY: Doubleday.

Beech, N., Gilmore, C., Cochrane, E., & Greig, G. (2012). Identity work as a response to tensions: A re-narration in opera rehearsals. *Scandinavian Journal of Management, 28*(1), 39–47.

Berlant, L. (2007). Cruel optimism: on Marx, loss and the senses. *New Formations, 63*(1), 33.

Berlant, L. G. (2011). *Cruel optimism*. Durham: Duke University Press.

Bertaux, D., & Kohli, M. (1984). The life story approach: A continental view. *Annual Review of Sociology, 10*(1), 215–237.

Betta, M., Jones, R., & Latham, J. (2010). Entrepreneurship and the innovative self: A Schumpeterian reflection. *International Journal of Entrepreneurial Behavior & Research, 16*(3), 229–244.

Bloom, P., & Cederstrom, C. (2009). 'The sky's the limit': Fantasy in the age of market rationality. *Journal of Organizational Change, 22*(2), 159–180. doi:10.1108/09534810910947190

Bouchikhi, H. (1993). A constructivist framework for understanding entrepreneurship performance. *Organization Studies, 14*(4), 549–570.

Bourdieu, P. (1984). *Distinction: A social critique of the judgment of taste*. Cambridge, MA: Harvard University Press.

Brown, W. (1995). *States of injury: Power and freedom in late modernity*. Princeton, NJ: Princeton University Press.

Calas, M. B., Smircich, L., & Bourne, K. A. (2009). Extending the boundaries: Reframing "entrepreneurship as social change" through feminist perspectives. *Academy of Management Review, 34*(3), 552–569.

Clough, P., Goodley, D., Lawthom, R., & Moore, M. (2004). *Researching life stories: Method, theory and analyses in a biographical age*. London: Routledge.

Cohen, A. P. (1992). The personal right to identity: A polemic on the self in the enterprise culture. In P. Heelas & P. Morris (Eds.), *The values of the enterprise culture: The moral debate* (pp. 179–193). London: Routledge.

Collinson, D. L. (2003). Identities and insecurities: Selves at work. *Organization, 10*(3), 527–547. doi:10.1177/13505084030103010

Culler, J. (1981). *The pursuit of signs: Semiotics, literature, deconstruction.* Ithaca: Cornell University Press.

Denzin, N. K. (1989). *Interpretive biography.* Newbury Park: Sage.

Department for Business, Innovation and Skills (BIS), UK (2011). www.bis.gov.uk/

Driver, M. (2009). From loss to lack: Stories of organizational change as encounters with failed fantasies of self, work and organization. *Organization, 16*(3), 353–369. doi:10.1177/1350508409102300

Du Gay, P. (1996). *Consumption and identity at work.* London: Sage.

Du Gay, P. (2003). The tyranny of the epochal: Change, epochalism and organizational reform. *Organization, 10*(4), 663–684.

Efrat, R. (2005). Bankruptcy stigma: Plausible causes for shifting norms. *Emory Bankruptcy Developments Journal, 22*, 481–520.

Ekman, S. (2013). Fantasies about work as limitless potential – How managers and employees seduce each other through dynamics of mutual recognition. *Human Relations, 66*(9), 1159–1181. doi:10.1177/0018726712461812

Elkins, J. R. (1985). Rites de passage: Law students telling their lives. *Journal of Legal Education, 35*, 27–55.

Flyvbjerg, B. (2006). Five misunderstandings about case-study research. *Qualitative Inquiry, 12*(2), 219–245. doi:10.1177/1077800405284363

Fournier, V. (1998). Stories of development and exploitation: Militant voices in enterprise culture. *Organization, 5*(1), 55–80.

Fournier, V., & Grey, C. (2000). At the critical moment: Conditions and prospects for critical management studies. *Human Relations, 53*(1), 7–32.

Garcia, P., & Hardy, C. (2007). Positioning, similarity and difference: Narratives of individual and organizational identities in an Australian university. *Scandinavian Journal of Management, 23*(4), 363–383. doi:10.1016/j.scaman.2007.09.002

Giddens, A. (1991). *Modernity and self-identity: Self and society in the late modern age.* Cambridge: Polity Press.

Goffman, E. (1963). *Stigma: Notes on the management of spoiled identity.* New York: Simon and Schuster.

Goffman, E. (1990). *The presentation of self in everyday life.* New York: Doubleday.

Goodley, D. (2004). *Researching life stories: Method, theory, and analyses in a biographical age.* London: Routledge.

Goss, D. (2005). Schumpeter's legacy? Interaction and emotions in the sociology of entrepreneurship. *Entrepreneurship Theory and Practice, 29*(2), 205–218. doi:10.1111/j.1540-6520.2005.00077.x

Goss, D., Jones, R., Betta, M., & Latham, J. (2011). Power as practice: A micro-sociological analysis of the dynamics of emancipatory entrepreneurship. *Organization Studies, 32*(2), 211–229. doi:10.1177/0170840610397471

Heelas, P., & Morris, P. (1992). Enterprise culture: its values and value. In P. Heelas & P. Morris (Eds.) *The values of the enterprise culture: The moral debate* (pp. 1–25). London: Routledge.

Hjorth, D. (2007). Lessons from Iago: Narrating the event of entrepreneurship. *Journal of Business Venturing, 22*(5), 712–732. doi:10.1016/j.jbusvent.2006.10.002

Hoedemaekers, C. (2009). Traversing the empty promise: Management, subjectivity and the other's desire. *Journal of Organizational Change, 22*(2), 181–201. doi:10.1108/09534810910947208

Humphreys, M., & Brown, A. D. (2002). Narratives of organizational identity and identification: A case study of hegemony and resistance. *Organization Studies, 23*(3), 421–447.

Jones, C. A., & Spicer, A. (2009). *Unmasking the entrepreneur.* Cheltenham, UK: Edward Elgar.

Kenny, K. (2010). Beyond ourselves: Passion and the dark side of identification in an ethical organization. *Human Relations, 63,* 857–873. doi:10.1177/0018726709345042

Kenny, K. (2012). 'Someone big and important': Identification and affect in an international development organization. *Organization Studies, 33*(9), 1175–1193. doi:10.1177/0170840612448156

Mallett, O., & Wapshott, R. (2012). Mediating ambiguity: Narrative identity and knowledge workers. *Scandinavian Journal of Management, 28*(1), 16–26.

Mann, B. H. (2002). *Republic of debtors: Bankruptcy in the age of American independence.* Cambridge, MA: Harvard University Press.

Marquand, D. (1992). The enterprise culture: Old wine in new bottles. In P. Heelas & P. Morris (Eds.), *The values of the enterprise culture* (pp. 61–72). London: Routledge.

Merrill, B., & West, L. (2009). *Using biographical methods in social research.* London: Sage.

Nicholson, L., & Anderson, A. R. (2005). News and nuances of the entrepreneurial myth and metaphor: Linguistic games in entrepreneurial sense-making and sense-giving. *Entrepreneurship Theory and Practice, 29*(2), 153–172.

Offe, C. (1976). *Industry and inequality: The achievement principle in work and social status.* London: Edward Arnold.

Ogbor, J. O. (2000). Mythicizing and reification in entrepreneurial discourse: Ideology-critique of entrepreneurial studies. *Journal of Management Studies, 37*(5), 605–635. doi:10.1111/1467-6486.00196

Rindova, V., Barry, D., & Ketchen, D. (2009). Entrepreneuring as emancipation. *Academy of Management Review, 34*(3), 477–491.

Rose, N. (1989). *Governing the soul.* London: Routledge.

Rose, N. (1996). *Inventing our selves: Psychology, power, and personhood.* Cambridge: Cambridge University Press.

Rudd, A. (2007). Kierkegaard, MacIntyre and narrative unity – Reply to Lippitt. *Inquiry, 50*(5), 541–549. doi:10.1080/00201740701612416

Silverman, E. K. (2001). *Masculinity, motherhood, and mockery: Psychoanalyzing culture and the Iatmul Naven rite in New Guinea.* Ann Arbor: The University of Michigan Press.

Skeggs, B. (2004). *Class, self, culture.* London: Routledge.

Skillen, T. (1992). Enterprise – Towards the emancipation of a concept. In P. Hellas & P. Morris (Eds.), *The values of the enterprise culture* (pp. 73–82). Oxford: Basil Blackwell.

Steedman, C. (1986). *Landscape for a good woman.* London: Virago.

Steedman, C. (2000). Enforced narratives. In T. Cosslett, C. Lury, & P. Summerfield (Eds.), *Feminism and autobiography: Texts, theories, methods* (pp. 25–43). London: Routledge

Steyaert, C. (2007). 'Entrepreneuring' as a conceptual attractor? A review of process theories in 20 years of entrepreneurship studies. *Entrepreneurship and Regional Development, 19*(6), 453–477. doi:10.1080/08985620701671759

Steyaert, C., & Katz, J. (2004). Reclaiming the space of entrepreneurship in society: Geographical, discursive and social dimensions. *Entrepreneurship and Regional Development, 16*(3), 179–196. doi:10.1080/0898562042000197135

Taylor, C. (1985). *Philosophy and the human sciences* (Vol. 2). Cambridge: Cambridge University Press.

9 Critiquing and renewing the entrepreneurial imagination

Neil A. Thompson

Introduction

Few concepts in the history of entrepreneurial thought rival that of the entrepreneurial imagination. Imagination has been referenced in entrepreneurship's early development from heterodox economics literature and continues to be cited in the present (Cornelissen, 2013; Gartner, 2007; Sarasvathy, 2002; Thompson, 2017; Witt, 2007). It has long been evoked to explain the creation of products, creative action, sensemaking of futures and pasts and decision making (Schumpeter, 1934; Shackle, 1979). There is an indication, however, that imagination is beginning to fall from grace in the cognitive domain of entrepreneurship studies. As Grégoire, Corbett, and McMullen's (2011) review demonstrates, during the last decade entrepreneurial cognition research has largely examined cognitive resources (e.g. heuristic, effectual or causal modes of decision-making, mindful alertness, emotional energy, ambiguity absorption), perceptual processes (motivations, content and structure of cognitive maps, mental prototyping, incongruence and incompleteness of representations, cognitive frames), and expertise (prior knowledge, information processing) with scant empirical references to imagination. Where references to imagination do still exist, it is often immediately surpassed by reference to social psychological concepts – such as perspective taking (McMullen, 2010), inferential reasoning (Cornelissen, 2013), or counter-factual thinking. What is more, scholars across many disciplines (Daston, 1998), with entrepreneurship being no exception (Hjorth, 2007; Hjorth, Jones, & Gartner, 2008; Hsieh, Nickerson, & Zenger, 2007), have expressed an uneasiness with a concept that can be all too easily related to fetishizing or fantasizing – something unruly that needs to be suppressed once entrepreneurial ideas have formed and exploitation begins.

Given the extent to which entrepreneurial imagination is referenced in the history of entrepreneurship thought, and its possible fall from grace, it is surprising that it has thus far escaped from being a focal point of a critical review. Few entrepreneurship scholars have interrogated the concept and even fewer have undertaken the difficult task of theorizing upon the entrepreneurial imagination directly. As a consequence, there remains a rich opportunity to revisit the various fundamental assumptions of the entrepreneurial imagination. The purpose of this chapter is thus twofold: first, I critically examine current assumptions about the entrepreneurial imagination to pinpoint underlying philosophical assumptions, and, second, I renew theorizing in light of the burgeoning philosophy of imagination literature.

This chapter begins with a rendition of past and present conceptualizations of the entrepreneurial imagination upon which scholars base their claims. I base my critical review upon three alternative social ontologies making headway in entrepreneurship studies – processual, relationality and aesthetics. The results of my critique suggest that imagination is: a continuous process used to form perceptions of (alternative) realities (processual critique); a shared phenomenon that is socially situated and contingent upon social interaction (relational critique); and is reality-oriented through sensory perception (aesthetic critique). Following this argumentation, I renew theorizing upon the entrepreneurial imagination using an up-to-date collection of philosophical works, building from philosopher Mary Warnock (1978, 1994) as a central reference point (herself building on foundations of Romanticism, phenomenology and existentialism). Imagination is recast in terms of its primary and secondary modes that produces, situates and shares images within ongoing social practices (Gartner, Stam, Thompson, & Verduijn, 2016; Thompson, 2017). The chapter ends with a discussion about the relevance of entrepreneurial imagination for future entrepreneurship scholarship. In particular, I make the argument that a 'return to imagination' in cognitive-oriented research will help further growing aims of situating, embedding and embodying entrepreneurial cognition. In particular, I argue that re-incorporating imagination moves discussions of situated cognition from exclusively reflexivity and towards generative capacities of the mind, whilst still emphasizing mystery, doubt and possibility that underlie all entrepreneurial endeavours.

Revisiting the entrepreneurial imagination: three critiques

It is hard to understate the extent to which imagination and entrepreneurship have been intertwined, both in the academy and in popular culture. The aim of this portion of the chapter is to take a rare critical eye of entrepreneurial imagination to understand the common conceptualizations and assumptions. In doing so, however, I do not execute a systematic literature review, rather I touch upon the persistent and central ideas that scholars today reference when they evoke entrepreneurial imagination. In Section 1, I give a brief historical sketch of the entrepreneurial imagination and its connection to contemporary references. Section 2 builds a critique of these common conceptualizations along processual, relational and aesthetic grounds, which motivates my re-theorizing of entrepreneurial imagination in the subsequent Section 3.

Imagination in entrepreneurship studies

Early heterodox economic scholars regarded images and imagination as critical contributors to visualization and realization of entrepreneurial opportunities, decision making and the creation of new organizations. In this lineage of early work, perhaps the most well-known is Schumpeter (1934), who emphasized imagination as an activity through which entrepreneurs articulate new concepts and metaphors to grasp meaning and instigate change economies. In his view, imagination allows one to put oneself in the place of another person's motives (or sentiments). Thus, the imagination is a vehicle of social change, as articulated in his notion of creative destruction. Schumpeter (1934, p. 86 emphasis added) writes, 'a new and another kind of effort of will is therefore necessary in order to wrest, amidst the work and care of the daily round, scope and time for conceiving and working out the new combination and *to bring oneself to look upon it as a real possibility and not merely as a day-dream'*. In a similar vein, Shackle (1979) and Buchanan and Vanberg (1991) argue that uncertainty is at the root of all future expectations since 'we can choose only what is still unactualized; we can choose amongst imaginations and figments. Imagined actions and policies can have only imagined consequences, and it follows that we can choose only an action whose consequences we cannot directly know, since we cannot be eyewitnesses of them because they are events in the future' (Shackle, 1968). The principle of uncertainty provides entrepreneurs (and all humans) a cognitive opening to develop hitherto unexplored visions of the future, such that entrepreneurial choice and decision making is intertwined 'amongst imagined experiences' (Shackle, 1964, p. 12).

Another influential theorist, Kirzner (1973), is often thought of as standing in opposition to Schumpeterian and Shacklean views of imagination (Alvarez & Barney, 2007). And yet, while it is true that Kirzner initially had little reference to the imagination in his theory of arbitrage opportunities – i.e. they are confined to error recognition abilities (a single-period market decision) – he later professed that entrepreneurship in conditions of uncertainty involves multi-period market decisions that require 'a more accurately envisaged future' (Kirzner, 1982, p. 150). In fleshing out his well-known concept of "alertness" he claims 'the human agent is at all times spontaneously on the lookout for hitherto unnoticed features of the environment (present or future), which might inspire new activity on his part' such that entrepreneurial imagination 'consists in seeing through the fog created by the uncertainty of the future' (Kirzner, 1997, p. 51). Kirzner (1999) himself outlined how his theory is not necessarily inconsistent with a Schumpeterian perspective, arguing that both views stress that 'it is [the entrepreneur's] ability to *shoulder uncertainty aside* through recognizing opportunities in which imagination, judgement and creativity can successfully manifest themselves' (Kirzner, 1998, p. 109). Finally, Lachmann (1986) makes the claim that markets are the outward manifestation of an endless stream of information continuously converted into new knowledge and new expectations. In his perspective, the forward-looking entrepreneurial imagination is the central mechanism from which new combinations of knowledge are derived.

Contemporary entrepreneurship research has kept the notion of imagination alive by reference to it as driving an individual ability to envision opportunities and reconceive of existing social order. Gartner (2007, p. 624) argues that the entrepreneurial imagination is the 'generation of hypotheses about how the world might be, look and act'. Many contemporary scholars follow suit by arguing entrepreneurs use their imaginations to envision and recognize opportunities (Baron,

2006; Bjerke & Ramo, 2011; Cornelissen & Clarke, 2010; Davidsson, 2015; Hjorth, 2013; Klein, 2008; Sarasvathy, 2003; Witt, 2007). Foss and Foss (2008) note that while experiential knowledge is fundamental in the initial phase of venture formation, entrepreneurs may only be able to identify some elements of an opportunity, so they need to invoke imagination and search for and process information in order to more fully identify and evaluate the opportunity. Similarly, Cornelissen (2013, p. 704) contends that imagination seems to fuel the emotions and guide the inferential reasoning of entrepreneurs, allowing them to spot or create new opportunities by 'blending different sets of ideas into a single guiding image, which, in turn, may trigger all sorts of inferential leaps'. Sarasvathy (2002) is a proponent of imagination such that entrepreneurs bring imagination into economic processes by sculpting visions and enacting the world they would want to live in. With this principle in mind, she emphasizes the urgent need to integrate imagination into economic theory (see Bronk (2009) for such an attempt).

Three critiques of the entrepreneurial imagination

In this section, I take a long overdue critical eye of such conceptualizations of the entrepreneurial imagination to develop a three-pronged critique – processual, relational and aesthetic.

The processual critique challenges contemporary conceptions of the entrepreneurial imagination as a cognitive ability associated mainly with the recognition of opportunities. In contemporary literature, imagination is commonly perceived to be operant in nascent ideation and early problem-solving stage of the entrepreneurship process (see Zhuo, 2008). While the imagination may be important for combining knowledge to come up with new venture ideas (Davidsson, 2015) or to envisage opportunities (Gartner, 2007), it is thought to give way to alternative cognitive processes (convergent, causal, effectual, inferential or analytical thinking) that are more necessary in the phases of opportunity evaluation and exploitation (Grégoire, Barr, & Shepherd, 2010). However, confining the imagination to a (bracketed) phase of the entrepreneurial process contradicts early theorists' argumentation that all entrepreneurial decision-making – whether a decision to engage in entrepreneurial activities, attempt to acquire investment capital or target a particular customer group – involves imagining likely scenarios and sentiments of others under conditions of uncertainty. In line with processual perspective of entrepreneuring (Hjorth, Holt, & Steyaert, 2015; Verduyn, 2015), imagination is continuous and ever-present, with the resulting multiplicity of images (what one imagines) under constant reproduction and change throughout daily entrepreneurial life (Dimov, 2007). Entrepreneurial imagination is in constant use; thus, it is not restricted to ideation or opportunity recognition phases. For example, Popp and Holt (2012) build an argument for entrepreneurship as an unfolding imaginative process embedded in social contexts. The authors illustrate the emergence of entrepreneurship as a revelatory 'poetic power' that comes into being through the imaginative act of 'making present' – bringing forward that which is not yet present (see also Chiles, Elias, Vultee, & Zarankin, 2013; Dolmans, van Burg, Reymen,

& Romme, 2014). Accordingly, a processual view of the entrepreneurial imagination challenges the common assumption that imagination can be contained to one (early) phase of the entrepreneurship process.

The second critique takes aim at the assumption that the entrepreneurial imagination is confined to an individual entrepreneur's head. Being a fundamentally distinctive cognitive process, imagination is commonly referenced as an exercise of free will or unobstructed (cognitive) agency. However, a growing relational ontology of entrepreneurship has successfully criticized the presumption that the individual mind and the social world are ontologically and analytically two separate units that may interact without affecting their distinctiveness (Bradbury & Lichtenstein, 2000; Fletcher, 2006; Mutch, Delbridge, & Ventresca, 2006). As such, a relational critique uproots the presupposition that individual imaginative minds are the locus of creative ideas and opportunities. Instead, entrepreneurial imagination is a socially emergent and situated phenomenon in which the successive words and actions of others alters the nature and content of each participant's imagining. A relational critique, therefore, claims that individualist conceptions of the entrepreneurial imagination understate the fact that the human mind is interdependent upon social relations, narratives and discourses. In other words, imagining is inseparable from the collaborative entrepreneurial process arising from shared activities, or practices (Schatzki, 2006), in which entrepreneurs imagine together with clients, suppliers, investors, etc. changes to objects and practices in a context of uncertainty. This resonates with Ramoglou and Tsang's (2016) arguments that entrepreneurs use imagining within social contexts to formulate projections of possibly real, yet empirically 'unactualised propensities'. Consequently, defining the entrepreneurial imagination as an individual cognitive process belies the notion that imagination both shapes as well as is shaped by others over the course of interaction.

The final critique pushes back against the tendency to view the entrepreneurial imagination as removed from or opposed to material realism. Much, if not all, of past and contemporary conceptualizations of the entrepreneurial imagination have strong undercurrents of subjectivism and idealism, whereupon which the social world exists as a matter of subjective perception and, as such, all changes to the social world originates from entrepreneurial visions. For example, the products of imagination, images, are thought to form the plan from which an enterprise emerges, thus it is an image, not the ontological phenomena they may reflect, that shapes entrepreneurial behaviour. This 'subjectivist logic', however, reinforces a tendency to view the entrepreneurial imagination as insensitive to or removed from socio-material realities. Alternatively, an aesthetic critique of the entrepreneurial imagination foremost draws attention to the absence of the senses – seeing, hearing, feeling, tasting and smelling – and their importance in grounding cognitive activities in actions and materiality. From an aesthetic tradition, cognitive and bodily ways of knowing and thinking about the world are not distinct phenomena but essentially intertwined (Strati, 2007), responsible for provoking the emotions and creative actions of entrepreneurs (Hjorth & Steyaert, 2008; Linstead & Hopfl, 2004). For example, the imagination of a restaurateur-entrepreneur is bound to the important dimensions of smell, sound, touch and sight of (imagined) cuisine, and the subconscious passion that can emerge from them. This is a notion that is under-developed in current literature leaving an untapped, rich opportunity to theorize how the interconnectedness of body and mind are shaping and shaped by entrepreneurs as they pursue endeavours.

In conclusion, processual, relational and aesthetic ontological orientations of the study of entrepreneurship largely undermine contemporary notions of the entrepreneurial imagination. Cornelissen (2013, p. 707) argues that the 'singular focus on the static, condensed simultaneity of a single thought or symbol' should give way to 'study the plastic, dynamic nature of imagery and imagination and how emergent inferences, in turn, are realized within the institutional, technological, and economic constraints of a market or industry'. However, few researchers to date have heeded this call. There is a pressing need to renew connections to philosophy of imagination to develop these notions of entrepreneurial imagination in light of these criticisms. This oversight is surprising considering many entrepreneurship scholars proclaim the imagination as important while, on the other hand, the philosophy of imagination remains a rich and burgeoning area of study (see Kind, 2016). In the next section, I turn to and utilize the philosophy of imagination literature in order to address difficult questions related to the ontology of images and imagining.

Towards a renewed theory of the entrepreneurial imagination

The philosophy of imagination literature is an active area of philosophy exploring questions related to the nature of imagination; its relation to mental imagery, reasoning, learning, perception, memory, and dreaming; its role in creativity and the creation of music, art and fiction; and its implications for morality amongst others. While there is ongoing debate and there are various perspectives of the imagination, influential philosophers such as Mary Warnock (1978) conclude that the concept plays a much more fundamental in human life than commonly perceived. In this section, I review the notions of primary and secondary imagination, images and creative expression from this literature (for more complete review see Thompson, 2017). In section 2, I integrate this theorizing with entrepreneurship studies to develop a renew theory of the entrepreneurial imagination.

Primary and secondary imaginations, images and creative expression

According to Warnock (1978), the imagination is best thought of as constituting two modes, primary and secondary, that operate together to form images. The primary imagination describes the fundamental ability to continuously and subconsciously blend and unify aspects of one's sensory experience with memories to form instantaneous perceptions of the world (Engell, 1981). This mode of imagination essentially designates a provisional reconciliation of body and mind, wherein perceptions are the product of combinations of senses, emotions and memories. Importantly, sensory experiences and memories are wrought by social and material processes, received via the senses, which makes the primary imagination empirically and socially anchored. For example, real-time perception of certain objects (e.g. a computer) are laden with meanings (e.g. utility as a tool) that is possible through a combination of the senses (e.g. seeing, touching, and hearing the computer) and past experiences (e.g. memories of its use). Perceptions, therefore, are not solely based on past experience or knowledge, nor from immediate sensory experiences. Instead, it is the blending of senses and memories that forms perception. Accordingly, the active primary imagination subconsciously blends and constructs a more dynamic, open-ended and meaningful reality than that of sensory experience or memory alone (Warnock, 1978).

The secondary imagination is a continuation of the primary, but it is consciously and voluntarily activated. As a person activates their secondary imagination, they allow the functioning of the primary imagination to bring forth images of something not currently present. In other words, people use their secondary imagination to force the initial conditions of imagining, but let the rest of the imaginative exercise unfold without interference. For instance, to imagine a new entrée, a restaurateur-entrepreneur does not make herself imagine the exact details of the possible dish in question. Rather, having forced the initial conditions (i.e. she wishes to imagine a new dish), she allows the imagination to operate in primary mode (normally delegated only to perception) to create an image that can be accessed consciously. Left to itself, her primary imagination develops an image of an entrée not present but in a reality-oriented way. The secondary imagination can be, therefore, thought of as 'perceiving in hypothetical mode' (Murphy, 2004) relying on the same operation of the primary mode (blending memories and senses), only for perceiving that which is not present. Consequently, the secondary imagination is distinguished from fantasizing (or what Coleridge would call 'fancy') because it establishes a link between what is perceived to be 'real' or 'true' and that which is considered totally 'fictive' or 'false'.

As mentioned, the 'object' of the interplay between primary and secondary imaginations are defined as images that themselves have unique ontological characteristics. First, images are characteristically fleeting in that they 'dissipate' when one stops activating secondary mode and/or being receptive to it (Casey, 1974). Second, images are also characteristically vague in that they do not communicate detail or exact likeness, like a photograph, rather they are suggestive of a certain essence or aesthetic 'feel' (Sartre, 1940), such as image-touch, image-taste, image-sound, image-sight and image-smell (Warnock, 1978). For instance, the restaurateur-entrepreneur evoking her secondary imagination senses in her mind's eye the aesthetics of a possible new entrée (i.e. its taste, smell and visual appeal), rather than perceive of a picture of itself. Finally, to materialize images, people undertake creative acts – talking, gesturing, writing, dancing, drawing, painting and so on – in an effort to express and communicate their suggestive content. Crucially, creative expression provides the social link between images of one person to another, such that they inspire others to imagine and share their images, which has recursive implications for one another's further imagining (Thompson, 2017). For example, the restaurateur-entrepreneur imagining a new entrée uses creative expressions (perhaps gestures, talk and sketches) to communicate to another person the content of the image (its imagined aesthetic taste, smell and look). This other person not only uses imagination in primary mode to understand these suggestive expressions, but can also use her own imagination in secondary mode (and subsequence creative expressions) to alter or edit this image. As a consequence, through interactive sequences of novel talk and actions, creative expressions make images publicly available, and thus shared phenomena.

Renewing the entrepreneurial imagination

As can be seen, the entrepreneurial imagination precludes assumptions of episodic, individual and purely cognitive elements. In this section, I reconsider imagination for entrepreneurship studies by way of an example between co-founders attempting to incorporate feedback from a client on a product design.

The entrepreneurial imagination begins, just like in all humans, with the primary imagination and one's attempt to perceive the material and social world. Accordingly, interactions between the co-founders coincide with the use of primary imagination to subconsciously understand and consciously participate in various social practices. A meeting between the entrepreneurs, for example, has certain understandings of the purpose of a meeting (incorporate client feedback) and how and where meetings are carried out. From this common basis, the entrepreneurs each share a base perception of client feedback as well as their immediate social and material context (e.g. office space in specific locale). Now, suppose one of the entrepreneurs participating in the meeting wishes to deal with client feedback by rethinking the design of their prototype product. To do so, she may activate her secondary imagination, allowing the primary mode to form an image of some altered product design. This image does not exist as a detailed and completed image in her mind's eye. Rather, it reflects her primary imagination's blending of memories and senses in which images are more aesthetic than complete. Next, using creative expression, she attempts to communicate this image using gestures, talk, and other objects (like drawing on a whiteboard) with other co-founders in the room. These creative expressions have implications for the primary imagination of all participating entrepreneurs, as they sense visually and audibly the creative expression from the first entrepreneur. Hence, the primary imagination not only blends and fuses this new sensory input to form immediate perceptions, but allows for all participants of the meeting to also imagine, with some degree of difference, what the first entrepreneur is imagining.

As the meeting continues, each entrepreneur takes turns in actively imagining, communicating and refining an image of a new product design that was initially instigated by client feedback. At this point, the contributions of one entrepreneur in the production of an image are lost in the recursive flow of imagining and creative expression, such that a shared image emerges (manifest perhaps physically on a whiteboard, computer, paper, etc.). Hence, as the entrepreneurs jointly imagine and express images, they manipulate their bodies and materials to express and communicate images in ways that diverge from the routine enactment of social practices. This exposition of entrepreneurial imagination can be repeated in different and subsequent situations, for example, when the team of entrepreneurs redevelops a business model or presents to potential investors. In these subsequent scenarios, the entrepreneurs attempt to communicate to each other or to investors some future imagined scenarios, customer experiences or aesthetic qualities of their product design, using creative expressions to try and stimulate others to imagine in a similar way. This may entail further feedback from which the entrepreneurial team may renew their joint imagining.

Discussion

The notion of entrepreneurial imagination has a long tradition in the history of entrepreneurship studies. Nevertheless, few scholars have conducted a review of common assumptions. In this chapter, I critique the entrepreneurial imagination literature by adopting a processual, relational and aesthetic stance. My review concludes that the entrepreneurial imagination is by and large conceived of: as operant only for early ideation of opportunities; is an individual-level phenomenon; and is isolated as solely a subjective cognitive process. I build from the philosophy of imagination literature to rethink the entrepreneurial imagination, which has three main contributions to entrepreneurship studies.

First, I show the value of building a constructive dialogue between entrepreneurship studies and philosophy. In particular, engaging with the philosophy of imagination literature, which remains a burgeoning area of thought, helps to challenge some common ontological conceptions of the entrepreneurial imagination. I have shown that prior conceptualizations have isolated imagining as a solely individual cognitive process that is active only for ideation. These overarching assumptions leave little room for a more phenomenologically driven understanding of imagination, as it is developed in philosophy. Indeed, the entrepreneurial imagination as a concept to date reflects the methodological individualism prominent in the history of entrepreneurial thought (Drakopoulou Dodd & Anderson, 2007; Watson, 2013), additive with a radical subjectivist account of images, visions and opportunities. Turning towards philosophy has the value of challenging and uprooting these taken-for-granted accounts.

The second contribution of this chapter is addressing taken-for-granted assumptions by renewing theorizing upon entrepreneurial imagination. I argue that imagining is an ongoing, shared and reality-oriented phenomenon that is a central component of perception, as well as an ability to perceive in hypothetical mode. In particular, drawing from the work of Warnock (1978) and Thompson (2017), I argue that imagination has two fundamental modes, primary and secondary, which operation together to form images. Rather than fall back into idealism and subjectivism, this literature demonstrates that image production is socially and materially anchored. Moreover, I address the ontology of images to argue that they are not analogous to pictures in the mind, but are more fleeting, vague and attuned with aesthetic perceptions. As one takes creative expression to 'materialize' and share them with others, participants jointly imagine, communicate and share images that are manifest in new artefacts (e.g. business models, products, strategies, etc.). Using the secondary imagination, however, is a conscious decision. As Weick (2005) argues, entrepreneurs (like all people) who fail to imagine other people, possible situations and alternative designs fail to be open to change and uncertainty. And yet, imagination is almost exclusively seen as a positive category in entrepreneurship literature, where it is likely that exercising the imagination may lead to anxieties based upon imagined negative scenarios that have a (miscalculated) chance of occurring. Future research could make new gains by exploring this negative or nuanced role of imagination.

Third, this chapter makes a contribution to current entrepreneurship research by arguing for the renewed relevance of the entrepreneurial imagination. Dew, Grichnik, Mayer-Haug, Read, and Brinckmann (2015) argue that entrepreneurial cognition cannot be 'boxed-in' as a mental condition or state rather it is tied into actions and objects, embodied with the senses. Hence, it is not located in individuals' heads, but is shaped by social, physical and/or cultural contexts. In this vein, I have renewed thinking about the entrepreneurial imagination by situating it in ongoing social practices, which includes sensory experience, bodily movement and memories. Hence, returning to imagination, using the conceptualization developed here, furthers growing aims of situating, embedding and embodying entrepreneurial cognition by attending to the human ability to both perceive of immediate situations as well as perceive of possible futures. Accordingly, imagination helps to further discussions of situated entrepreneurial cognition by highlighting this important generative capacity of the mind, without straying into radical subjectivism.

In conclusion, despite a long history of references to entrepreneurial imagination to explain a variety of phenomena, such as ideation, opportunities, decision-making and creative action, the concept remains surprisingly underdeveloped. My critical review argues that the entrepreneurial imagination remains rooted in its methodological individualism and radical subjectivist past, which has complicated it use in a growing body of research developing the notion of situated entrepreneurial cognition. By making a connection to the philosophy of imagination literature, I have outlined a processually, relationally and aesthetically sensitive conception of the entrepreneurial imagination. As a consequence, I have argued that returning to imagination will help to further situate entrepreneurial cognition by attending to the human ability to not only perceive of immediate situations but imagine that which does not yet exist.

References

Alvarez, S. A., & Barney, J. B. (2007). Discovery and creation: Alternative theories of entrepreneurial action. *Strategic Entrepreneurship Journal*, *1*(November), 11–26. http://doi.org/10.1002/sej

Baron, R. (2006). Opportunity recognition as pattern recognition. *Academy of Management Perspectives*, *20*, 104–120. http://doi.org/10.5465/AMP.2006.19873412

Bjerke, B., & Ramo, H. (2011). *Entrepreneurial imagination: Time, timing, space and place in business action*. Cheltenham, UK. Northampton, MA, USA: Edward Elgar Publishing Limited.

Bradbury, H., & Lichtenstein, B. B. (2000). Relationality in organizational research: Exploring the space between. *Organization Science, 11*(5), 551–564. http://doi.org/10.1287/orsc.11.5.551.15203

Bronk, R. (2009). *The romantic economist*. Cambridge: Cambridge University Press.

Buchanan, J. M., & Vanberg, V. J. (1991). The market as a creative process. *Economics & Philosophy, 7*(2), 167–186.

Casey, E. S. (1974). Toward a phenomenology of imagination. *Journal of the British Society for Phenomenology, 5*(1), 3–19. http://doi.org/10.1080/00071773.1974.11006346

Chiles, T. H., Elias, S., Vultee, D., & Zarankin, T. G. (2013). The Kaleidic world of entrepreneurs: Developing and grounding a metaphor for creative imagination. *Qualitative Research in Organizations and Management: An International Journal, 8*(3), 276–307.

Cornelissen, J. P. (2013). Book reviews: Portrait of an entrepreneur: Vincent van Gogh, Steve Jobs, and the entrepreneurial imagination. *Academy of Management Review, 38*(4), 700–709.

Cornelissen, J. P., & Clarke, J. (2010). Imagining and rationalizing opportunities: Inductive reasoning and the creation and justification of new ventures. *Academy of Management Review, 35*(4), 539–557.

Daston, L. (1998). Fear and loathing of the imagination in science. *Daedalus, 127*(1), 73–95.

Davidsson, P. (2015). Entrepreneurial opportunities and the entrepreneurship nexus: A reconceptualization. *Journal of Business Venturing, 30*(5), 674–695. http://doi.org/10.1016/j.jbusvent.2015.01.002

Dew, N., Grichnik, D., Mayer-Haug, K., Read, S., & Brinckmann, J. (2015). Situated entrepreneurial cognition. *International Journal of Management Reviews, 17*(2), 143–164. http://doi.org/10.1111/ijmr.12051

Dimov, D. (2007). Beyond the single-person, single-insight attribution in understanding entrepreneurial opportunities. *Entrepreneurship Theory and Practice, 31*(5), 713–731.

Dolmans, S. A. M., van Burg, E., Reymen, I. M. M. J., & Romme, A. G. L. (2014). Dynamics of resource slack and constraints: Resource positions in action. *Organization Studies, 35*(4), 511–549. http://doi.org/10.1177/0170840613517598

Drakopoulou Dodd, S., & Anderson, A. R. (2007). Mumpsimus and the mything of the individualistic entrepreneur. *International Small Business Journal, 25*(4), 341–360. http://doi.org/10.1177/0266242607078561

Engell, J. (1981). *The creative imagination: Enlightenment to romanticism*. Cambridge, MA: Harvard University Press.

Fletcher, D. E. (2006). Entrepreneurial processes and the social construction of opportunity. *Entrepreneurship & Regional Development, 18*(5), 421–440. http://doi.org/10.1080/08985620600861105

Foss, K., & Foss, N. (2008). Understanding opportunity discovery and sustainable advantage: The role of transaction costs and property rights. *Strategic Entrepreneurship Journal, 2*, 191–207.

Gartner, W. B. (2007). Entrepreneurial narrative and a science of the imagination. *Journal of Business Venturing, 22*(5), 613–627.

Gartner, W. B., Stam, A. M. C. E., Thompson, N. A., & Verduijn, J. K. (2016). Entrepreneurship as practice: Grounding contemporary practice theory into entrepreneurship studies. *Entrepreneurship and Regional Development, 28*(9–10), 813–816.

Grégoire, D. A., Barr, P. S., & Shepherd, D. (2010). Cognitive processes of opportunity recognition: The role of structural alignment. *Organization Science, 21*(2), 413–431. http://doi.org/10.1287/orsc.1090.0462

Grégoire, D. A., Corbett, A. C., & McMullen, J. S. (2011). The cognitive perspective in entrepreneurship: An agenda for future research. *Journal of Management Studies, 48*(6), 1443–1477. http://doi.org/10.1111/j.1467-6486.2010.00922.x

Hjorth, D. (2007). Lessons from Iago: Narrating the event of entrepreneurship. *Journal of Business Venturing, 22*(5), 712–732. http://doi.org/10.1016/j.jbusvent.2006.10.002

Hjorth, D. (2013). Absolutely fabulous! Fabulation and organisation-creation in processes of becoming-entrepreneur. *Society and Business Review, 8*(3), 205–224. http://doi.org/10.1108/SBR-02-2013-0020

Hjorth, D., Holt, R., & Steyaert, C. (2015). Entrepreneurship and process studies. *International Small Business Journal, 33*(6), 599–611. http://doi.org/10.1177/0266242615583566

Hjorth, D., Jones, C., & Gartner, W. B. (2008). Introduction for 'recreating/recontextualising entrepreneurship'. *Scandinavian Journal of Management, 24*(2), 81–84. http://doi.org/10.1016/j.scaman.2008.03.003

Hjorth, D., & Steyaert, C. (2008). *The politics and aesthetics of entrepreneurship.* Cheltenham: Edward Elgar Publishing.

Hsieh, C., Nickerson, J. A., & Zenger, T. R. (2007). Opportunity discovery, problem solving and a theory of the entrepreneurial firm. *Journal of Management Studies, 44*(7), 1255–1277.

Kind, A. (2016). *The Routledge handbook of philosophy of imagination.* London, UK: Taylor & Francis.

Kirzner, I. M. (1973). *Competition and entrepreneurship.* Chicago: Chicago University Press.

Kirzner, I. M. (1982). Uncertainty, discovery and human action: A study of the entrepreneurial profile in the misesian system. In I. M. Kirzner (Ed.), *Method, process and Austrian economics* (pp. 139–160). Washington, DC: Heath.

Kirzner, I. M. (1997). Entrepreneurial discovery and the competitive market process: An Austrian approach. *Journal of Economic Literature, 35*(1), 60–85.

Kirzner, I. M. (1998). Entrepreneurship. In P. J. Boettke (Ed.), *The Elgar companion to Austrian economics.* Cheltenham, UK; Northampton, MA, USA: Edward Elgar Publishing, Incorporated.

Kirzner, I. M. (1999). Creativity and/or alertness: A reconsideration of the Schumpeterian entrepreneur. *The Review of Austrian Economics, 11*(1), 5–17. http://doi.org/10.1023/A:1007719905868

Klein, P. (2008). Opportunity discovery, entrepreneurial action and economic organization. *Strategic Entrepreneurship Journal, 2*, 175–190.

Lachmann, L. M. (1986). *The market as an economic process.* Boston, MA, USA : Wiley-Blackwell.

Linstead, S., & Hopfl, H. (2004). *The aesthetics of organization.* London: Sage.

McMullen, J. S. (2010). Perspective taking and the heterogeneity of the entrepreneurial imagination. In R. Koppl, S. Horwitz, P. Desrochers (Eds.), *What is so Austrian about Austrian economics?* (Vol. 14, pp. 113–143). Bingley, UK: Emerald Group Publishing Limited. http://doi.org/doi:10.1108/S1529-2134(2010)0000014009

Murphy, K. M. (2004). Imagination as joint activity: The case of architectural interaction. *Mind, Culture, and Activity, 11*(4), 267–278. http://doi.org/10.1207/s15327884mca1104_3

Mutch, A., Delbridge, R., & Ventresca, M. (2006). Situating organizational action: The relational sociology of organizations. *Organization, 13*(5), 607–625. http://doi.org/10.1177/1350508406067006

Popp, A., & Holt, R. (2012). The presence of entrepreneurial opportunity. *Business History*, *55*(July 2015), 1–20. http://doi.org/10.1080/00076791.2012.687539

Ramoglou, S., & Tsang, E. W. K. (2016). A realist perspective of entrepreneurship: Opportunities as propensities. *Academy of Management Review*, *41*(3), 410–434. http://doi.org/10.5465/amr.2014.0281

Sarasvathy, S. D. (2002). Entrepreneurship as economics with imagination. *Business Ethics Quaterly*, *3*, 95–112. http://doi.org/10.5840/ruffinx200238

Sarasvathy, S. D. (2003). Entrepreneurship as a science of the artificial. *Journal of Economic Psychology*, *24*, 203–220. http://doi.org/10.1016/S0167-4870(02)00203-9

Sartre, J.-P. (1940). *L'Imaginaire: Psychologie phénoménologique de l'imagination*. Paris: Gallimard.

Schatzki, T. R. (2006). On organizations as they happen. *Organization Studies*, *27*(12), 1863–1873.

Schumpeter, J. A. (1934). *The theory of economic development*. Cambridge, MA: Harvard University Press.

Shackle, G. L. S. (1964). *General thought-schemes and the economist*. Edited by E. Woolwich. London: Woolwich Polycentric Press.

Shackle, G. L. S. (1968). *Expectations, investment, and income* (2nd ed.). Oxford: Clarendon Press.

Shackle, G. L. S. (1979). *Imagination and the nature of choice*. Edinburgh, UK: Edinburgh University Press.

Strati, A. (2007). Sensible knowledge and practice-based learning. *Management Learning*, *38*(1), 61–77. http://doi.org/10.1177/1350507607073023

Thompson, N. A. (2017). Imagination and creativity in organizations. *Organization Studies*, in press.

Verduyn, K. (2015). Entrepreneuring and process: A Lefebvrian perspective. *International Small Business Journal*, *33*(6), 638–648. http://doi.org/10.1177/0266242614559059

Warnock, M. (1978). *Imagination*. Berkeley, CA: University of California Press.

Warnock, M. (1994). *Imagination and time*. Oxford, UK; Cambridge, MA, USA : Wiley.

Watson, T. J. (2013). Entrepreneurial action and the Euro-American social science tradition: Pragmatism, realism and looking beyond 'the entrepreneur'. *Entrepreneurship & Regional Development*, *25*(1–2), 16–33. http://doi.org/10.1080/08985626.2012.754267

Weick, K. E. (2005). Organizing and failures of imagination. *International Public Management Journal*, *8*(3), 425–438. http://doi.org/10.1080/10967490500439883

Witt, U. (2007). Firms as realizations of entrepreneurial visions. *Journal of Management Studies*, *44*(7), 1125–1140.

Zhuo, J. (2008). New look at creativity in the entrepreneurial process. *Strategic Entrepreneurship Journal*, *2*, 1–5.

10 Examining the contributions of social science to entrepreneurship

The cases of cosmopolitanism and orientalism

Katerina Nicolopoulou and Christine Samy

Introduction

Entrepreneurship is still largely seen as an emerging field, and its theoretical development has proven over time to be gradual but inconclusive, leaving the field permeable in terms of its boundaries (Busenitz et al., 2003). The field has seen a host of emerging social science approaches, such as the use of 'grand narratives', typically in the form of the theory of capitals (Bourdieu, 1986) applied in the study of various aspects of the entrepreneurial process, amongst others, in garnering resources for addressing entrepreneurial opportunities (Karatas-Ozkan & Chell, 2010; Pret, Shaw, & Drakopoulou Dodd, 2015). An alternative perspective has focused on the integration of insights from a social science-informed perspective, in order to study in depth the context of entrepreneurial activity (Shane & Venkataraman, 2001) and the interaction between context and process involved in entrepreneurship through a relational, or social constructionist approach (Hosking & Hjorth, 2004; Chell & Baines, 2000; Jack & Anderson, 2002).

Theoretical framing

In order to offer our perspective in this field-wide conversation, we are proposing to position our thesis within the overarching framework of research oriented towards addressing the 'grand societal challenges' (George, Howard-Grenville, Joshi, & Tihanyi, 2016) and the ways in which these priorities have been shaping research funding initiatives such as the GCRF as well as the Newton Fund. The basic tenet of this position is that global challenges address global problems which call for solutions that can be drawn from the space of pluralism and inter-disciplinarity. Such challenges, according to George et al. (2016) pose research problems that are not only managerial, but also scientific. The Going Global initiative organized annually by the British Council had introduced, in 2015, the idea of supporting the resolution of societal challenges through revisiting the study and application of humanities and social sciences as frameworks of thinking and potential repertoires/spaces of solutions. Within the same logic, the emergence of the Sustainable Development Goals as a global 'benchmark' against which to develop business solutions affords an opportunity to consider more holistically priorities of enterprising. The entrepreneurship community has also followed this trend – the 2016 ICSB global forum had been dedicated to the engagement of the field with the Sustainable Development Goals and ways in which new entrepreneurship forms could emerge to address what effectively could be termed as global challenges. The 2016 Special Forum of the Journal of Management Studies (Markman, Russo, Lumpkin, Jennings, & Mair, 2016) on Sustainability, Ethics and Entrepreneurship is another example of that. Researchers such as Jack, Dodd, and Anderson et al. (2008) as well as Welter (2011) have hinted at the notion that, as a response to the consideration of context in entrepreneurship, the interaction with disciplines such as sociology and anthropology can be of importance, as those can afford the theoretical tools to explore in depth the variety and nuances of 'context'.

Context matters

The circumstances, the events and the space around any activity can hinder or facilitate the entrepreneurial process. Aoyama (2009, p. 497) claims that entrepreneurs' decisions and practices are shaped by economic, societal and cultural surroundings. Other studies have emphasised that contextual aspects as culture, social support and trainings play an imperative role in the entrepreneurial process (Fischer & Nijkamp, 2009). Low and MacMillan (1988) highlight that entrepreneurship is a process that can be commenced in different contexts. The way that entrepreneurial processes unfold is dependent on the context; these processes develop differently in diverse settings and do not develop consistently across regions (Mueller, 2006). Lately, there has been a shift in the entrepreneurship discussion "*away from the entrepreneur as an island of exchange towards entrepreneurship as a contextual process*" (Kalantaridis & Bika, 2006, p. 110). Scholars have called for further research on the interaction between the entrepreneur with the different spheres of context (Zahra, 2007; Welter, 2011; Shane, 2012; Wright, 2012; Gaddefors & Anderson, 2017).

Context can be defined as "*circumstances, conditions, situations, or environments that are external to the respective phenomenon and enable or constrain it*" (Welter, 2011, p. 167). In his study, Leighton (1988, p. 74 and 76) concluded that "*studying entrepreneurs as individuals is a dead end*" while "*environment, culture, etc., the context of entrepreneurial behaviour is important*". Given the significance of context in influencing and shaping the entrepreneurial processes (Mair, Marti, & Ventresca, 2012), it is essential to for researchers to also discuss the place and space in which entrepreneurs are embedded. Lefebvre (1991) introduced the notion that space is deeply connected with social action; he clarified that space is not simply a social product but rather a producer as well as a controller of social action (Lefebvre, 1991, p. 358). Space works as a medium of social communication and it embodies differences of power. According to Gregory, Meusburger, and Suarsana (2015), space is understood as relative or relational space, and that space is "*conceptualized as a product of interrelations and interactions*". The authors add that space is not a closed system; it is always "in a process of becoming, always being made" (Massey, 1999, p. 28).

Last but not least, Said (2003, p. 23) argues "*that each humanistic investigation must formulate the nature of that connection in the specific context of the study, the subject matter, and its historical circumstances*". The argument against 'cultural imperialism' in the study of entrepreneurship, and for increased sensitivity to the culture of the nation and the psychology of its people, is also elaborately made by Dana (2000).

What we mean by social science – its scope and importance for entrepreneurship

For our work, we will be using the term social science in a two-pronged perspective; we are following the tenet of an institution like the London School of Economics, which presents an inquiry-based as well as action-oriented approach to engaging with social science i.e.: first, as its institutional mission and vision highlight, it is important to *understand the causes of things* and second, *put those into practice for the betterment of societies*. In that way, we make sure that the application of a social science-informed perspective not only is a theoretical exercise, but draws from, and informs, in return, real world action and practice. According to a definition from ESRC,

> *Social science is, in its broadest sense, the study of society and the manner in which people behave and influence the world around us. . . . Social science tells us about the world beyond our immediate experience, and can help explain how our own society works – from the causes of unemployment or what helps economic growth, to how and why people vote, or what makes people happy. It provides vital information for governments and policymakers, local authorities, non-governmental organisations and others.*
>
> (www.esrc.ac.uk/about-us/what-is-social-science/)

The ESRC defines in detail the disciplines covered within the range of social sciences eligible for funding by the council (www.esrc.ac.uk/about-us/what-is-social-science/social-science-disciplines/). It is beyond the scope of this chapter to conduct a systematic literature review of the exact coverage within the entrepreneurship field of all the social science subjects identified in the list. However, we believe that this topic merits further study, particularly because conceptualising the positioning of research as such, is important before moving to the concrete evidence-based research which can inform policy-making, a key concern for the funding councils. It would be interesting, for example, to see how many published entrepreneurship articles have drawn from environmental planning, human geography, development studies, social anthropology, international relations and social work. We are mentioning here some of the categories of social science, as listed within the ESRC website, which also seem to less likely to be prominent in terms of an interdisciplinary approach, when combined with the study of entrepreneurship. Our own life experience and research trajectory (working and living between different countries, contexts and institutions) have motivated us as authors to look further afield in order to effectively consider approaches which can support the use and applicability of social science for entrepreneurship. This concerns, in particular, the debates about context in entrepreneurship, as outlined in the theoretical framing and context sections. Here we can draw on two particular examples, i.e., orientalism and cosmopolitanism as context and disposition for entrepreneurship.

The case of cosmopolitanism as disposition for entrepreneurship

Alcaraz, Sugars, Nicolopoulou, and Tirado (2016, p. 315) highlight the elements of a framework for cosmopolitanism, based on premises of culture, morality and governance:

> *Succinctly explained, cosmopolitanism discards nationhood as the frame for cultural identity, citizenship, ethical concerns or governance. It brings a triple proposal:*
>
> * *it is a radical celebration of cultural difference and of embracing diversity;*
> * *an urge for moral concern and responsibility for the "distant other"; and*
> * *the quest to find mechanisms and institutions for global governance.*
>
> *This scholarly work ultimately points out that in the new global landscape, multiple agents (including businesses) need to care for the global common good and share co-responsibility.*
>
> (Maak, 2009; De Bettignies & Lépineux, 2009;
Maak & Pless, 2009)

The cosmopolitan perspective can be understood as 'being at home in all parts of the world' and assumes that humans are to be considered citizens of a single community (Held, 2005), whilst it emphasises the decreased importance of *nationality* (Delanty, 2006). Work on *cosmopolitanism and management* (a comprehensive review completed by Levy, Peiperl, & Jonsen, 2013) includes concepts such as globally mobile managers and professionals (Sanchez-Runde, Nardon, & Steers, 2012); business leaders as citizens of the world (Maak & Pless, 2009); 'global mindsets' (Levy, Beechler, Taylor, & Boyacigiller, 2007) and 'cultural intelligence' (Vertovec & Cohen, 2002). In the field of management, Halsall (2009) highlights the elements of *concepts, connections, competence, choice, flexibility and detachment* (operating above context, and with fluid loyalty) as key components of cosmopolitanism in its application for organisations and corporate executives. Woodward, Skribs, and Bean (2008) argue that a globalised reality does not make everyone necessarily a cosmopolitan, as somebody can espouse cosmopolitan values, even if they are not world travelers; indeed, Levy et al. (2013) identify the category of 'ordinary cosmopolitans': individuals who are mostly outward-looking in terms of their preferences, although not necessarily globally mobile.

In this particular book chapter, we are following the understanding of *disposition* as an aligned perspective between Bourdieu's Theory of Practice (1977) and Woodward et al. (2008); according to Woodward et al. (2008, p. 211), disposition interacts with practice, thus enabling social agents to obtain 'a particular set of cultural understandings of the world'. Whilst a number of authors have already discussed disposition in the entrepreneurship field, mostly following a Bourdieuan approach (Anderson, Dodd, & Jack, 2010; Terjesen & Elam, 2009), the particular understanding of a 'cosmopolitan' disposition for the field of entrepreneurship is new, yet it can have implications in transnational, international and diversity-based approaches to entrepreneurship as well as business venturing (Nicolopoulou, Kakabadse, Sakellariou, & Alcaraz, 2016).

Diversity-related factors usually concern age, nationality and gender and their effect in entrepreneurial actions, choices, motivations and behaviours of enterprises operating within a certain national context or community, or internationally, and merit further academic investigation (Carter, Ram, Trehan, & Jones, 2013; Collins, 2003): their dynamics can manifest in increased population diversity, or in superdiversity (Ram et al., 2011; Sepulveda, Syrett, & Lyon, 2011) or class, as a global elite currently appears to be dealing with recovered parts of the economy, and business growth (Nicolopoulou, Kakabadse, Sakellariou, & Alcaraz, 2014). Previous studies which have addressed the link between cosmopolitanism with entrepreneurship include Robertson and Wind (1983), who highlighted a positive relationship between cosmopolitanism and innovation, Tyfield and Urry (2009) who studied the example of China and identified how engagement with innovation focusing on forms of low-carbon technologies and sustainability has been an expression of cosmopolitanism, as well as Singapore (Yeoh, 2004), featuring as the twenty-first century 'cosmopolis' fueled by the strength of IT revolution, culture, arts and social innovation within an increasing 'transnational' space. Pecould (2004) used the established notion of an 'ethnic enclave' highlighting the focus of entrepreneurial activity from an 'outside-in' rather than 'inside-out' perspective to describe a cosmopolitan disposition in entrepreneurship, as the openness to the worldly 'otherness' in terms of looking for the business opportunity, can be seen as essentially a cosmopolitan feature. Volery (2007) distinguished opportunity identification as an 'ethnically' based strategy (based on the notion of 'collective identity formation'), whilst also identifying the pursuit and exploitation of opportunity as a 'metropolitan' strategy (an expression of the 'outward' motion). Drori, Honig, and Wright (2009), highlighted the challenges of transnational entrepreneurs in accessing finance and maintain productive links both in the host context a well as the original country of origin. Cosmopolitanism has also been considered as a disposition in entrepreneurship by Nicolopoulou, Kakabadse, Nikolopoulos, Alcaraz and Sakellariou (2016); this work was focused on the development of entrepreneurship by transnational elites in Dubai, UAE, as an example of a cosmopolitan city, and highlighted the interaction between the context (city) and disposition of individual entrepreneurs – mostly transnational entrepreneurs or nationals ones with transnational activities.

Specifically focusing on the cultural view of cosmopolitanism as developed by Vertovec and Cohen (2002, pp. 7–13), cosmopolitanism for entrepreneurship is identified in terms of a 'disposition' of intellectual openness in relation to the 'other', as well as 'practice' or 'competence' as this can be developed through the right training and exposure. Nicolopoulou et al. (2016) conclude that a cosmopolitan disposition (Woodward et al., 2008) is an asset for entrepreneurship. In an increasingly interconnected world where networks and transnational capital are increasingly important, understanding the cosmopolitan disposition and ways in which it can facilitate entrepreneurial development within and above specific contexts could be a significant insight in terms of related global challenges of diversity and inclusion as well as sustainable economic growth.

The case of orientalism and links to entrepreneurial context

According to Peter Chua (2008), a limited number of social researchers have reflected on and analysed *orientalism* as embedded in the widely used philosophies of Western theorists. Chua (2008) argues that only a few researchers have studied the question of identity and lived experiences as shaped by orientalist representations and their related cultural regulations. Chua (2008) points out to one argument that relates to the orientalist practices of ethnographers narrating everyday lives of people as the 'other' and the extent to which their representations could be misleading:

> *As a consequence, these researchers have argued that formative sociology has participated in promoting orientalism in its underlying assumptions, fundamental concepts, epistemological models, and methodological procedures involving canonical ethnographies and historical and cross-national comparisons.*
>
> (Chua, 2008, p. 1186)

Edward Said opens his book *Orientalism* with a translated quote from Karl Marx stating *"They cannot represent themselves; they must be represented"*, which reflects how he perceives the term orientalism. "Orientalism" is a noun form of the adjective "oriental" which reflects something related to the Eastern countries, but in the context of Said, it mirrors the distorted image of the culture of the Eastern countries as Asia, North Africa as well as the Middle-East and its people. Said (2003, p. 2) defines "orientalism" as:

> *Anyone who teaches, writes about, or researches the Orient and this applies whether the person is an anthropologist, sociologist, historian, or philologist either in its specific or its general aspects, is an Orientalist, and what he or she does is Orientalism.*

In other words, Edward Said uses the word "orientalism" to refer to Western interpretations of the Eastern nations. Said's inquiry was based on the Eastern nations relative to Europe, as he observed the interpretations of the East and the Middle

East in European discourses. It is worth mentioning that Said explains orientalism as "the epistemological and ontological distinction between the West and the East" (2003, p. 3), with the outlook that the Middle East and Asia in art and literature are less civilised than the West. This, in return, indicates a tendency to interpret the role of the West as more experienced and powerful to apply their expertise to the oriental region, based on a transfer of knowledge from the affluent 'Western' context and its scholars.

This bears importance for entrepreneurship and the context in which it is developed. For example, according to global reports on entrepreneurial activity, as well as African etrepreneurs, is rising (Sanders, 2017, Wennekers & Thurik, 1999, (Herrington, Kew, Kew, & Monitor, 2010). Conversely, we can detect a negligence of the context in researching entrepreneurship in different parts across Africa. Entrepreneurship as a field is, in general, selective about the philosophical stances and paradigms used to position its discourse about other nations and their entrepreneurial behaviors. There are some popular dogmas through which we view entrepreneurship globally, which reflect 'Western' thoughts and ideas that entrepreneurship is a path to economic success, prosperity and social development (Peacock, 2016). Nonetheless, following Said's premises, such approaches fundamentally echo an ideological agenda. Entrepreneurship scholars are starting to recognise that ideology and other taken for granted axioms have an influence on knowledge construction (Bygrave, 1989; Ogbor, 2000).

Burrell and Morgan's (1979) work emphasised the role of philosophy in research and raised awareness about the impact of research paradigms on knowledge construction (Burrell & Morgan, 1979). Similar to Foucault (1984), Edward Said considers knowledge to be power and argues that, in academia, Europe has a hold over the power. For Said, such a power goes through an individual channel, whilst for Foucault it can be more systemic or institutional. 'Imagined geographies' is another concept coined by Edward Said (2003), which denotes that the perception of space is created through certain images, texts, discourses and ideologies. We believe that the texts, the literature and the reports we read shape our opinions and draw an "imagined" mental picture for what entrepreneurship is in the 'oriental' nations, which might not be necessarily real. Therefore, context-based studies are required to understand the entrepreneurial phenomenon, and its role in building cities, economic development and poverty reduction. Such considerations bear significance for an engagement of social sciences in resolving global challenges, as those could be targeted by international stakeholders and the funding councils.

Developing propositions for the field of entrepreneurship

In order to further support our framework of social science contributions in the field of entrepreneurship, we are proposing the development of three propositions, following the scheme of Guba and Lincoln (1994) in 'Competing Paradigms in Qualitative Research':

Proposition 1: Ontological implications of applying social science in the field of entrepreneurship

More recently, some entrepreneurship scholars are calling for a constructivist ontology (as well as epistemology) advocating that it *"may shed new light on parts of the opportunity phenomenon that the discovery perspective is unable to illuminate"* (Wood & McKinley, 2010). From an ontological point of view, engaging with social science in the field of entrepreneurship creates potentially new pathways towards definitions, practices and methods involved in its development. Considerations of identity, skills and culture as implied in the concept of cosmopolitanism and of the cosmopolitan disposition as a diversity factor for the development of transnational forms of entrepreneurship are one way in which such pathways could be shaped; on the other hand, understanding the 'hegemonic' frameworks (institutions, knowledge transfer, dominant narratives) within which entrepreneurship is practiced, whether in the East or the West, is another pathway towards a new ontology of entrepreneurship informed by the concept of orientalism.

Proposition 2: Epistemological implications for the field of entrepreneurship and how social science can further inform those

What can we know and how we know it are key questions to epistemology. According to Bygrave (1989), entrepreneurship is a process of interactions which occurs and further develops over time. Thus, this process cannot be understood by an approach which simply depends on collecting data at one particular period of time. Besides, various authors support that knowledge on entrepreneurship is created through understanding *"how individuals and collectives subjectively and inter-subjectively, construct their entrepreneurial actions as unfolding processes"* (Lindgren & Packendorff, 2003; Fletcher, 2006; Drakopoulou Dodd & Anderson, 2007). Ahl (2006) acknowledged the need to develop further the entrepreneurship research "object" and shift from an individualist emphasis on studying entrepreneurs to include more factors such as context, culture and content. Linking to the point made in our previous section, Said's stance resembles Foucault's in that "knowing" and "power" are closely associated: knowledge belongs to those who have power and those who have power can impress their own form of knowledge on others. From an epistemological standpoint, cosmopolitanism as a social science–informed approach signifies the need to re-evaluate issues of agency and process within a specific context when enterprise development is considered.

Proposition 3: Methodological implications

According to Alvesson (2002, p. 60), "the point of social science is not to get it right but to challenge guiding assumptions, fixed meanings and relations, and to reopen the formative capacity of human beings to others and the world". Social sciences emphasise that individual and social phenomena have to be studied "through the subjective minds of individuals, not by observable behaviour" (Lindgren & Packendorff, 2009, p. 30). Fletcher (2006), for example, made use of social constructionist premises when analysing the process of opportunity formation. She reasoned that the entrepreneurial process is collectively constituted and not fully considered in descriptive and linear process models of opportunity recognition. As mentioned by Lindgren and Packendorff (2009, p. 40), "established lines of thought as causality, generalisation, prediction and statistical significance can be seen as ideologically based in an ideal, only where reality can be described in an objective and true manner".

The entrepreneurship field is largely dominated by functionalistic methodologies and positivistic views of reality (Grant & Perren, 2002). Researchers argue that entrepreneurship research focuses excessively on positivist views of enquiry (Bygrave, 2007) and that, commonly, research in this discipline adopts a positivist epistemology (Berglund, 2007). According to Dana and Dana (2005), an inquiry based on inductive qualitative methodologies, already a prevailing paradigm in sociological and anthropological research, could be a useful alternative. Those could include thick descriptions of agents and their interactions with context (Geertz, 1973). More recently, Gaddefors and Anderson (2017) mentioned that the current methodological individualism of the prevailing paradigms in the field (Verduijn, Dey, Tedmanson, & Essers, 2014) does not leave explanatory room for the role of social context. Similarly, according to Patton (1982):

> *The methodological mandate to be contextually sensitive, inductive, and naturalistic means that researchers must get close to the phenomenon under study. The institutional researcher who uses qualitative methods attempts to understand the setting under study through direct personal contact . . . through physical proximity for a period of time and through the development of closeness.*
>
> (Patton, 1982, p. 10)

Edward Said claims that all experiences and places can be described as a book. Subsequently, reality can be described and descriptions overcome authority as sources of reality. This narrative-based approach highlights an increased need to consider qualitative inquiry as a predominantly relevant paradigm when the influence of social science is considered for entrepreneurship. *"No production of knowledge in the human sciences can ever ignore or disclaim its author's involvement as a human subject in his own circumstances"* (Said, 2003, p. 11). It has been established that researchers from the West have made the most contributions to the entrepreneurship field (Luor, Lu, Yu, & Chang, 2014). Thus, in order to understand discourses within which our knowledge of entrepreneurship and entrepreneurial behaviour is constructed, the notion of context is important; for example, within the 'oriental' nations, we have to understand the issue of representation. Nonetheless, according to Said, it is dubious whether a true representation is possible at all (Said, 2003, p. 273). If all representations are rooted in the language and culture of the one who makes representations *"then we must be prepared to accept the fact that a representation is eo ipso implicated, intertwined, embedded, interwoven with a great many other things besides the 'truth' which is itself a representation"* (Said, 2003, p. 273).

An increasing number of empirical studies, methodological innovations and theoretical developments are now being published on the sociology of orientalism (Chua, 2008, p. 1179). Said puts emphasis on *"texts"* as they are embedded in our systems, *"in short, they are in the world, and hence worldly"* (Said, 1975, p. 35). For Said, texts have the same situatedness as speech (Machátová, 2007). Texts have connections to the context, physical setting, to the society and the culture. Based on this, several theoretical perspectives are applied to texts in methods or approaches that incorporate semiotics, cultural theory, and feminist theory. A deeper engagement with a narrative-based, textual approach can better inform nuances about culture; in terms of a cosmopolitan-focused understanding of entrepreneurship, such cultural nuances can be important as unique characteristics of an entrepreneurial disposition. As Elliot (2005) states, narratives show the connection between agency and the broader social context. Those would also satisfy the call for deeper cultural understanding of the context within which entrepreneurship takes place (Dana, 2000). A narrative method to understand contexts is prominent in the body of research in sociology (Elliot, 2005) as well as in psychology (Creswell, 2007). Narrative is discourse that offers a rich linear order which links events in an expressive manner, in so doing, offering understandings on societies' experiences (Hinchman & Hinchman, 1997). It is worth mentioning that, recently, a narrative approach has been used in entrepreneurship research as seen in special issues (Venkataraman, Sarasvathy, Dew, & Forster, 2013) which provide dedicated forums and the intellectual space to develop such a conversation. Nonetheless, a recent study on data collection methods used over 29 years from 1985 to 2013 in entrepreneurship (McDonald, Ching Gan, Fraser, Oke, & Anderson, 2015) highlights to us the evidence: entrepreneurship research is dominated by the survey method (54%) in their 3,749 articles in the consensus sample. At 16%, case studies were the next most common, and interviews accounted for almost 15%, while other qualitative methods counted for only 7% of the studied articles. They concluded that there are no other data-gathering methods used in entrepreneurship research to any noteworthy extent (McDonald et al., 2015). It is important to inform our conversation through such findings.

Discussion and concluding remarks

In the present chapter, we have attempted to problematise and examine cosmopolitanism and orientalism as two social science–informed concepts in order to discuss disposition and context in the development of entrepreneurship; culture is a related concern, in that the division between East and West was a key differentiating factor in terms of related underlying assumptions and logic for the development of entrepreneurship. Additional concerns are: operating beyond or above a national context, the cultural implications involved in a cosmopolitan disposition and factors of diversity for developing entrepreneurship.

This has been a first attempt to delve into these complex social science–informed constructs and target the fleshing out of potential implications for the development of entrepreneurship, as a way to problematise and enrich the entrepreneurship field. We purport that such an interdisciplinary approach as implied in the engagement with the complex matrix of nuances involved within these two concepts has the potential to inspire multiple lines of inquiry, narrative and interpretation for the creation of pathways that can inform Societal Grand Challenges (George et al., 2016).

Said (2003) and Prasad (2003) pointed to the orientalist discourse in organisational research which categorises non-Western business practices as old-fashioned cultural practices which are a hurdle to organisational efficiency and effectiveness. Thomas and Mueller (2000) argue that entrepreneurship research was generated by 'Western' intellectuals, from the United States and Western Europe. Consequently, Thomas and Mueller (2000, p. 289), clarify that its transferability to contexts where the task and 'psychic environments' are different is debatable. For example, the experience of 'Western' nations regarding rural entrepreneurship tends to focus on increasing levels of prosperity, rather than alleviating absolute poverty as in rural cities in the Arab world. Correspondingly, postcolonial feminist perspectives highlight how Westernised images of "Otherness" impact the legitimacy and agency of Arab female entrepreneurs (Essers & Tedmanson, 2014). Scholarly work that uses theories and methodologies applied effectively in organisation and entrepreneurship fields suggest that the path to success has homogeneous values and consistently highlights the hegemonic position that the West knows better.

From a cosmopolitanism-informed perspective, it is the emphasis on the three foundational elements of the concept that are of importance for this conversation (Alcaraz et al., 2016, p. 315):

(a) Cultural difference and embracing diversity
(b) Moral concern and responsibility for the 'distant other'
(c) The quest to find mechanisms and institutions for global governance.

It is within the frame identified by those three elements that entrepreneurship in its different forms, including its more socially progressive aspects (social, sustainable, eco-social), can develop. Engagement with all of these perspectives can redefine the relationship between context and the entrepreneur as agent and can therefore shape new possibilities about the ways in which the development of enterprise can serve several additional agendas beyond purely the creation of wealth.

Further engagement with both concepts, their ramifications for theory and practice as well as other social science–informed concepts within a pluralistic, interdisciplinary framework can only be of benefit to the domain of entrepreneurship. Related empirical studies to explore these notions within different populations can create the necessary evidence base to support the practical resolution of the Societal Grand Challenges at local, regional and global scales.

References

Ahl, H. (2006). Why research on women entrepreneurs needs new directions. *Entrepreneurship Theory and Practice, 30*, 595–621.

Alcaraz, J., Sugars, K., Nicolopoulou, K., & Tirado, F. (2016). Cosmopolitanism or globalization: The Anthropocene turn. *Society and Business Review, 11*(3), 313–332. https://doi.org/10.1108/SBR-10-2015-0061

Alvesson, M. (2002). *Postmodernism and social research.* Buckingham: Open University.

Anderson, A. R., Dodd, S. D., & Jack, S. (2010). Network practices and entrepreneurial growth. *Scandinavian Journal of Management, 26*(2), 121–133.

Aoyama, Y. (2009). Entrepreneurship and regional culture: The case of Hamamatsu and Kyoto, Japan. *Regional Studies, 43*(3), 495–512. doi:10.1080/00343400902777042

Berglund, H. (2007). Researching entrepreneurship as lived experience. In H. Neergaard, & J. Parm Ulhoi (Eds), *Handbook of Qualitative Research Methods in Entrepreneurship* (pp. 75–93). Cheltenham, UK and Northampton, MA. USA: Edward Elgar.

Bourdieu, P. (1986). The forms of capital. In J. G. Richardson (Ed.), *Handbook of theory and research for the sociology of education* (pp. 241–258). New York, NY: Greenwood Press.

Burrell, G., & Morgan, G. (1979). *Sociological paradigms and organizational analysis: elements of the sociology of corporate life.* London: Heinemann.

Busenitz, L., West III, P., Shepherd, D., Nelson, T., Chandler, G., & Zacharakis, A. (2003). Entrepreneurship research in emergence: Past trends and future directions. *Journal of Management, 29*, 285–309.

Bygrave, W. D. (1989). The entrepreneurship paradigm (I): A philosophical look at its research methodologies. *Entrepreneurship Theory and Practice, 14*(1), 7–26.

Bygrave, W. D. (2007). The entrepreneurship paradigm (I) revisited. In H. Neergaard & J. Parm Ulhøi (Eds.), *Handbook of qualitative research methods in entrepreneurship* (pp. 17–48). Cheltenham, UK: Edward Elgar Publishing.

Carter, S., Ram, M., Trehan, K., & Jones, T. (2013). *Diversity and SMEs : Existing Evidence and Policy Tensions : ERC White Paper No.3.* Working paper. Enterprise Research Centre, Warwick. Available at https://strathprints.strath.ac.uk/44679/

Chell, E. & Baines, S. (2000). Networking, entrepreneurship and microbusiness behavior. *Entrepreneurship & Regional Development, 12*(3), 195–215.

Chua, P. (2008). Orientalism as cultural practices and the production of sociological knowledge. *Sociology Compass, 2*, 1179–1191. doi:10.1111/j.1751-9020.2008.00129.x

Collins, J. (2003). Cultural diversity and entrepreneurship: Policy responses to immigrant entrepreneurs in Australia. *Entrepreneurship & Regional Development, 15*(2), 137–149.

Creswell, J. W. (2007). *Qualitative inquiry & research design: Choosing among five approaches* (2nd ed.). Thousand Oaks, CA: Sage Publications Inc.

Dana, L. P., & Dana, T. E. (2005). Expanding the scope of methodologies used in entrepreneurship research. *International Journal of Entrepreneurship and Small Business, 2*(1), 79–88.

Dana, L-P. (2000). *Economies of the Eastern Mediterranean Region: Economic miracles in the making.* Singapore, London and Hong Kong: World Scientific.

De Bettignies, H. C., & Lépineux, F. (2009). Can multinational corporations afford to ignore the global common good? *Business and Society Review, 114*(2), 153–182.

Delanty, G. (2006). The cosmopolitan imagination: Critical cosmopolitanism and social theory. *The British Journal of Sociology, 57*(1), 25–47.

Drakopoulou Dodd, S., & Anderson, A. R. (2007). Mumpsimus and the mything of the individualistic entrepreneur. *International Small Business Journal, 25*(4), 341–360.

Drori, I., Honig, B., & Wright, M. (2009). Transnational entrepreneurship: An emergent field of study. *Entrepreneurship Theory and Practice, 33*(5), 1001–1022.

Elliot, J. (2005). *Using narrative in social research: Qualitative and quantitative approaches*. Thousand Oaks, CA: Sage Publications Inc.

Essers, C., & Tedmanson, D. (2014). Upsetting 'others' in the Netherlands: Narratives of Muslim Turkish migrant businesswomen at the crossroads of ethnicity, gender and religion. *Gender, Work & Organization, 21*, 353–367.

Fischer, M. M., & Nijkamp, P. (2009). Entrepreneurship and regional development. *VU University Amsterdam, Faculty of Economics, Business Administration and Econometrics, Amsterdam*, Working Paper: Series Research Memoranda 0035.

Fletcher, D. E. (2006). Entrepreneurial processes and the social construction of opportunity. *Entrepreneurship & Regional Development, 18*(5), 421–440.

Foucault, M. (1984). Space, knowledge and power. In P. Rabinow (Ed.), *The Foucault reader* (pp. 239–256). Harmondsworth, UK: Penguin.

Gaddefors, J., & Anderson, A. R. (2017). Entrepreneurship and context: When entrepreneurship is greater than entrepreneurs. *International Journal of Entrepreneurial Behavior & Research, 23*(2), 267–278. https://doi.org/10.1108/IJEBR-01-2016-0040

Geertz, C. (1973). *The interpretation of cultures: Selected essays*. New York: Basic Books.

George, G., Howard-Grenville, J., Joshi, A., & Tihanyi, L. (2016). Understanding and tackling societal grand challenges through management research. *Academy of Management Journal, 59*(6), 1880–1895. Research Collection Lee Kong Chian School of Business. http://ink.library.smu.edu.sg/lkcsb_research/5045

Grant, P., & Perren, L. (2002). Small business and entrepreneurial research: Metatheories, paradigms and prejudices. *International Small Business Journal, 20*(2), 185–211.

Gregory, D.,Meusburger, P,, & Suarsana, L. (2015). Power, knowledge, and space: A geographical introduction. In *Geographies of Knowledge and Power. Knowledge and Space* (Vol. 7, pp. 1–18). Dordrecht: Springer. 10.1007/978-94-017-9960-7_1.

Guba, E., & Lincoln, Y. (1994). Competing paradigms in qualitative research. In N. Denzin & Y. Lincoln (Eds.), *Handbook on qualitative research* (pp. 105–118). Thousand Oaks, CA: Sage Publications Inc.

Halsall, R. (2009). The discourse of corporate cosmopolitanism. *British Journal of Management, 20*, 136–148.

Held, D. (2005). Principles of cosmopolitan order. In G. Brock & H. Brighouse (Eds.), *The political philosophy of cosmopolitanism* (pp. 10–27). Cambridge, MA: Cambridge University Press.

Herrington, M., Kew, J., Kew, P., & Monitor, G. E. (2010). *Tracking entrepreneurship in South Africa: A GEM perspective*. South Africa: Graduate School of Business, University of Cape Town.

Hinchman, L., & Hinchman, S. (1997). *Memory, identity, and community: The idea of narrative in the human sciences*. New York: State University of New York.

Hosking, D. M., & Hjorth, D. (2004). Relational constructionism and entrepreneurship: Some key notes. In D. Hjorth & C. Steyaert (Eds.), *Narrative and discursive approaches in entrepreneurship studies* (pp. 255–273). Cheltenham: Edward Elgar.

Jack, S.L. & Anderson, A.R. (2002). The effects of embeddedness on the entrepreneurial process. *Journal of Business Venturing, 17*(5), 467–487.

Jack, S.L., Dodd, S.D., & Anderson, A.R. (2008). Change and the development of entrepreneurial networks over time: a processual perspective. *Entrepreneurship & Regional Development, 20*(2), 125–159.

Kalantaridis, C., & Bika, Z. (2006). In-migrant entrepreneurship in rural England: Beyond local embeddedness. *Entrepreneurship and Regional Development, 18*(2), 109–131.

Karatas-Ozkan, M., & Chell, E. (2010). *Nascent entrepreneurship and learning*. Cheltenham, UK: Edward Elgar.

Lefebvre, H. (1991). *The production of space*. Translated by D. Nicholson-Smith. Oxford, UK: Blackwell (French original 1974).

Leighton, D. (1988). Summary. In R. Peterson & K. Ainslie (Eds.), *Understanding entrepreneurship* (pp. 73–78). Dubuque, IA: Kendall/Hunt.

Levy, O., Beechler, S., Taylor, S., & Boyacigiller, N. (2007). What we talk about when we talk about 'global mindset': Managerial cognition in multinational corporations. *Journal of International Business Studies*, *38*(2), 231–258.

Levy, O., Peiperl, M., & Jonsen, K. (2013). *Cosmopolitanism in a globalised world: A multidisciplinary approach*. Istanbul: Academy of International Business.

Lindgren, M. & Packendorff, J. (2003). A project-based view of entrepreneurship: Towards action-orientation, seriality and collectivity. In: C. Steyaert & D. Hjorth (Eds.). *New movements in entrepreneurship* (pp. 86–102). Cheltenham: Edward Elgar.

Lindgren, M. & Packendorff, J. (2009) Social constructionism and entrepreneurship: Basic assumptions and consequences for theory and research. *International Journal of Entrepreneurial Behaviour & Research*, *15*(1), 25–47.

Low, M., & MacMillan, I. (1988). Entrepreneurship: Past research and future challenges. *Journal of Management*, *14*(2), 139–161.

Luor, T., Lu, H.-P., Yu, H., & Chang, K. (2014). Trends in and contributions to entrepreneurship research: A broad review of literature from 1996 to June 2012. *Scientometrics*, *99*(2), 353–369. http://doi.org/10.1007/s11192-013-1203-5

Maak, T. (2009). The cosmopolitical corporation. *Journal of Business Ethics*, *84*(3), 361–372.

Maak, T., & Pless, N. (2009, September). Business Leaders as Citizens of the world: Advancing humanism on a global scale. *Journal of Business Ethics*, *88*(3), 537–550.

Machátová, B. (2007). *Edward W. Said: Postcolonial studies and the politics of literary theory*. Diplomová práce. Univerzita Karlova, Filozofická fakulta, Ústav anglistiky a amerikanistiky. Vedoucí práce Armand, Louis.

Mair, J., Marti, I., & Ventresca, M. (2012). Building inclusive markets in rural Bangladesh: How intermediaries work institutional voids. *Academy of Management Journal*, *55*(4), 819–850.

Markman, G.D., Russo, M., Lumpkin, G.T., Jennings, P.,& Mair, J. (2016). Entrepreneurship as a platform for pursuing multiple goals: A special issue on sustainability, ethics, and entrepreneurship. *Journal of Management Studies*, *53*(5), 673–694.

Massey, D. (1999). Philosophy and politics of spatiality: Some considerations. In D. Massey (Ed.), *Power-Geometries and the Politics of Space-Time* (Hettner-lecture, Vol. 2, pp. 27–42). Heidelberg, Germany: Heidelberg University, Department of Geography.

McDonald, S., Ching Gan, B., Fraser, S., Oke, A., & Anderson, A. (2015). A review of research methods in entrepreneurship 1985–2013. *International Journal of Entrepreneurial Behavior & Research*, *21*(3), 291–315. https://doi.org/10.1108/IJEBR-02-2014-0021

Mueller, P. (2006). Entrepreneurship in the region: Breeding ground for nascent entrepreneurs? *Small Business Economics*, *27*, 41. https://doi.org/10.1007/s11187-006-6951-7

Nicolopoulou, K., Kakabadse, N., Sakellariou, K., & Alcaraz, J. (2014). Cosmopolitanism and the elite disposition as diversity factors in enterprise development. Paper presented at the *British Academy of Management Conference*, Belfast.

Nicolopoulou, K., Kakabadse, N. K., Nikolopoulos, K.-P., Alcaraz, J. M., Sakellariou, K. (2016). Cosmopolitanism and transnational elite entrepreneurial practices: Manifesting the cosmopolitan disposition in a cosmopolitan city. *Society and Business Review*, *11*, 257–275, http://dx.doi.org/10.1108/SBR-01-2016-0001

Ogbor, J. O. (2000). Mythicising and reification in entrepreneurial discourse: Ideology-critique of entrepreneurial studies. *Journal of Management Studies*, *37*(5), 605–635.

Patton, M. (1982). Qualitative methods and approaches: What are they. In E. Kuhns & S. V. Martorana (Eds.), *Qualitative methods for institutional research* (pp. 3–16). San Francisco: Jossey-Bass.

Peacock, E. (2016). Western Bias at the Global Entrepreneurship Congress. *Global Policy Journal*. www.globalpolicyjournal.com/blog/22/03/2016/western-bias-global-entrepreneurship-congress [Accessed 2 August 2017].

Pecould, A. (2004). Entrepreneurship and identity: Cosmopolitanism and cultural competencies among German-Turkish businesspeople in Berlin. *Journal of Ethnic and Migration Studies*, *30*(1), 3–20.

Prasad, A. (Ed.). (2003). *Postcolonial theory and organizational analysis: A critical engagement*. New York, NY: Palgrave Macmillan.

Pret, T., Shaw, E., & Drakopoulou Dodd, S. (2015). Painting the full picture: The conversion of economic, cultural, social and symbolic capital. *International Small Business Journal*, *34*(8), 1004–1027.

Ram, M., Jones, T., Edwards, P., Kiselinchev, A., Muchenje, L., & Wodesenbet, K. (2011). Engaging with super-diversity: New migrant businesses and the research-policy nexus. *International Small Business Journal*, *31*(4), 337–356.

Robertson, T., & Wind, Y. (1983). Organizational cosmopolitanism and innovativeness. *The Academy of Management Journal*, *26*(2), 332–338. www.jstor.org/stable/255980

Said, E. (1975). The text, the world, the critic. *The Bulletin of the Midwest Modern Language Association*, *8*(2), 1–23. doi:10.2307/1314778

Said, E. (2003). *Orientalism*. London: Penguin Books.

Sanchez-Runde, C., Nardon, L., & Steers, R. (2012). Accounting for culture in the development of global leaders. In: Canals J. (Ed.) *Leadership Development in a Global World*. The Palgrave Macmillan IESE Business Collection. London: Palgrave Macmillan.

Sanders, R. (2017). *The rise of Africa's small & medium size enterprises* (1st ed.), Bloomington, Indiana: Xlibris.

Sepulveda, L., Syrett, S., & Lyon, F. (2011). Population superdiversity and new migrant enterprise: The case of London. *Entrepreneurship & Regional Development*, *23*(7–8), 469–497.

Shane, S. & Venkataraman, S. (2001). Entrepreneurship as a field of research: A Response to Zahra and Dess, Singh and Erickson. *Academy of Management Review*, 26(1), 13–16.

Shane, S. (2012). Reflections on the 2010 AMR Decade Award: Delivering on the promise of entrepreneurship as a field of research. *The Academy of Management Review*, *37*(1), 10–20.

Terjesen, S & Elam, A. (2009). Transnational entrepreneurs' venture internationalization strategies: A practice theory approach. *Entrepreneurship Theory and Practice*, *33*(5), 1093–1120. doi: 10.1111/j.1540-6520.2009.00336.x

Thomas, A., & Mueller, S. (2000). A case for comparative entrepreneurship: Assessing the relevance of culture. *Journal of International Business Studies*, *31*(2), 287–301. www.jstor.org/stable/155638

Tyfield, D., & Urry, J. (2009). Cosmopolitan China? Lessons from international collaboration in low-carbon innovation. *The British Journal of Sociology*, *60*(4), 793–812.

Venkataraman, S., Sarasvathy, S., Dew, N., & Forster, W. (2013). Of narratives and artifacts. *Academy of Management Review*, *38*, 163–165.

Verduijn, K., Dey, P., Tedmanson, D., & Essers, C. (2014). Emancipation and/or oppression? Conceptualizing dimensions of criticality in entrepreneurship studies. *International Journal of Entrepreneurial Behavior & Research, 20*(2), 98–107. https://doi.org/10.1108/IJEBR-02-2014-0031

Vertovec, S., & Cohen, R. (2002). Conceiving cosmopolitanism. In S. Vertovec & R. Cohen (Eds.), *Conceiving cosmopolitanism: Theory, context and practice* (pp. 1–22). Oxford: Oxford University Press.

Volery, T. (2007). Ethnic entrepreneurship: A theoretical framework. In L. P. Dana (Ed.), *Handbook of research on ethnic minority entrepreneurship* (pp. 30–41). Cheltenham: Edward Elgar.

Welter, F. (2011). Contextualizing entrepreneurship – Conceptual challenges and ways forward. *Entrepreneurship Theory and Practice, 35*(1), 165–184. doi:10.1111/j.15406520.2010.00427

Wennekers, S., & Thurik, R. (1999). Linking entrepreneurship and economic growth. *Small Business Economic, 13*, 27–55.

Wood, M. S., & McKinley, W. (2010). The production of entrepreneurial opportunity: A constructivist perspective. *Strategic Entrepreneurship Journal, 4*(1), 66–84.

Woodward, I., Skribs, Z., & Bean, C. (2008). Attitudes towards globalisation and cosmopolitanism: Cultural diversity, personal consumption and the national economy. *The British Journal of Sociology, 59*(2), 207–226.

Wright, M. (2012). Entrepreneurial mobility, resource orchestration and context. In F. Welter, D. Smallbone, & A. Van Gils (Eds.), *Entrepreneurial processes in a changing economy: Frontiers in European entrepreneurship research* (p. 6). Cheltenham: Edward Elgar Publishing.

Yeoh, B. (2004). Cosmopolitanism and its exclusions in Singapore. *Urban Studies, 41*(12), 2431–2445.

Zahra, S. A. (2007). Contextualizing theory building in entrepreneurship research. *Journal of Business Venturing, 22*(3), 443–452. http://dx.doi.org/10.1016/j.jbusvent.2006.04.007

11 A unified account of the firm

Deontic architecture

Brian R. Gordon and Russ McBride

> *The mind striving after unification of the theory cannot be satisfied that two fields should exist which, by their nature, are quite independent.*
> – Albert Einstein, Lecture delivered to the Nordic
> Assembly of Naturalists at Gothenburg, July 11, 1923

A note on the philosophical approach to understanding the firm

A scientific theory enables scholars working in an area to do a few rather useful things. In particular, scientific theories are useful for determining what is likely to happen (prediction), why things happened the way that they did (retrodiction) and what can be expected to occur if certain preconditions are meet (causal explanation). Armed with a good theory, it is possible, in principle, to figure out how to intervene in the causal structure of the world to make things happen in ways that we want. We usually call this engineering or applied science. Scientific theories, in other words, provide epistemic and pragmatic benefits. Or at least that is what we hope for, knowing full well that science as a practice is fallible and imperfect.

What then are we to make of the role of philosophy in all of this? What does a philosophical approach add to the practice of science or to prediction, retrodiction, and causal explanation? One answer is that philosophy does not provide anything *special*, although this doesn't preclude it from making an important contribution. What philosophers are doing, when they are philosophizing about some phenomenon of interest, is basically what any other theorist does when trying to understand a phenomenon. The philosopher builds theories that attempt to explain, predict, and provide tools for agents seeking to intervene and bring about desired ends. Perhaps they do so at a higher level of abstraction and with a keener eye towards logical precision, but otherwise not much of a difference. What we call science is only the refinement of 'natural philosophy', a preoccupation of philosophers since the Ancient Greeks.

Others have suggested a rather different role for philosophy. Instead of being essentially coincident with the practice of science, philosophers are thought to do something complementary. Scientists, in their rush to predict, explain, and provide useful knowledge, sometimes get ahead of themselves and sometimes get a little careless or sloppy in their theorization. Philosophy's role, on this account, is to help the scientists do better theorization – uncovering implicit assumptions, clarifying terms, showing implications, etc. And this is valuable, or so it is argued, for the same reasons division of labor usually is; scientists specialize in field-specific theories and philosophers specialize in helping scientists make those theories clearer and more cogent – so everyone wins. To push an analogy in line with the topic of entrepreneurship, if scientists are like the executives of a firm, then philosophers are like the board of directors; they leave the day-to-day work to the scientists, but help out with governance and the 'big' decisions.

Our position is that both of these characterizations are undoubtedly right. In part, this is because philosophers do different things when they engage with science. Some philosophers choose to theorize with more attention to foundations while others see their role as something more like that of the board of directors (although we doubt very many philosophers at all would actually use that kind of metaphor to describe what it is that they are doing). Moreover, it is clear that both are valuable; they each make science better because they make for better theorizing (Weick, 1995a). In any case, it is often hard in practice to see a non-blurry distinction between these two. Science advances because it takes notice of anomalies and corner cases and seeks to build theory that can accommodate the facts about the phenomena as they are understood (Kuhn, 1996).

For our part, we think of ourselves and our project as one of building theory with attention to foundational issues. We want to get the ontology right, which is to say that we think it is important to be clear about what we believe are the fundamental entities and processes at work in organizations as a phenomenon of study. If you're not clear about what an organized social entity, like a firm, actually is, it's hard to get either the theories correct or the downstream predictions, retroductions, or causal explanations correct. Go ahead, call us funny names if you will (philosopher, scientist, etc.); it's the work of building useful theory that matters, at least to us.

I   The model of unification

Prior to Newton, there was a scattered panoply of explanations for the movement of physical objects. Newton's *Principia* unified celestial mechanics (the movement of the planets and the sun) and terrestrial mechanics (the movement of objects on Earth) by postulating a common structure underlying them (the gravitational inverse square law).[1] This single, common underlying explanation applied to all physical objects in all domains – not just those objects on Earth or those in the heavens – a fact which bolstered both the theory's importance and the strength of the evidence in favor of it.

Most firms arise from entrepreneurial efforts and a full understanding of entrepreneurship cannot be complete without an understanding of the vehicle of mature entrepreneurship – the firm. But today there is a scattered panoply of explanations of firms and their behavior,[2] including the programmatic view of capabilities introduced by March and Simon (1993) and Nelson and Winter (1982), the roles and rules framework articulated by March (1994), the nexus of contracts view of Jensen and Meckling (1976), and the dynamic capabilities framework of emerging out of Nelson and Winter (1982) and Teece, Pisano, and Shuen (1997). The difficulty lies not in the criticisms that have accumulated against such views over the years but, rather, for our concerns here, in the fact that each is an answer to a somewhat different question leading to diverse, often orthogonal understandings of the firm itself. Adam Smith (1776) opens the *Wealth of Nations* lauding what he sees as the essence of the firm – the productive power derived from division of labor. For Coase (1937), the firm is a result of the realization that markets do not operate costlessly. Alchian and Demsetz (1972) see the firm as an answer to the question of how to solve the information-shirking problem of team production. Nelson and Winter (1982) see the firm is the result of solving the problem of how to coordinate sequences of agent behavior and organizational routines that evolve over time. Which is it? At stake is nothing less than an understanding of the firm itself.

Against this cacophony, we suggest instead the existence of a single, common structure underlying all of them, implied by the philosophy of social ontology – what we call, deontic architecture. We have far less work to do than a Newtonian unification as there has been much more foreshadowing of the role of deontics in the firm. But making clear exactly how deontic architecture unifies the various theories of the firm has not yet been described. And just as Newton's answer struck him initially as "so great an absurdity", so too, the answer we propose initially appears implausible. Our plan is to erode that initial sense of implausibility over the course of this chapter by showing how each of the approaches to the firm discussed here can be 'reconstructed' in terms of deontic architecture. We hope that such an effort illustrates both the importance of deontic architecture and highlights the evidence in favor of it.

II   The plan

Unification of diverse phenomena is one important kind of scientific progress, Newton's unification of terrestrial and celestial mechanics being a paradigmatic example. Darwin's theory of evolution is another. As Kitcher (1981) argues, in both cases, science advanced not because we learned more details about one particular facet of the world, but, rather, because the theories in question were able to subsume a number of ostensibly different classes of phenomena and demonstrate how they actually reflected the operation of a single underlying principle. Newton's and Darwin's successes, in turn, have become important precedents, suggesting that theoretical unification itself is a legitimate goal of scientific inquiry. A theory that is able to show how *prima facie* disparate phenomena actually reflect a singular underlying principle represents an important advance in our understanding because it simplifies and subsumes more phenomena under the same explanatory framework (Kitcher, 1981).

Social scientists working on the nature of the firm have developed many approaches over the past century (March & Simon, 1993; Morgan, 2006; Scott & Davis, 2007), each prioritizing different aspects of firms: firms as social institutions; as entities comprised of individuals; and as embedded within the larger political, economic, and social structures of our societies. *Prima facie*, these theories – and the underlying frameworks upon which they are based – have little in common with one another. The range of phenomena such theories have tried to explain has been broad. Coase (1937), for example, set in motion a concern with the boundaries of the firm and the market, asking why different economic activities are governed by different kinds of economic vehicles. March and Simon (1993) set out to explain the nature of firm-level capabilities in terms of more elementary pieces. Penrose (1959) sought to understand why firms grow and why they pursue particular growth trajectories over others, leading to work focused on how management is able to dynamically reconfigure firm capabilities in the pursuit of growth and competitive advantage (Teece et al., 1997).

There is a maze of important discussions about how well these theories succeeded as answers to the questions they posed. We shall sidestep such discussions and remain more or less neutral about each theory's success. The question we are asking is, not whether each theory is true, but: *What would have to be the case in order for the theory to be true?* Like Newtonian mechanics, is it possible that there is a deeper, unifying framework here – one capable of unifying perhaps not *every* extant theory of the firm, but at least those described here?

In this chapter, we propose just such a unification, introducing deontic architecture and showing how this can help make sense of a number of ostensibly unrelated phenomena that have been discussed in the context of: a) organizational capabilities; b) roles and role hierarchies; c) theories of the firm based on the idea of a nexus of contracts; d) and dynamic capabilities.

Our approach here is built around the idea of a *deontic architecture*. A deontic architecture is a structured collection of deontics. *Deontics* are rights, duties, authorizations, permissions, obligations, and the like. An employment contract, for examples, establishes an explicit collection of rights and duties an employee has relative to his or her employer – the right to a specified salary, the right to a work area, the obligation to satisfy the described job responsibilities, etc. Other rights and duties that affect the employee are implicit, developed by the employee, created or modified ad hoc by the employer, or derived from other sources (the local culture, the regional legal code, professional norms etc.). A *deontic bundle* is that specific system of deontics for an individual occupying a particular locus or role in some social structure, like a firm. The deontics internal to a firm bind multiple individuals together into interdependent groups and circumscribe the social entity as a functional unit. The argument we shall advance is that these deontics are guides for appropriate action, channeling the agent's reasoned actions and decisions towards ends that are encouraged by the 'guardrails' of the deontology. More specifically, we suggest that deontics define societally sanctioned roles for individual agents while larger social entities – like firms and other forms of organization – can themselves be understood as deontic architectures built, in part, out of these more basic roles that constitute them.

Our contention is that an understanding of the essence of an organization as a deontic architecture, a structured collection of deontics, can provide a unifying theoretical framework for understanding a diverse array of organizational and firm-related phenomena. To make our point more concretely, we will describe how deontic architecture can: a) Provide a better way of thinking about the foundations of organizational capabilities and action (Felin & Foss, 2005, 2009; Barney & Felin, 2013); b) How roles and role hierarchies are developed by organizations (March, 1994); c) What it means to think of firms as a nexus of contracts (Bratton, 1989b); and, finally, d) How firms are able to dynamically reconfigure their organizational capabilities (Teece et al., 1997; Augier & Teece, 2009).

We begin by introducing these four different historical areas of research by scholars interested in organizations and firms, each of which is the focus of a large literature. Volumes can (and have) been written about each. We have no illusions of providing a complete, fair and balanced review of the work in these areas. Our intention is simply to introduce the core elements of these approaches and to point out some of the critical issues that remain unresolved. Next we then introduce the basics of the deontic architecture framework. We then come back to each of these four areas to perform an 'analytical reconstruction' of each using the deontic architecture framework. The goal is to illustrate how deontic architecture can help us better understand the four phenomena at issue and resolve some of the puzzles that current theories handle only problematically, if at all.

III Organizational and firm-level phenomena

A The programmatic view of organizational capabilities

In neoclassical economics, a firm is understood as a production function that transforms a vector of inputs into a vector of outputs. The actual processes involved in turning factor market inputs into product market outputs are abstracted in these theories so that the internal processes and dynamics of the firm are treated as a 'black box', inside of which no description is offered.

Of course the similarity of the production function to a computer which takes inputs, process the input, and then return outputs, did not go unnoticed and opened attempts to describe the black box activity in terms of deterministic computer processing. The capabilities perspectives articulated by March and Simon (1993) and Nelson and Winter (1982) explicitly sought to explain *how* firms generate specific outputs from a particular set of factor market inputs by opening up the organizational black box and looking at the mechanics of production and organization.

The central idea that emerges in both of these approaches is that firm-level capabilities can be understood in terms of more basic elements that at their core are simple automata that execute deterministic programs when triggered by the appropriate stimulus. Action at the organizational level, we are told, is the result of a complex concatenation of rule-based elements, each operating by "matching of appropriate action to recognized situations" (March & Simon, 1993, p. 11).

March and Simon (1993) and Nelson and Winter (1982) each argued that organizational capabilities operate on the same principles as individual skills, borrowing heavily from the newly emerging paradigm of cognitive science that was arising at the time – a paradigm that Simon himself was instrumental in formulating as one of the early pioneers of cognitive psychology and artificial intelligence. March and Simon's (1993) theory of organizational capabilities was deeply influenced by the parallel work Simon was pursuing in cognitive science on the nature of cognition; the theories in many ways were isomorphic.

As Simon himself noted, production systems "have an obvious affinity to the classical stimulus-response (S → R) connections in psychology" (1999a, p. 676). And in the same way that an individual's complex behavior could ultimately be explained in terms of the operations of concatenated stimulus-response systems, March and Simon (1993) and Nelson and Winter (1982) argued that an organization's capabilities ultimately constituted the programs that were the microfoundations which underwrote the organization's actions as an productive entity (cf. Felin & Foss, 2005, 2009; Barney & Felin, 2013).

Accounting for *how* capabilities change and *how* new, *de novo*, capabilities are created has always been a weakness of the capabilities approach. March and Simon (1993) and Nelson and Winter (1982; see too Winter, 2012, 2013) have each provided an account based on what can broadly be considered evolutionary (though not necessarily Darwinian in a strict sense) processes. At the core of March and Simon's (1993) approach is the construct of *search*. In novel, i.e. non-routinized, circumstances, whether they arise out of endogenously or exogenously driven changes, these routinized programs lie fallow. Absent the normal triggering flows of information, the capabilities are not exercised. The absence of a triggering stimuli doesn't mean an absence of action, however. An *aspiration* of a certain level of organizational performance is itself an internal prompt to action of an *ad hoc*, improvisational kind (March & Simon, 1993). Aspiration alone can spur organizational search for effective novel action patterns which, if proven successful, are the genesis of novel organizational capabilities.

March and Simon (1993, pp. 198–200) elaborate on this process with a 'warehouse' model that, while metaphorical in parts, represents a fairly well developed process account. The 'machinery' of organizational action – the programs and subroutines that generate action – are stored in memory. When whole programs are triggered, things work smoothly and proceed in a routinized manner. When unmet aspirations spur a search for novel action patterns, the processes unfold differently. Instead of whole programs, it is subroutines and sub-subroutines that are invoked, in a process "characterized by a great deal of 'randomness'" (1993, p. 199). And much like a rat in a Skinner Box, in the tradition of stimulus-response psychology from which the idea of Simon's production systems derived, operant conditioning (the reinforcing of successful action via *ex post* reward) allows for the slow determination of new courses of action and ultimately the elaboration of new programs of immense complexity, March and Simon (1993) argue. Similar evolutionary models of the origin of novel capabilities are at the core of approach pioneered by Nelson and Winter (1982; see too Winter, 2012, 2013 and Aldrich & Ruef, 2006).

The Lingering Problems:

Such accounts of change, innovation, and the origin of novel capabilities based on random mutations that occur on the glacial pace of evolution are hard to square with accounts of entrepreneurship that take vision, imagination, and judgement seriously (Buchanan & Vanberg, 1991; Kirzner, 1999; Chiles, Bluedorn, & Gupta, 2007; Foss & Klein, 2012; Zenger, 2016). Accounts which highlight the decidedly non-random, rapid, purposeful pursuit of opportunities that are as much created as they are discovered (Alvarez & Barney, 2007), are hard to reconcile. In section V, we will show how the deontic architecture solves this problem.

B   *Roles and role hierarchies*

March and Simon (1993) also talk a good deal about hierarchy. And while this discussion is certainly congruent with their discussions of organizational capabilities, it should not be taken as identical. These discussions cover different territories. The theory of capabilities that March and Simon put forward attempts to explain how the macro-level phenomenon of routinized and programmatic organizational action is accomplished via an architecture of lower-level elements. It is a project in microfoundations (Felin & Foss, 2005, 2009; Barney & Felin, 2013; Winter, 2012). The discussion of hierarchies and roles (March & Simon, 1993; March, 1994) picks out a surface-level feature of organizations – the observation that individual members of an organization typically have relatively well-defined sets of responsibilities and tasks within the overall economy of the firm and that the individuals within the firm typically have a formally defined set of interactions and authority relationship with other members of the organization – and attempts to provide a functional explanation for why this should be so.

March and Simon (1993) suggest that hierarchies highlight three different aspects of the work done by organizations. First, they argue that most of the work done in an organization is accomplished by relatively small teams or groups of individuals who may work closely together in an interdependent manner requiring a fair amount of planning and close coordination but whose work is relatively independent and only loosely coupled with the work done by other individuals, teams, and groups within the economy of the organization. Simon described this kind of organization as 'nearly decomposable' (1999b). While the information flows and task interdependencies comprise a dense network within teams or groups, the flow of information and the task interdependencies between divisions is typically much lower and the interactions subject to more standardization and formalization.

Second, March and Simon (1993) note that there is a rather well-elaborated system of authority relationships, with individuals reporting to other individuals who are 'higher up' in authority – where authority is usually understood to involve both i) oversight and control functions, where individuals are evaluated and rewarded (or punished) for their efforts and contributions by a higher ranking individual, and ii) fiat, where an individual is agreed to forgo some measure of autonomy within the organization and accept that their activities (to a certain degree) can be directed by the a higher ranking individual (Barnard, 1938; Nelson & Winter, 1982).

Third, March and Simon (1993) argue, to a first approximation at least, that the orchestration of efforts within an organization reflects something of a means-end type relationship, where overarching goals are factored into subgoals and further sub-subgoals (and so on) and individuals are assigned to teams and groups responsible for the execution of specific deliverables within the plan represented by the means-ends decomposition of work. This is a reflection of what Chandler (1962) described as "structure following strategy."

One explanation that March and Simon (1993) provide for the hierarchical nature of organizational work is that this way of orchestrating efforts is efficient (in a loosely understood way) given the bounded rationality of the individuals who comprise the organization. Individuals have limited knowledge, limited skills, and limited cognitive powers; there are limits to what they know and what they can accomplish, and factorization of work enables individuals to specialize and improve their effectiveness within particular task-domains. A second explanation is that this kind of means-ends organization of work parallels the more basic processes of problem-solving that are a basic component of human cognitive faculties. Organizations are arranged hierarchically, this argument asserts, because human problem solving, in general, is accomplished via means-ends decomposition of large complex problems into sub-problems, each of which can be tackled relatively independently.

March (1994) develops a complementary account of roles and role hierarchies in his discussion of the 'logic of appropriateness' in the context of organizational decision making. For March, a logic of appropriateness, where individuals make decisions on the basis of what is expected of them given their roles within an organizational hierarchy, is contrasted with a 'logic of consequences', where decisions are made on estimations of the outcomes of alternative lines of action as these impact preferences and/or utilities. March (1994) argues that much of the decision making actually observed in organizational settings is better explained by a logic of appropriateness than it is by a logic of consequences. This behavioral account is in contradiction to the traditional account of decision making in economics and decision science and while the processes involved in a logic of appropriateness requires "thought judgement, imagination, and care. . . . [this is] quite different from the processes of rational analysis (1994, p. 61).

The basic premise of March's account of role-based decision making is that individuals within an organization make decisions based on the identities that they assume and enact within that context. And for March, the core of such identities can be expressed in the set of rules that the role-holder uses to make decisions. "When individuals fulfill . . . identities" he notes, "they follow rules or procedures that they see as appropriate to the situation" (1994, p. 57). And what are these rules? Not surprisingly, they turn out to be the same kind of stimulus-response elements that played a central role in March and Simon's (1993) account of organizational capabilities: "The reasoning process is one of . . . matching rules to recognized situations" (1994, p. 58).

Roles matter, according to March's (1994) account, because they are the basic element of hierarchical order. The features of hierarchy that March and Simon (1993) outline, in other words, are best understood in terms that are cashed out by a formal network of roles, where each role is assigned certain tasks within the overall economy of the organization and where each role fits into a complex of authority relationships and information flows that may be formal or informal and more or less temporary and ad hoc or permanent and routinized. March notes:

> Formal and informal organizational rules are woven into, utilize, and help define organizational identities and roles. Tasks are organized around sets of skills, responsibilities, and rules that define a role. Roles and their associated rules coordinate and control organizational activities.
>
> (1994, pp. 60–61)

The Lingering Problems:
The weakness in the theory of role and role hierarchies is the same that we noted for the theory of capabilities – namely, the difficulty of providing an account of novelty, innovation, and the origin of novel roles and role hierarchies. March (1994) does suggest three different primary processes by which new roles arise and existing roles change. He suggests that: i) individuals can learn from experience and incorporate what they learn into future contexts, essentially rewriting the triggers and/or the programmatic responses that are encoded in the production systems that constitute the rules that comprise the roles they play in the organization, ii) that rules and roles will evolve in something like the processes of natural selection, where feedback from the environment impacts which rules and roles are carried forward into the future based on how they perform in past situations, and iii) that individuals envision and write roles for others as they plan for the future, in what constitutes a type of programming exercise.

The problem with these accounts is that, where they are forward-looking (as opposed to contexts where rules and roles change because of evolutionary processes) they fall into trouble trying to provide an account of how a new rule can be specified in the absence of a well-defined triggering condition or action pattern. If a production system can be specified, there is no problem. A new rule is just a new action program attached to a specified input trigger. But when either or both of those elements of a production system are vague or ill-specified, the account fails to provide a way to explain how a new rule comes to be specified. Despite this, new organizations – with new roles and role hierarchies – come into being all the time. And many of these involve organizations pursuing novel opportunities (Buchanan & Vanberg, 1991; Kirzner, 1999, Alvarez & Barney, 2007; Chiles et al., 2007; Foss & Klein, 2012) where it is not easy to see how the entrepreneurial action entailed in the pursuit of these new opportunities can be easily squared with production systems rooted in older production system specifications in any straightforward way (contra Winter, 2012) – especially when the pursuit involves the invention of new technologies, products, business models, or value chains.

How does this model attempt to account for the creation of de novo roles and role hierarchies? Even in cases where the production systems themselves would, in principle, be fairly standard – so that it is safe to assume that there were existing social models that could be used in the specification of the production system rules – it is not necessarily clear that the model outlined by March (1994) can provide the needed speed and flexibility to account for the fact that firms are quite adept at creating new roles 'on the fly'. New teams and new startups can be launched quickly; there isn't necessarily an enormous lag between the time when a group of individuals commits to a venture and when the individuals begin to operate within a set of structured roles and authority relationships – even in an ad hoc and ephemeral situations (see Barnard, 1938).

Evolutionary processes, where new roles evolve out of older models that individuals bring with them from prior experience, work too slowly to provide the kind of rapid deployment of roles and hierarchy that we see in these contexts. And the same is true for models based on experiential learning and socialization (Berger & Luckmann, 1966). What is still needed is an account of how the kind of rapid deployment of new roles and new rules in de novo contexts that March (1994) suggests takes place actually occurs.

C   *The firm as a nexus of contracts*

Prior to Alchian and Demsetz (1972) and Jensen and Meckling (1976), firms were anomalous entities in a sea of well-structured microeconomic theory which described things like the coordination of resources in markets and the effects of competition on supply, demand, and profitability. The internal workings of firms – as the exceptions – were treated as idiosyncratic black boxes within which microeconomic theory did not reach. The internals of firms were instead described by management theory which was grounded in a view of the firm as a structured hierarchy of power relations. Management organized the factors of production, dominated the bureaucracies via authority, and justified its authority on the basis of organizational expertise, specialized knowledge (Bratton, 1989b), and entrepreneurial vision (Knight, 1921). Such an account is provided by deontic architecture, as we will describe in section V.

The nexus of contracts approach suggests that the firm is essentially nothing more than a set of interlocking contracts distinguished from the broader markets in which it is embedded only in terms of the density of interlocks rather than by some important qualitative distinction (Jensen & Meckling, 1976). This move away from the management-centered approach accomplished a number of important feats. First, for a century prior, corporate law had tilted between theories of the state-derived legitimacy and authority (where firms were seen as state-facilitated entities, serving the interests of the state); theories of hierarchy and managerial authority; and theories of contracts. The nexus of contracts view pushed things solidly toward contracts (Bratton, 1989a) as the primary ordering principle.

Second, it gave neoclassical economics analytical purchase inside the black box of firms where, it was argued, the very same principles of economics could be applied as in the market. The rational actors inside a firm were postulated to act just like the rational actors outside a firm, pursuing their self-interests in a utility-maximizing way.

Third, as the microeconomic wave moved "into" the firm it de-emphasized traditional conceptions of hierarchical power relations and authority structures. Instead, management was seen as an ongoing process of contract negotiation and formation with employees who choose what conditions they would associate with a firm and what conditions they would more or less cede decision authority to a manager (Barnard, 1938). From this perspective, an employee is not bound to the authority of higher-level management as much as they are a part of a freely designed, voluntary exchange agreement, a contract. Alchian and Demsetz (1972) were so comfortable rejecting managerial authority that they said the firm,

> "has no power or fiat, no authority, no disciplinary action any different in the slightest degree from ordinary market contracting between two people. I can "punish" you only by withholding future business or by seeking redress in the courts for any failure to honor our exchange agreement" (p. 777).[3]

Fourth, the firm as a productive entity is itself de-emphasized as an important object in the economic landscape. The individual agent is the preeminent point of causation and theoretical discussion by virtue, primarily, of the agent's contract-making which, again, provides traction on the firm as a standard subject of microeconomic analysis. While production was traditionally understood as the special provenance of the firm, nexus of contract thinking blurred the lines between the firm and the market, arguing that production was primarily orchestrated via contracts and that the firm was no special boundary for the these means of coordination.

If everything is a contractual agreement, explicit or otherwise, why bother arranging these contracts in a firm when they could be formed in the markets directly without a firm? The answer, as Coase (1937) noted, is that the formation and monitoring of such contracts is not without cost. One chooses a firm when the transaction costs of establishing such agreements in the free markets are greater than the costs of doing so inside a firm. But cost considerations endogenously vary with scope, scale, and technology, learning, and co-specialization among other factors. Firm boundaries, from this perspective, then, are the result of impinging forces and considerations rather than constituting some causal feature of the economic landscape on their own.

The Lingering Problems:

The contract 'unit' is not an especially tractable construct with which to theorize. Almost every contract is different. There's little hope for comparing contracts without some more fine-grained unit of analysis. Understanding contacts as a formalization of relations between individuals that are engaged in utility-maximization makes it difficult to see how the goals of the firm find their place.

This brief overview above, though, is enough to appreciate the wide overlap between the nexus of contracts view and the deontic architecture view which can solve these problems. Contracts are, of course, *essentially a collection of rights and duties* that are described explicitly in formal contracts and implicitly in informal contracts. What contracts specify is precisely the obligations and rights of each party. A deontic architecture view makes possible a more fine-grained analysis of contracts because the unit of analysis, instead of being the contract, are the deontic components that in aggregate comprise the contract. This approach sees the contract itself subsumed into the broader network of deontics that structure and order the action of the individuals coordinating their efforts in pursuit of organization-defined goals. At the same time, deontic architecture provides for a reconstruction of what it means to order the collective efforts of individual efforts in ways that illuminate how authority is constructed and wielded within organizations. On one view, deontic architecture can be seen as a powerful extension to transaction cost economics. How exactly this works shall be explained in section V.

D   Dynamic capabilities of the firm and organizational transformation

Organizations transform themselves in response to exogenous changes in the competitive environment and in response to endogenous decisions to pursue entrepreneurial opportunities. Nelson and Winter's (1982) inquiry into the nature of routinized action suggested that this process of change and transformation – in some circumstances – could itself be routinized and institutionalized as an organizational capability of its own (see too Eisenhardt & Martin, 2000; Winter, 2003; Teece, 2012). In Winter's (2003) formalization, the organization's current routines and capabilities – the capabilities that it exercises when exploiting its current opportunity set (March, 1991) – are termed 'zero-level' capabilities. Dynamic capabilities are then understood to be the organizational capabilities that modify and transform existing 'zero-level' organizational capabilities or create de novo 'zero-level' capabilities.

Teece (2012) has suggested that it can be a mistake to think about dynamic capabilities in exactly the same way that we think about ordinary 'zero-level' capabilities. In particular, in contradiction to 'zero-level' capabilities, where the microfoundations are typically understood in terms of the knowledge embedded in actions of a large number of individuals in the form of the production systems or 'roles and rules' that dictate what is to be done in various circumstances, a firm's dynamic capabilities are often tied to the idiosyncratic, ad hoc actions, beliefs, and visions of the individuals occupying positions of senior leadership within the organization. What makes for a dynamic capability in this perspective is not that it is itself embedded in a capability – as is the case for Nelson and Winter (1982) and Winter (2003) – but what it *does*, i.e., that it is able to generate change in response to exogenous factors or endogenous decisions to pursue new opportunities. In this respect, dynamic capabilities can be understood as the process account underlying organizational transformation more generally, in the sense outlined by Weick and Quinn (1999).

The Lingering Problems:

A now-familiar question presents itself here. How is the organization capable of instituting these broad transformational changes in its underlying 'zero-level' capabilities? In Weick and Quinn's (1999) terminology, how is the organization able to 'transition' or 'rebalance' the focus of its operational capabilities in either episodic or continuous contexts? What are the mechanisms by which intention and vision are transformed into new action patterns in contexts where the change occurs in time frames that make it hard to conceptualize the process in terms of evolutionary or experiential learning processes? The dynamic capabilities literature makes the case that these kinds of transformational change can and do happen on a regular basis. What is needed is an account of the mechanisms that makes this possible. Deontic architecture provides it.

IV   An introduction to deontic architecture

Although efforts to understand social structures date back at least to Plato and Aristotle, efforts to understand the ontology of the social and what exactly a social entity is are a relatively recent effort led by philosophers like Bratman (1987, 2014), Searle (1995, 2010), Tuomela (2007, 2013), Gilbert (1992, 2015), and Epstein (2015) among others.[4] All the business sciences study social phenomena and are, in this way, involved in the study of social reality. Social ontology is an attempt to provide a foundation for all of the social sciences, an attempt to ground the study of social reality in a robust, coherent, unified framework.

Social ontology suggests that social reality requires a different set of explanatory frameworks from those of the physical sciences. As a sub-discipline unto itself dedicated to understanding the nature of social entities there is not, as in any sub-discipline, perfect agreement about the answer to the question about what a social entity is, but there is a majority view about what the shape of the answer to that question looks like. On 'the standard model' (Guala, 2007) social entities depend upon the collective recognition of the existence of that social entity by the members of society. A social entity, like a governmental department, an American football team, or a C corporation, is a kind of elaborate fiction, one that becomes real by virtue of our collection recognition and belief about it.

Most social ontologists ascribe to what we can refer to as the 'Deontological Thesis' (McBride, 2015), the thesis that what we collectively recognize, when we recognize the existence of a social entity, are deontics – rights, duties, obligations, authorizations, permissions, etc. There are two broad categories of deontics, the positive deontics of rights, authorizations, permissions, etc., which afford additional abilities, and the negative deontics of duties, obligations, commitments, etc., which restrict behavior, demand additional efforts, or demand acquiescence. Social structures are, on this view, essentially, built from deontology, that is, built from rights and duties, obligations and permissions, and so forth, so that the creation of a new social structure is fundamentally the creation of a new set of deontics and the transformation of an existing organization is a transformation of the networks of deontics that order and orchestrate the coordinated functioning of the individuals who comprise the social group.

A couple of examples will make this clear. When a minister issues the declaration: "I now pronounce you husband and wife" what *exactly* comes into existence that did not exist a few seconds prior? A new social entity – a marriage. But there is no *physical difference* between the current state and the state a few seconds prior. What changed was the deontology. Negative deontics (duties) and positive deontic (rights) that didn't previously exist came into existence as if by magic. Each partner in the marriage is now *required* to make medical decisions for the other in emergencies, *permitted* to file a joint income tax return, and if they live in an urban area of China they *obligated* to have no more than two children. They have the *right* to a tax credit, the *right* to couple's discounts, and the *right* to the other's assets after death. A marriage, as a social entity, is, in an important sense, essentially decomposable into the deontics that comprise it.

If every social entity consists essentially of deontics, then a firm is of course essentially comprised of *its* deontics. What *is* a corporation then, essentially? What exactly is created when a corporation comes into existence by virtue of a piece of paper, a small payment, and a stamp of approval from the Department of Corporations? Again: *deontology*. The officers named in the corporation are now empowered with a variety or rights, duties, obligations, authorizations, entitlements, and responsibilities that did not previously exist. The department of Corporations is now obligated to ensure compliance with various obligations. The State Franchise Tax Board is now obligated to ensure the collection of state taxes, and the IRS for federal taxes. The officers have a basket of powers they did not previously possess. The officers can, in the name of representing the firm, now open bank accounts, engage in financial transactions on behalf of the firm, enter contracts, and indeed enter into and exercise almost all the rights of a real person but with a different (limited) set of liabilities. "We have a capacity to create a reality by representing it as existing. The only reality that we can so create is a reality of deontology. It is a reality that confers rights, responsibilities, and so on" (Searle, 2010, p. 89).

There are real powers the corporation now has and the officers of the firm are emboldened with these new powers to engage in the process of creating subsidiary deontic structures that further the goals of the firm. Some examples: the firm can enter into rental contracts for its office space, it can serve as the recipient and guarantor of a loan, it can establish and dissolve internal departments, and it can issue additional stock. The officers can of course hire employees who are in turn empowered with a quiver of rights and obligations given their role in the company and the terms of their contract. In a growing firm, the duties, responsibilities, and powers of the firm to act in the market grow. A timeline of deontics branches outward as the rights and duties that are established expand.

From the perspective of social ontology, a firm is one type of organization and every social organization is fundamentally a collection of rights, permissions, and authorizations, on the one hand, and duties, obligations, and commitments, on the other hand. En masse, these are deontic powers. The structure and the distribution of those deontics determine the fundamental structure of the firm. The internal deontics determine the internal structure, and the external deontics determine the form of the connections to the rest of the social world. Examples of internal structures include employee contracts and the voting privilege of a director from the board. External deontics includes the initial formation of the corporation which establishes a small framework of rights and duties in the eyes of the relevant federal and state governments, the right to open a bank account in the firm's name, etc. But it also includes things like a partnership agreement with a distribution partner and the obligation to share market demand numbers with a competitor, based on a history of such exchanges.

To advance the view that deontics make the firm what it is, that the specific rights and duties actually comprise all formal and informal agreements, is to claim that the essential structure of the firm itself is captured uniquely by the unique structure of the rights and duties that the firm instantiates. If a firm is to succeed, management has to create (intentionally or otherwise) the appropriate of rights and duties for the appropriate individuals within its team and the appropriate external deontics to facilitate the goals of the organization (e.g., giving technology decisions to the marketing person doesn't help, nor does giving the accountant the duty to solder circuit-boards).

If a firm is essentially a detailed, idiosyncratic deontic structure then differently structured firms are different insofar as their deontic structures are different. The different governance structures and different informal obligations and rights and different agreements and patterns of engagement with the external social world are all a distinct arrangements of deontics. If correct, this forces a reinterpretation of the classic question, "What is division of labor?", the more modern variant of which looks more generally at the firm-level version of this question: "What is the source of firm heterogeneity?" The answer in short, is, "whatever brought about that particular collection of deontics." And this often entails entrepreneurs copying off-the-shelf organization structures that seem relevant to their business model in addition to the construction of novel, idiosyncratic deontics tuned to the organization's goals.

V   Deontic architecture as a framework for a unified theory of the firm

Our basic contention is that the deontic architecture framework that we introduced in section IV can provide a theoretical unification for a number of ostensibly different organizational level phenomena, including the microfoundations of organizational capabilities, role hierarchies, the nexus of contracts view of the firm, and dynamic capabilities. What is common, we claim, in each of these areas is that agents choose how to act (in both strategic and entrepreneurial action) in part, on the basis of the set of deontics that constitute the socially constructed role that the agent enacts when and while acting in an organizational capacity. In each case, the granular substantive content of the deontics that constitute the agent's organizationally-defined role play a central role in shaping and channeling the agent's actions by serving as something like a 'key premise' in the decision-processes that the agent employs as they seek to answer Weick's central organizational questions of 'What now?' and 'What's next?' (Weick, Sutcliffe, & Obstfeld, 2005).

It is this channeling and shaping of individual-level decision making via organizationally constructed deontics that makes the agent's actions constitutive of organizational-level action and not simply individual-level action in an organizational context (King, Felin, & Whetten, 2010). And it is the overall network or interrelated specific, particular, and granular deontics – what we term the deontic architecture – that shapes decision-making of the individuals participating in any concrete instance of organizing. This provides the structuring sinews which comprise and constitute the organization as an accomplishment (Tsoukas & Chia, 2002).

The vast diversity of human life is made more complex and diverse because of social institutions like firms. The social life of ants, wolves, whales, and non-human primates, for example, may be complex, but they are nothing in comparison to vast complexity of human social reality. Animals are driven mostly by basic needs. Humans have another layer of behavioral motivation – the enormous socially constructed deontological conduits that encourage and chaperone us into all sort of behaviors that simply do not exist in the more basic social worlds inhabited by the other social species of our planet. Social institutions exist precisely to motivate an enormous collection of behaviors that otherwise make no sense to the individual. You *can* get someone to sit in an office cubicle all day because doing so *represents* things in their social structure. It *means* that the person is fulfilling his *duties* as part of a position in a social structure, which *means* that he will receive compensation, adoration, rewards, or avoidance of castigation. Social reality is the vast invisible network of deontology that shapes human behavior by providing reasons for action that exceed the relatively localized force of the animal drives (cf. Searle's "desire-independent reasons for action", 1995, 2010).

Deontic-mediated imaginative decision-making processes

How should one understand the role of deontics in decision-making? We have suggested that they play a role in choices that is somewhat analogous to the role of a 'key premise', but this needs some elaboration.

March (1994) argues, as described earlier, that there are two modes of decision-making. The first he terms the 'logic of consequences'. In this model, decisions are understood as choices made on the basis of the anticipated outcomes of alternative lines of possible action, where the choice between the alternatives is made by examining how the anticipated outcomes affect the agent's preferences or desires. As Nanay (2016) notes, this model is definitive of rational decision-making in the belief-desire psychology paradigm.

The second mode of decision-making in March's (1994) framework is what he terms 'the logic of appropriateness'. In this mode, agents are understood to make choices not on the basis of anticipated outcomes of future lines of actions, but rather, on the basis of how any particular line of action fits with the agent's identity; in other words, on the 'correctness' of the action under consideration for the agent's role.

Deontics shape an agent's choices and actions in organizational contexts by outlining for the agent how their socially instantiated role is to be enacted in terms of specific sets of rights, permissions, duties, and obligations. It is in this sense that we talk about deontics as premises within decision-making processes. The deontics lay out for the agent a very specific set of obligations to perform certain kinds of actions in certain contexts and they provide for the agent a set of resources (in terms of rights, permissions, etc.) that the agent can avail themselves to as they seek to accomplish the objectives of the deontically determined lines of action that define their organizational role.

In the model we put forward here, deontic-based decision processes are not determinative in the same way as the kind of production systems (Lewis, 1999; Simon, 1999a) that underlie March and Simon's (1993) model of organizational capabilities are postulated to operate. The core theoretical mechanism underlying the capabilities model is instead closely related to the traditional stimulus-response arc of behaviorist psychology (Simon, 1999a). The S-R process, even when understood to reflect the probability of a response (rather than the necessity of a response) given an input, is essentially a deterministic system. The decision-process model we adopt here, on the other hand, is based on a framework of imaginative decision making (Craik, 1943; Nanay, 2016).

In the imaginative model of decision-making, the agent is understood to simulate future alternative lines of actions and results that arise under the various envisioned scenarios and use those results to choose between the alternatives. As Nanay says, "when we decide between two possible actions, we imagine ourselves in the situation that we imagine to be the outcome of these two actions and then compare these two imaginings" (2016, p. 134). These simulations don't compel action in anything like the way that an S-R type production system is postulated to determinatively evokes action sequences in response to input conditions. They don't really compel the agent to behave in any way at all, really.

Our agents are rational and evaluative – in a boundedly rational sense – but free in the sense of having the ability to decide for themselves whether or not to engage in action on the basis of their strategic priorities (Swidler, 1986). This is so even when their action is bound, shaped, and channeled by deontics that are imposed or voluntary (McBride, 2015).

Deontics matter in agent decision-making because they provide the agent a set of guides for what is expected of them and a set of tools for helping them think through how to accomplish their directives in a given contexts. This is what we mean when we suggest that deontics both shape and channel an agent's action. Deontics, in the form of duties (responsibilities, prohibitions, and obligations) and rights (the usable resources, authorizations, and permissions) avail themselves to the agent as critical 'guardrails' that determine available courses of action.

Deontics have granularity and specificity. Even individuals working in similar positions (defined by a functional role) can be subject to quite different specific deontic packages, differentiating the work they do from other agents within the organization. The specific 'articulation' of content matters.

The way that deontics impact decision-making, then, is by providing constraints, resources, and evaluative ideals that the agent can flexibly deploy in their goal-oriented reasoning. In this way, our model of the role of deontics parallels the role played by cultural elements, more generally, in Swidler's (1986) model of strategic action. "Culture is not a unified system that pushes action in consistent direction" Swidler argues, but "rather, it is more like a 'tool kit' or repertoire . . . from which actors select differing pieces for constructing lines of action (1986, p. 277).

Deontics, then, play the role akin to premises in decision-making because they delineate how an action should be performed or what outcomes the agent should be targeting (March & Simon, 1993) while simultaneously articulating the means and resources that the agent can use as they go about their work. And they do all this by shaping and constraining the imaginative simulations that the agent uses to decide how to act in both proximate and longer-term contexts of action – in the ways outlined by Craik (1943) and Nanay (2016).

One final note, here, is that deontics shape reasoning in ways congruent with both modes of decision-making highlighted by March (1994). Deontics, in other words, define appropriate action for an agent occupying a specific role by articulating how an 'ideal' agent should behave and what outcomes the agent should strive to produce. At the same time, deontics can be understood within a logics of consequences as articulating the evaluative rubrics that the agent uses when deciding what line of action to pursue. That is, they sketch out for the agent an idealized template of the consequences of action that the organization seeks from the agent qua holder of a specific role within the overall economy of the organizations means-ends directed strivings.

How novel deontic architectures are created

It is not enough to be able to provide an account explaining how an existing deontic framework shapes and channels the strategic action of agents acting in organizational contexts. Organizations operate in a constant state of flux and transformation (Nelson & Winter, 1982; Weick & Quinn, 1999; Tsoukas & Chia, 2002) and new organizations are created in the pursuit of entrepreneurial opportunities (Foss & Klein, 2012). We must also be able to explain how new deontic architectures are created and how existing deontic architectures are transformed.

At the core of our approach is the idea that deontics are fundamentally cognitive and that they are created – and in some sense constituted – discursively. The discursive foundation of deontics has two aspects. First, agents understand what they are supposed to do and how they are supposed to act in any given organizational context in light of the set of responsibilities, obligations, rights, permissions, etc. that define the specific role(s) that they are to enact. These deontic 'rule sets' are not constituted by stimulus-response (S-R) type production systems of the kind suggested by Simon (1999a; see also Lewis, 1999). Rather, they are best understood as something that is formulated and transmitted primarily through language, conversation, narrative, and other symbolic or semiotic modes (Searle, 1969, 2010; see too Ford & Ford, 1995; Ford, 1999; Phillips, Lawrence, & Hardy, 2004; Weick et al., 2005; Lawrence & Suddaby, 2006).

Second, arising in conversations, deontics emerge as the settled formulation of what the agent needs to get done and what social resources the agent can avail themselves of as they go about their coordinated organizational work. As such, they are better understood as vague, flexible, and fluid, constantly adapting to the changing contexts of the work and the needs of the actors to get work done and figure out what needs to get done (Weick et al., 2005; Felin & Foss, 2009; Salvato, 2009). But even more importantly, they should be understood as literally talked into being by the agents themselves as they go about their work in organizational contexts.

Deontic architectures – and the roles and rules that constitute them – are not in any simple or direct sense, then, to be understood as determinate action grammars (Pentland & Rueter, 1994), production system-style programs (March & Simon, 1993), procedural memories (Cohen & Bacdayan, 1994), or action generators (Starbuck, 1983). They are, instead, best thought of as something like a web of stories – told and retold, woven and rewoven over time by the agents themselves – about how to act in the context of their organizationally defined pursuits. Stories that are told as ways of shaping the actions of the agents as the agents autonomously and strategically decide on what needs to be done and how they will attempt to go about accomplishing what they are pursuing (once they have, indeed, chosen to pursue a collective goal (Barnard, 1938; Nelson & Winter, 1982).

Unifying theoretical accounts of the firm

The deontic architecture framework introduced in this paper provides a unified account of the firm. In this section, we show how the framework can provide an account of the core features of: a) organizational capabilities; b) roles and role hierarchies; c) nexus of contracts approaches; and d) dynamic capabilities. We also show how the deontic architecture framework can provide insight into those aspects of these four areas that have not been well accounted for in existing theoretical treatments. And we emphasize throughout this section, in particular, how the deontic architecture framework provides a more natural account of dynamism, transformation, and origin – aspects that have sometimes been less well theorized in existing treatments of these fundamental organizational phenomena.

A   The programmatic view of organizational capabilities

Deontics shape and channel the behavior of an individual by providing them with a set of resources that they can use to reason through situations. They form, as Swidler (1986) suggested, something of a flexible toolkit the agent can draw upon when faced with the problem of determining what exactly is going on at any point of time and deciding upon what line of strategic action they need pursue if they are to simultaneously meet their socially determined obligations and achieve their collectively determined and mandated goals. The deontic bundle specific to an agent, in this sense then, articulates the key premises for a role-defined logic of appropriate action. At the same time, by specifying specific, particular, and concrete (granular) role-specific outcome desiderata, this same deontic bundle supplies the delineation of goal-states that the agents strive for as they engage in their organizationally defined roles. The deontic bundle shapes the agent's logic of consequences, channeling action towards organizationally defined outcomes. The deontic bundle, in this way, motivates and directs the behavior in both modes of decision making – the logic of appropriateness and the logic of consequences. And it does so at simultaneously.

As noted, one of the weakness of the capabilities approach, as developed by March and Simon (1993) and Nelson and Winter (1982) has been finding an account of both routinized and improvisational modes of action in organizational contexts. In March and Simon's account, for instance, routine organizational action is ultimately cashed out in terms of performance programs built on something like a S-R production system architecture while improvisational and innovative action is explained by recourse to the processes of action search within an economy of exogenous consequences that guide learning at the level of the individual and the group. Not only are these two modes of action predicated on what amounts to two quite different kinds of cognitive processes, but the account suggests that improvisation and innovation are essentially random. While acknowledging that organizational action can sometimes be myopic, it is important to remember that it is often purposeful too (Wiltbank, Dew, Read, & Sarasvathy, 2006).

The deontic architecture framework provides a simple account for both modes of action. In both contexts, an agent's actions are guided by the specific content of their deontic bundle – by the specific articulations of just what exactly the agent's obligations are in particular contexts and what exactly are their responsibilities. While often vague and sometimes even ambiguous to varying degrees, these outcome desiderata and processual norms help the individual decide how exactly they should and could act as they pursue their role-specific objectives (cf., Ouchi, 1979; Simons, 1994). These deontic bundles anchor the agent's reasoning, suggesting strongly that certain ways of acting or certain outcomes are valued and/or even mandated by the organization in particular contexts. In this way, the deontic bundle actively shapes the agent's understandings and expectations about just what it is that is required of them if they are to be successful in an the role that they are living (cf. King et al., 2010). And it is these understandings and expectations – as articulated in the agent's deontic bundle and unpacked by the agent in the social contexts of ongoing organizational action – that we argue guides the agent's actual choices and actions in both more routinized and more improvisational and innovative contexts.

B   Roles and role hierarchies

In the deontic architecture framework, a role is understood as essentially a bundle of deontics that attach to an individual agent in an organizational context. This means that roles are created when a collection of specific, particular, and granular deontics are assembled as a collective bundle that is assignable to an individual. In principle, this means that roles exist independently of the individual agents that inhabit them. A role can exist even if it is never filled. Likewise, a role is not necessarily somehow diminished, altered, or transformed just because an agent fails to uphold any specific deontic element or acts in contradiction to a specific deontic. A deontic role, in other words, exists independently of any individual agent who might hold that role or the agent's success or failure in that role.

Deontics define roles by defining an interlocking set of rights, responsibilities, obligations, permissions, etc. that the role occupier is expected and intended to further in the context of the ongoing activities of the organization. As the specific content of the deontics change, the role itself changes. The actual change can vary from incremental, or adaptive, that may not even be recognized, to fairly radical and transformational changes to the basic charter, causing significant rewrites of the deontic roles of related agents as a result.

The deontic architecture framework suggests that role hierarchy creation can be best understood as the chartering of an interrelated collection of roles, each of which is created via the discursive articulation of specific deontic bundles. This chartering is sometimes primarily a top-down affair, where the senior leadership delineates deontic bundles in response to the need for a division of labor and a network of authority relations within the organization. But deontics are often established from the 'bottom-up' and from the 'outside-in' as an agent goes about establishing how they will go about their organizationally relevant pursuits in coordination and interdependence with other agents in the organization. Nelson and Winter (1982) described this feature of role articulation as a 'truce' while Barnard (1938) spoke of 'zones of indifference'.

By cashing out roles and role hierarchies into bundles of deontics assignable to agents, the deontic architecture framework suggests that 'organizational becoming' (Tsoukas & Chia, 2002) and sensemaking (Weick, 1995b; Weick et al., 2005) are both reflections of the same underlying exercise to some extent. In each case, the goal is to articulate a set of guides for action that the agent can use when determining their strategies. By framing this process as a discursive articulation of a bundle of specific, particular, granular, and role-specific deontics, the deontic architecture framework begins to cash out what it means to create a new role or role hierarchy or to transform existing roles and role hierarchies in a concrete and actionable manner.

Adam Smith opens The Wealth of Nations (1776) applauding the radical improvement in productivity that role specialization provides: "The greatest improvement in the productive powers of labour . . . seem to have been the effects of the division of labour." We now have the ability to say what exactly division of labor is. A role is a specific collection of rights and duties. A division of labor is a division of roles. Productivity occurs when a diversity of rights and duties that might otherwise occur in the same person are divided into multiple roles across different individuals enabling gains from the learning attendant to specialization. The productivity of each role is enhanced by specialization and when such roles are combined under a single firm to an appropriate aggregate the result is radically enhanced productivity. A role just is a specific collection of rights and duties and a role specialization is, then, the unique assignment of rights and duties to determine unique roles.

C Nexus of contracts

The nexus of contracts theory suggests that a firm differs little from the markets in which it is embedded in that both are essentially collections of contracts and both are analyzable through microeconomics. The arrival of the theory had important implications for law, economics, management, and strategy (Bratton, 1989a).

The nexus of contracts view is not without its criticisms, of course. A number of problems, for example, arise from that fact that contracts can be both imperfectly executed – one party may "shirk" its responsibilities (Alchian & Demsetz, 1972) – and the fact that one can never cover every eventuality in a contract which results in ambiguous areas in the contract and also "residual rights" that remain outside of the purview of that (or possibly any) firm contract. Every contract is incomplete with regard to some concern.

Deontics are, as suggested, the very "atoms" of any contract. Rights, responsibilities, obligations, and permissions are exactly what are made explicit in a formal contract in order to coordinate both parties' behavior and expectations. And they are exactly what remains implicit in an implicit contract. Deontic architecture, then, is not so much an alternative as it is means of providing greater granularity and traction for the nexus of contracts view.

This more fine-grained granularity means that some long-standing problems in the nexus of contracts view can be addressed by deontic architecture. One problem is the inability of the nexus of contracts view to denote many of the agent-guiding structures that exist outside of a contract between two parties. There is a vast panoply of expectations – implicit obligations, promises, duties, or expectations of past behavior – that fall outside of the realm of contracts proper, even informal contracts. Insofar as deontics exist at the root of such structures, they can be individuated, described, and made tractable.

The second problem is the tension between the nexus view and the classic theory of management structured around authority and control hierarchies. A full discussion of power and control hierarchies from a deontic perspective is beyond the scope here[5] but the relevant implications flow quickly from one basic fact about deontics: one person's right is another person's duty. The CEO has the *right* to restructure the R&D division which means that the employees of the R&D division are under *obligation* to move their equipment, cancel research projects, eliminate costs, or hire hundreds of more employees to redouble efforts on a project, at the discretion of the CEO. In general, as one moves up the hierarchy the employees have more rights and as you move down the employees have fewer rights. And in general (in a hierarchical organization), obligations aim upwards to top-level management and the board of directors, and rights aim downwards. It is easy to run through exercises analyzing the rights and duties of any given role in an organization. Hierarchies are essentially composed of rights and duties that shape the structure of the hierarchy, even if the formal contracts between employees and the firm specifies no hierarchy. Deontics allows you to specify the managerial authority hierarchy in a way that neither nexus of contracts nor classical economics does.

The third problem is the inability of the nexus view to explain the transition from an entrepreneurial venture to a firm. The interesting thing about this transition is that the structure of the deontics moves from one where there are agreements interconnected and distributed among the founders to one where all the internal agreements instead now point *from* the individual agents *to* the firm (McBride & Westgren, 2018). There are at least three reasons why this phenomenon is difficult to approach from a nexus of contracts view. (a) The deontics – the obligations, duties, rights, etc. – that structure the relations between founders are often not contractualized. (b) Many of the deontics (and in ventures with one founder, *all of the deontics*) are *self-imposed*. Unless the nexus view is willing to entertain the possibility of contracting with oneself it cannot explain the self-imposed duties that characterize motivated founders and the overwhelming bulk of their behavior. What's a self-imposed duty? Steve Jobs *committing himself* to building the first consumer personal computer (and then enrolling others into that vision), or Elon Musk *committing himself* to building an electric car company. To commit oneself is, of course, to impose a duty upon oneself.

Fourth, there is a gap in the discussions of the nexus view and residual control rights. Returns that are not contractually pre-determined and fall outside of established contracts (with, e.g., debt holders) fall to the owners of the firm (Stout, 2012). But the owners also get discretionary control over the deployment of the firm's assets and human capital (Foss & Klein, 2012). These two aspects of ownership do not, however, exhaust the rights that accrue to the owners of the firm and management teams to which they delegate day-to-day control. Ownership also entails the ability to determine *deontics*. Insofar as deontics are the most important means of structuring the interconnected flow and shaping human behavior, control rights over the firm's deontics is arguably one of, if not the most, important components of the firm's modes of behavioral control.

One overall advantage of this deontic architecture approach is that it provides a theory with all the advantages of the nexus of contracts, but with a more fine-grained set of explanatory elements and so is essentially an explanatory "super-set" relative to the nexus view. The rights are the "atoms" for the molecules-as-contracts.

D   Dynamic capabilities of the firm and organizational transformation

Dynamic capabilities can be understood as the mechanisms by which the organization deliberately and purposefully transforms its underlying functional architecture – understood in terms of capabilities, roles, and role hierarchies. What distinguishes the kinds of transformation that are commonly understood as the result of dynamic capabilities versus those more incremental and local transformations that are characteristic of adaptation and change (cf. Felin & Foss, 2009; Salvato, 2009) is arguably the scale, coherence, and simultaneity of the changes. Local, adaptive, and evolutionary change can arise from problem-solving by individual agents in non-central leadership roles in response to exogenous circumstances or purposive attempts to 'do better' or 'do differently' – but these rarely cascade far enough across the organization to constitute a global reconfiguration of activities or purpose. What distinguishes a dynamic capability from these more local and adaptive forms of change is that the former are wrought by the organization's senior leadership in a deliberate attempt to make just these kinds of ramifying structural reconfigurations of activity and purpose.

The deontic architecture framework suggests that these kinds of broad-based structural changes can be made, effectively rewriting some aspects of the deontics common to large collections of roles within an organization en masse via the discursive efforts of the organization's senior leadership (cf. Ford & Ford, 1995; Ford, 1999; Lawrence & Suddaby, 2006). The capabilities of the organization at any point in time – its 'zero order' capabilities (Winter, 2003) – constitute an organization's production set (Nelson & Winter, 1982). Rewriting key elements of the deontic bundles held in common by organization as a whole (or significant subsets of the organization) provides senior leadership a tool for 'deforming' the production set in its entirety. Different 'rule sets', which is to say different deontics, entail different capabilities. Deliberate efforts to change components or elements of the overarching, general obligations, responsibilities, duties, and rights, etc. held in common across the organization or important subsets of the organization, then, is a means for enacting the kinds of transformational changes that are definitive of dynamic capabilities.

VI   Conclusion

A necessary component of any entrepreneurial venture is the dynamic, ongoing effort to design and build a vehicle that creates and captures economic value – the firm. We reconceptualize what that vehicle is. Deontics constitute all social entities and so constitute the firm as well. A deontic architecture view should, then, be able to explain, expand, and patch holes in existing theories of the firm. As a proof of concept to that effect we looked at four of the most prominent approaches to the firm and how a deontic architecture approach analytically reconstructs and amends them.

A firm consists of internal and external deontics. Internal deontics include roles which are themselves bundles of deontics. External roles include, primarily, agreements with external agents and organizations. The internal and external deontics together form the deontic architecture of the firm. A key entrepreneurial task facing any firm is the building of the deontic architecture in such a way that, with the right resources, the agents are able to achieve the firm's goals. Once established, the deontics serve as the central levers of control for directing the behavior and decision-making activity of agents both internal and external to the firm. Directing the structure of human activity is the central task of every firm and building out a comprehensive architecture of ongoing human activities that is coordinated in such a way so as to create or capture economic value is the overarching goal. To build a comprehensive architecture of human activities in a firm is to build a deontic architecture.

Notes

1   Like all scientific discoveries, the details are much messier than the tidy story that outlives them. Proving that an inverse square law would lead to elliptical orbits of the planets started as a cafe challenge from Christopher Wren to Halley and Hooke, after all of them had a few too many cups of coffee, we can imagine. Halley failed but told Newton of the challenge. Both Newton and Hooke claimed that they had already done the calculations but conveniently neither could find their respective notes anywhere. The end result of Newton 'recreating' his calculations is the famous *Principia*. Hooke and Newton fought

over who made the actual discovery until their dying days. Oddly, neither Newton, nor Kepler, nor Boulliau initially believed the inverse square law for objects, though all of them entertained parts of it. Kepler advanced the inverse square law in his explanation for how light dissipates, but believed that the planets were kept in motion by strange magnetic emissions from the sun which dissipated in direct inverse of the distance (rather than inverse square). Boulliau countered, for the sake of argument, using Kepler's own reasoning about light (Gleick, 2004).

2   There is also, of course, a sizable literature on the *theory of the firm*, which largely concerns itself with the question of why firms exist at all within a market economy, how the boundaries of firms are set, and how economic activity, within and across firms and markets, is coordinated via different governance mechanisms. Seminal work here includes Coase (1937), Alchian and Demsetz (1972), and Williamson (1985) among many others. Some of this work is addressed in the current endeavor in our discussion of nexus of contracts approach, but, in the main, our concerns are somewhat different.

3   It should be noted that the institutional variant (e.g., Williamson, 1985) of the nexus of contracts view is distinct from the neoclassical version and clashes with management theory less brazenly.

4   Management science, entrepreneurship, strategy, finance, and organizational behavior are, in an important sense, similar to economics or political science in that they are all social sciences rather than natural sciences. The proper domain for the study of social ontology is arguably sociology but for whatever reason sociology has often abstained from work on the foundations of its own discipline. There are various efforts to correct this from within sociology proper, but right now the field with the most momentum behind work on the foundations is social ontology.

5   For an example of one such discussion, see Searle (2010), chapter 7.

Bibliography

Alchian, A., & Demsetz, H. (1972). Production, information costs, and economic organization. *The American Economic Review*, *62*(5), 777–795.

Aldrich, H. E., & Ruef, M. (2006). *Organizations evolving* (2nd ed.). London: Sage.

Alvarez, S. A., & Barney, J. B. (2007). Discovery and creation: Alternative theories of entrepreneurial action. *Strategic Entrepreneurship Journal*, *1*, 11–26.

Augier, M., & Teece, D. J. (2009). Dynamic capabilities and the role of managers in business strategy and economic performance. *Organization Science*, *20*, 410–421.

Barnard, C. I. (1938). *The functions of the executive*. Cambridge, MA: Harvard University Press.

Barney, J., & Felin, T. (2013). What are microfoundations? *Academy of Management Perspectives*, *27*, 138–155.

Berger, P. L., & Luckmann, T. (1966). *The social construction of reality: A treatise in the sociology of knowledge*. Garden City, NY: Anchor.

Bratman, M. (1987). *Intentions, plans, and practical reason*. Cambridge, MA: Harvard University Press.

Bratman, M. (2014). *Shared agency: A planning theory of acting together*. Cambridge, MA: Oxford University Press.

Bratton, W. W. (1989a). The new economic theory of the firm: Critical perspectives from history. *Stanford Law Review*, *41*(6), 1471–1527.

Bratton, W. W. (1989b). The 'nexus of contracts' corporation: A critical appraisal. *Faculty Scholarship*, Paper 839. http://scholarship.law.upenn.edu/faculty_scholarship/839

Bryan, K. A. (2015). *Handout on theories of the firm* [class notes pdf]. http://kevinbryanecon.com/NotesonTheoryoftheFirm.pdf

Buchanan, J. M., & Vanberg, V. J. (1991). The market as a creative process. *Economics and Philosophy, 7*, 167–186.

Chandler, A. D. (1962). *Strategy and structure: Chapters in the history of the industrial enterprise.* Cambridge, MA: The MIT Press.

Chiles, T. H., Bluedorn, A. C., & Gupta, V. K. (2007). Beyond creative destruction and entrepreneurial discovery: A radical Austrian approach to entrepreneurship. *Organization Studies, 28*, 467–493.

Coase, R. H. (1937). The nature of the firm. *Economica, 4*, 386–405.

Cohen, M. D., & Bacdayan, P. (1994). Organizational routines are stored as procedural memory: Evidence from a laboratory study. *Organization Science, 5*, 554–568.

Conner, K. R., & Prahalad, C. K. (1996). A resource-based theory of the firm: Knowledge versus opportunism. *Organization Science, 7*, 477–501.

Craik, K. (1943). *The nature of explanation.* Cambridge, UK: Cambridge University Press.

Demsetz, H. (1988). The theory of the firm revisited. *Journal of Law, Economics, and Organization, 4*, 141–161.

Denrell, J., Fang, C., & Winter, S. G. (2003). The economics of strategic opportunities. *Strategic Management Journal, 24*, 977–990.

Dierickx, I., & Cool, K. (1989). Asset stock accumulation and sustainability of competitive advantage. *Management Science, 35*, 1504–1511.

Einstein, A. (1923). *Fundamental ideas and problems of the theory of relativity.* Nobelprize. org. www.nobelprize.org/nobel_prizes/physics/laureates/1921/einstein-lecture.html

Eisenhardt, K. M., & Martin, J. A. (2000). Dynamic capabilities: What are they? *Strategic Management Journal, 21*, 1105–1121.

Epstein, B. (2015). *The ant trap: Rebuilding the foundations of the social sciences.* Oxford: Oxford University Press.

Felin, T., & Foss, N. J. (2005). Strategic organization: A field in search of micro-foundations. *Strategic Organization, 3*, 441–455.

Felin, T., & Foss, N. J. (2009). Organizational routines and capabilities: Historical drift and course-correction toward microfoundations. *Scandinavian Journal of Management, 25*, 157–167.

Ford, J. D. (1999). Organizational change as shifting conversations. *Journal of Organizational Change Management, 12*, 480–500.

Ford, J. D., & Ford, L. W. (1995). The role of conversations in producing intentional change in organizations. *Academy of Management Review, 20*, 541–570.

Foss, N. J., & Klein, P. G. (2012). *Organizing entrepreneurial judgement: A new approach to the firm.* Cambridge, UK: Cambridge University Press.

Gilbert, M. (1992). *On social facts.* Princeton: Princeton University Press.

Gilbert, M. (2015). Joint commitment: What it is and why it matters. *Phenomenology and Mind, 9*, 18–26.

Gleick, J. (2004). *Isaac Newton.* New York: Vintage Press.

Grossman, S. J., & Hart, O. D. (1986). The costs and benefits of ownership: A theory of vertical and lateral integration. *Journal of Political Economy, 94*, 691–719.

Guala, F. (2007). The philosophy of social science: Metaphysical and empirical. *Philosophy Compass, 2*(6), 954–980.

Hayek, F. A. (1945). The use of knowledge in society. *American Economic Review, 35*, 519–530.

Jensen, M. C., & Meckling, W. H. (1976). Theory of the firm: Managerial behavior, agency costs, and ownership structure. *Journal of Financial Economics, 3*(4), 305–360.

King, B. G., Felin, T., & Whetten, D. A. (2010). Finding the organization in organizational theory: A meta-theory of the organization as a social actor. *Organization Science, 21*, 290–305.

Kirzner, I. M. (1999). Creativity and/or alertness: A reconsideration of the Schumpeterian entrepreneur. *Review of Austrian Economics, 11*, 5–17.

Kitcher, P. (1981). Explanatory unification. *Philosophy of Science, 48*, 507–531.

Knight, F. H. (1921). *Risk, uncertainty and profit*. New York: August M. Kelley.

Kogut, B., & Zander, U. (1992). Knowledge of the firm, combinative capabilities and the replication of technology. *Organization Science, 3*, 383–397.

Kogut, B., & Zander, U. (1996). What do firms do? Coordination, identity and learning. *Organization Science, 7*, 502–518.

Kuhn, T. S. (1996). *The structure of scientific revolutions* (3rd ed.). Chicago: University of Chicago Press.

Lawrence, T. B., & Suddaby, R. (2006). Institutions and institutional work. In S. R. Clegg, C. Hardy, T. B. Lawrence, & W. R. Nord (Eds.), *Handbook of organization studies* (2nd ed., pp. 215–254). London: Sage.

Lewis, R. L. (1999). Symbolic cognitive modeling. In R. A. Wilson & F. C. Keil (Eds.), *The MIT encyclopedia of the cognitive sciences* (pp. 141–142). Cambridge, MA: The MIT Press.

March, J. G. (1991). Exploration and exploitation in organizational learning. *Organization Science, 2*, 71–87.

March, J. G. (1994). *A primer on decision making: How decisions happen*. New York: Free Press.

March, J. G., & Simon, H. A. (1993). *Organizations* (2nd ed.). Oxford, UK: Wiley.

McBride, R. (2015). *Deontic binding*. Working paper.

McBride, R., & Westgren, R. (2018). *The critical move in deontic structure: Entrepreneurship architecture to firm architecture*. Working paper.

McCarthy, I. P., Lawrence, T. B., Wixted, B., & Gordon, B. R. (2010). A multi-dimensional conceptualization of environmental velocity. *Academy of Management Review, 35*, 604–626.

Morgan, G. (2006). *Images of organizations*. Thousand Oaks, CA: Sage Publications Inc.

Nahapiet, J., & Ghoshal, S. (1998). Social capital, intellectual capital, and the organizational advantage. *Academy of Management Review, 23*, 242–266.

Nanay, B. (2016). The role of imagination in decision-making. *Mind & Language, 31*, 127–143.

Nelson, R. R., & Winter, S. G. (1982). *An evolutionary theory of economic change*. Cambridge, MA: The Belknap Press.

Nonaka, I. (1994). A dynamic theory of organizational knowledge creation. *Organization Science, 5*, 14–37.

Ouchi, W. G. (1979). A conceptual framework for the design of organizational control mechanisms. *Management Science, 25*, 833–848.

Penrose, E. T. (1959). *The theory of the growth of the firm*. Oxford, UK: Blackwell.

Pentland, B. T., & Rueter, H. H. (1994). Organizational routines as grammars of action. *Administrative Science Quarterly, 39*, 484–510.

Phillips, N., Lawrence, T. B., & Hardy, C. (2004). Discourse and institutions. *Academy of Management Review, 29*, 635–652.

Polanyi, M. (1958). *Personal knowledge: Towards a post-critical philosophy*. Chicago: University of Chicago Press.

Prahalad, C. K., & Hamel, G. (1990, May–June). The core competence of the corporation. *Harvard Business Review*, 2–14.

Salvato, C. (2009). Capabilities unveiled: The role of ordinary activities in the evolution of product development processes. *Organization Science, 20*, 384–409.

Sarasvathy, S. (2001). Causation and effectuation: Toward a theoretical shift from economic inevitability to entrepreneurial contingency. *Academy of Management Review, 26*, 243–263.

Scott, W. R., & Davis, G. F. (2007). *Organizations and organizing: Rational, natural and open system perspectives.* London and New York: Routledge.

Searle, J. R. (1969). *Speech acts: An essay in the philosophy of language.* Cambridge: Cambridge University Press.

Searle, J. R. (1995). *The construction of social reality.* New York: The Free Press.

Searle, J. R. (1998). *Mind, language and society: Philosophy in the real world.* New York: Basic Books.

Searle, J. R. (2010). *Making the social world: The structure of human civilization.* Oxford, UK: Oxford University Press.

Simon, H. A. (1999a). Production systems. In R. A. Wilson & F. C. Keil (Eds.), *The MIT encyclopedia of the cognitive sciences* (pp. 676–677). Cambridge, MA: The MIT Press.

Simon, H. A. (1999b). *The sciences of the artificial* (3rd ed.). Cambridge, MA: The MIT Press.

Simons, R. (1994). *Levers of control.* Boston: Harvard Business Review Press.

Smith, A. (1776). *An inquiry into the nature and causes of the wealth of nations.* London: W. Strahan and T. Cadell.

Starbuck, W. H. (1983). Organizations as action generators. *American Sociological Review, 48,* 91–102.

Stout, L. (2012). *The shareholder value myth.* San Francisco: Berret-Koehler Publishers.

Swidler, A. (1986). Culture in action: Symbols and strategies. *American Sociological Review, 51,* 273–286.

Teece, D. J. (2012). Dynamic capabilities: Routines versus entrepreneurial action. *Journal of Management Studies, 49,* 1395–1401.

Teece, D. J., Pisano, G., & Shuen, A. (1997). Dynamic capabilities and strategic management. *Strategic Management Journal, 18,* 509–533.

Tsoukas, H., & Chia, R. (2002). On organizational becoming: Rethinking organizational change. *Organization Science, 13,* 567–582.

Tuomela, R. (2002). *The philosophy of social practices: A collective acceptance view.* Cambridge: Cambridge University Press.

Tuomela, R. (2007). *The philosophy of sociality.* Oxford: Oxford University Press.

Tuomela, R. (2013). *Social ontology: Collective intentionality and group agents.* New York: Oxford University Press.

Weick, K. E. (1995a). What theory is not, theorizing is. *Administrative Science Quarterly, 40,* 385–390.

Weick, K. E. (1995b). *Sensemaking in organizations.* Thousand Oaks, CA: Sage Publications Inc.

Weick, K. E., & Quinn, R. E. (1999). Organizational change and development. *Annual Review of Psychology, 50,* 361–386.

Weick, K. E., Sutcliffe, K. M., & Obstfeld, D. (2005). Organizing and the process of sensemaking. *Organization Science, 16,* 409–421.

Wernerfelt, B. (1984). A resource-based view of the firm. *Strategic Management Journal, 5,* 171–180.

Williamson, O. E. (1975). *Markets and hierarchies: Analysis and antitrust implications.* New York: Free Press.

Williamson, O. E. (1979). Transaction cost economics: The governance of contractual relations. *Journal of Law and Economics, 22,* 233–261.

Williamson, O. E. (1981). The economics of organization: The transaction cost approach. *American Journal of Sociology, 87,* 548–577.

Williamson, O. E. (1985). *The economic institutions of capitalism.* New York: Free Press.

Wiltbank, R., Dew, N., Read, S., & Sarasvathy, S. D. (2006). What to do next? The case for non-predictive strategy. *Strategic Management Journal, 27*, 981–998.

Winter, S. G. (2003). Understanding dynamic capabilities. *Strategic Management Journal, 24*, 991–995.

Winter, S. G. (2012). Capabilities: Their origins and ancestry. *Journal of Management Studies, 49*, 1402–1406.

Winter, S. G. (2013). Habit, deliberation, and action: Strengthening the microfoundations of routines and capabilities. *Academy of Management Perspectives, 27*, 120–137.

Zenger, T. (2016). *Beyond competitive advantage: How to solve the puzzle of sustaining growth while creating value.* Boston: Harvard Business Review Press.

12 Uncertainty under entrepreneurship

Dimo Dimov

Entrepreneurship represents a diverse set of economic activities. In our quest for a theory of entrepreneurship, we strive to identify a common denominator to these activities. There is consensus that this denominator is the bearing of uncertainty (Venkataraman, 1997), as originally discussed by Frank Knight (1921). Indeed, Knightian uncertainty is considered a defining feature of the context of entrepreneurial action (Sarasvathy, 2001).

But what does bearing uncertainty mean? The dictionary definition of 'bear' is to endure; endurance pertains to a situation or experience and it refers to how a person relates to it. It is therefore a subjective experience. In order to get a closer sense of endurance, let's consider the following hypothetical situation. We have an uncertain payoff and anyone willing to receive it should make an upfront sacrifice, at the very least in the form of an effort to attain the payoff. The laws that determine whether and how much payoff is received are not known to anyone, even to me as the author of this hypothetical scenario. Nevertheless, people can make their own inferences on the basis of their observation and interpretation of what is going on in deciding whether to give the challenge a try.

Clearly, we have a situation of fundamental or Knightian uncertainty. Therefore, anyone who takes the challenge and makes the sacrifice in anticipation of the payoff would, in essence, be acting entrepreneurially. But upon closer look, we can distinguish three types of people among this group of challenge-takers in respect to how they perceive the situation. First, there are those who study the payoff in great depth and conclude that it is indeed subject to fundamental uncertainty; i.e. they will never have the necessary knowledge. Second, there are those who see patterns and control levers in the payoff and thus act in full confidence (or elevated hope) that they can attain the payoff if they put sufficient effort. In reality, unbeknownst to them, they are operating under a false framework. Third, there are those who are completely ignorant of the laws behind the payoffs and simply go for the challenge. This can be action on impulse (e.g. Wiklund, Patzelt, & Dimov, 2016) or perhaps wilful or non-wilful ignorance, lack of curiosity.

It is interesting to consider that, while all three types appear to act entrepreneurially, given an external, objective assessment of the situation in which they have been placed, not all of them actually *bear* uncertainty. Indeed, only the first type can be deemed to be doing so as they have full appreciation of that uncertainty. In the other two types, there is no subjective experience of the uncertainty, either because it is not considered at all or because it has been replaced by a false sense of certainty.

The three types of action represent two extremes of a continuum and an intermediary position. At one end of the continuum is complete ignorance of the effort-outcome relationship; all that matters is that the potential payoff is valuable. At the other end of the continuum is the full consideration of the effort-outcome relationship, which rightly concludes that it is fundamentally uncertain. In between lies a consideration of the effort-outcome relationship that balances the frivolity of ignorance and the dejection of rationality. Curiously, there is another intermediary position, namely of a certain situation which one perceived wrongly to be uncertain. In that case, one would in fact be bearing uncertainty, even if that uncertainty is not really there.

The question then arises about the interplay between the objective and subjective assessment of a situation. On what basis can we conclude that a situation is indeed one of fundamental uncertainty? For the ease of the example above, this was considered a given, based on the simplistic way of defining it, but in reality such exogenous definition is not available to an actor. We have to reach this conclusion ourselves. But how do we actually do that?

Objective assessment calls for rigour and evidence. In the logic of scientific inquiry, in the search for patterns, there is a null hypothesis that presumes lack of any patterns or relationships. This hypothesis then needs to be rejected on the basis of evidence. It represents the default position of the scientist, scepticism. This evidence is always tentative, subject to norms of statistical inference and aggregation across studies. It is notable, however, that lack of evidence for a relationship does not mean evidence for a lack of relationship. In this sense, the null hypothesis can never be proven (e.g. Cook & Campbell, 1979); it is an assumption by default that serves a logical purpose, just like the method of assuming the opposite of what has to be proven. It is a residual category, after all attempts to find a relationship have been exhausted. There is no theoretical end to how much this is tried, but in practice it ends when scientists stop trying.

In regard to subjective assessment, entrepreneurs do not operate in the realm of scientific inquiry. There is no reason that they would adopt a sceptical position by default, as their interest lies in finding practical value rather than some absolute understanding for its own sake. Such pragmatic inquiry looks to transform an indeterminate situation into a determinate one (Dewey, 1938/1991). Therefore, they also operate with working hypotheses but these are assessed by whether they work, i.e. bring something beneficial rather than by whether they constitute a true representation of the situation (Romme, 2003). In this sense, to accept the situation as fundamentally uncertain is tantamount to having given up, because every try brings with it a working hypothesis, of making the situation determinate.

This line of thought leads to two conclusions. First, objective assessment of a situation as fundamentally uncertain is a matter of scientific interest. Thus, only a scientist would be interested in using and applying this label, based on his or her position as a detached external observer. Second, in terms of subjective assessment, fundamental uncertainty does not really exist since in any action it is supplanted by the working hypothesis that is being tried out.

These conclusions suggest, further, that the first type of people, i.e. those who truly bear the uncertainty, do not really exist. This is because, to retain their perception of fundamental uncertainty, they would not be acting at all; they remain detached observers. Every action either brings with itself a working hypothesis that provides a shrine of certainty while the action lasts, or is undertaken, under complete ignorance, for the sake of finding out what happens, in which case uncertainty is irrelevant.

It would seem, therefore, that our current conception of entrepreneurship as the bearing of uncertainty serves just an academic purpose as a topic for conversations that are detached from the reality of the acting entrepreneur. In other words, it belongs to the Ivory Tower. In the rest of this essay, I explore the implications of a conception of entrepreneurship that leaves the Ivory Tower behind and attempts to step into the ring of action, while also maintaining a certain level of abstraction.

The subjective assessment of a situation

Let's consider for a moment the subjective assessment of a situation from the point of view of the entrepreneur's knowledge of it as well as the potential knowledge he or she could gain from others. This captures both the incomplete and asymmetric nature of knowledge. I use a simplistic, self-explanatory framework, popularised by Donald Rumsfeld in 2002, but with recorded prior use in the engineering industry and related entry in the Oxford English Dictionary (unk-unks). We can divide the knowledge into (1) known knowns, (2) unknown knowns, (3) known unknowns, and (4) unknown unknowns.[1] (1) informs what the entrepreneur does, but the rest are things that he or she has to live with. In this sense, they could contribute to the bearing uncertainty, but do so in different ways.

Unknown knowns (2) are perhaps completely irrelevant from the point of view of the actor. They pertain to the knowledge of others that could be potentially useful to the entrepreneur. But accessing that knowledge depends on the entrepreneur making contact with these people; when this happens the particular knowledge exchanged converts into (1) or (3). Since there are always people who know something relevant, but perhaps whom the entrepreneur would never meet (indeed, they cannot meet everyone), it would be reasonable to assume that we have reached a situation where (2) cannot be reduced any further. In that situation, (2) becomes irrelevant.

Unknown unknowns (4) represents an external category. By definition, they cannot be known by anyone – this is the essence of incomplete knowledge and the basis of fundamental uncertainty. To appreciate these, one has to look at the situation from outside of it, as well as outside of time, in order to note the gaps. To those inside the situation, unknown unknowns are outside its realm. As such, they are irrelevant for entrepreneurial action, because there is nothing that can be done about them; reasoning about them is both arbitrary and speculative.

But to the extent that we know that some hitherto unknown things will happen and that they can affect us, bearing uncertainty in this case is about being at the mercy of time. But is there any activity that is not at the mercy of time? For instance, a marriage is at the mercy of time in the sense that people inevitably change and so does their relationship, sometimes for the better, sometimes for the worse. What matters is the expectation, indeed the reliance, that what we have in the present needs to be retained in the future. There is thus a sense in which the future can take away from what we have. This reflects the second law of thermodynamics, the entropy principle, which states that everything tends towards disorder in the absence of a force that aims to preserve the order. This same principle is reflected in finance in the notions of 'time value of money' and in the pricing of options (longer term makes them more valuable because a wider range of things can happen).

Known unknowns (3) represent perhaps the most interesting category. Similar to (2), some of this category can be converted into known knowns (1) as part of the actions that an entrepreneur undertakes. But there will always be elements of (3) that are not in play, i.e. they are not subject to immediate conversion. These are the ones that the entrepreneur has to live with in the sense that he or she is aware of them as currently indeterminate; they may turn out to hold positive or negative consequences. Here, again, the entrepreneur is at the mercy of time.

In order to distinguish further between (3) and (4), let's consider the following example. We are moving along a path through a forest and reach a steep corner around a big rock. We do not know what lies around the corner. In one scenario, we know that there are tigers in this forest. In this sense, the question arises whether there is a tiger around this particular corner. It becomes a known unknown.

In another scenario, we have no idea (and nor does anyone else) what creatures, if any, there are in the forest. In this sense, the question of what lies around the corner is an unknown unknown. We can of course imagine that there might be a tiger behind the corner. The only difference in the first situation is that our thinking has been channelled towards a tiger on the basis of prior knowledge and the idea of a tiger is less arbitrary or speculative. With an unknown unknown, our thinking about the tiger is of our making; we inflict this upon ourselves. We could easily be thinking about something more pleasant such as a rabbit or a tortoise.

Regardless of what prompts us to think about a possible creature around the corner – whether our prior knowledge or our imagination – the corner matters only in terms of the consequences it can inflict upon us. These can be bad or non-bad (which can comprise both neutral and good). Any hesitation to turn the corner is related to the possibility of bad consequences. If we are assured that nothing bad will happen, we will not be conscious of turning the corner. The notion of bad relates to the possibility of loss as the essence of risk (March & Shapira, 1987).

Viewed from this perspective of approaching the corner, (3) and (4) effectively merge into one single notion of not knowing what is behind the corner. This is a one-time event, to which probabilities do not really apply. This is because they apply to ensembles of events – either turning the corner many times in identical situations or many people turning the identical corners at the same time.

We can therefore reduce the notion of being at the mercy of time to the notion of turning a corner (or opening a door) in the sense that our journey over time can be seen as a series of corners to be turned. We can now zoom onto the subjective experience of turning the corner with the sense that this can be bad or non-bad.

The one-time experience of turning a corner

In the classic Schrodinger's Cat thought experiment – devised to probe the interpretation of the superposition of quantum states – there is a cat in a box with a radioactive material, a Geiger counter on which a hammer is suspended, and a glass container with cyanide positioned under the suspended hammer. It is known that at some point the radioactive material will decay, which will be detected by the Geiger counter, which will lower the hammer, which will break the container and release the cyanide, which will kill the cat. But, without opening the box, we cannot know whether this has happened. Until then, the cat is deemed both alive and dead.

Our turning the corner is tantamount to opening the box. Until we do, both the bad and non-bad scenarios are real and we have to entertain both of them. This is consistent with the notion that there are no future facts, i.e. every proposition about the future has fractional truth about it (Brumbaugh, 1966). Thus both the bad and non-bad scenarios are possibly true. The only way to remove this duality is . . . to turn the corner.

The more we think about what lies around the corner, the more agonizing the experience becomes and the more the uncertainty bears down on us; we have to endure it. But, at the same time, this may slow us down. And as we slow down and approach the corner, our heartbeat speeds up (but perhaps this is just me). And the faster our heart beats, the more we want to think about the corner. Until we are poised at the edge of a precipice. There is nowhere further to go without appearing around the corner and becoming at the mercy of whatever lies there in waiting. The feeling is not dissimilar to standing at the end of a high board, about to jump into a pool of cold water, many meters below. We have to push off, let go . . . and there is no coming back to the moment before. We cross a point of discontinuity.

It appears that the generator of the feeling of uncertainty in crossing this point is our thinking fuelled by emotion, our desire to conjure up the definite image of what is around the corner. Looking at the situation with a cool-headed rationality, we know that we cannot know. But this is overpowered by wanting to know before we can know.

In the next section, I will attempt to get closer to this feeling in order to understand what generates it. Because the point of discontinuity is bridged by time, however brief that moment might be, there is a sense then that it is the passing of time that brings a resolution of the uncertainty. We can therefore consider our being in that time, our endurance of it. To understand endurance, I will use Henry Bergson's masterful examination of time as pure duration in his doctoral thesis, *Time and Free Will: An Essay on the Immediate Data of Consciousness*.

Henry Bergson's *time and free will*

What is time, as defined within our own experience? Henry Bergson's work focuses on immediate experience, of being in the flux of things. We can think of the passing of time – for example, of one minute – as a series of 60 seconds (or even smaller units), and we can relate to each of these seconds our own state of consciousness, i.e. 60 moments. Seen in this way, time is a multiplicity of moments and we understand its duration by counting the moments.

For Bergson, counting entails dividing something into identical parts and then extending these parts in space, whereby we can lay them side by side. The units are considered identical and homogeneous and can thus be represented collectively by their quantity. This is essentially the meaning of 60 seconds, a collection of 60 identical moments, and we can see these extended on a line. In the counting of moments, there is no succession; all the states are held simultaneously and are extended or charted in space in order to differentiate them, and thereby count them. To do this, we effectively stand outside of the experience itself. Bergson calls this 'externality without succession'.

The concept of space is essential for carrying out the extension and counting: "Space is what enables us to distinguish a number of identical and simultaneous sensations from one another; it is thus a principle of differentiation other than that of qualitative differentiation, and consequently it is reality with no quality" (*The Multiplicity of Conscious States. The Idea of Duration*, paragraph 13).

Therefore, when we consider time in terms of counting the multiplicity of moments, there is an implicit conception of time that we apply: "When we speak of time, we generally think of a homogeneous medium in which our conscious states are ranged alongside one another as in space, so as to form a discrete multiplicity" (The *Multiplicity of Conscious States. The Idea of Duration*, paragraph 10). This, in turn, leads to the conclusion that, so conceived time is essentially space: "It is to be presumed that time, understood in the sense of a medium in which we make distinctions and count, is nothing but space" (*The Multiplicity of Conscious States. The Idea of Duration*, paragraph 10). When time is projected into space, duration becomes expressed as extensity. The attempt to measure replaces duration with space.

But, Bergson argues, the moments whose multiplicity constitutes time are immediate conscious experiences of a qualitative nature. These are psychic states whose causes are within us. Pure quality cannot be counted or even compared. At the most, we can talk about the intensity of psychic states – such as the intensity of feeling or of effort – but by admitting some degree of quantification, intensity implicitly presupposes some form of extension in space: "Representative sensation, looked at in itself, is pure quality; but, seen through the medium of extensity, this quality becomes in a certain sense quantity, and is called intensity" (*The Multiplicity of Conscious States. The Idea of Duration*, paragraph 10).

There are thus two kinds of multiplicity: 1) of material objects that can be counted and thus represented by a number; and 2) of states of consciousness, which cannot be counted without symbolical representation that requires the medium of space. These reflect two different kinds of reality: one heterogeneous, of sensible qualities, and the other homogeneous – space. Space enables us to count and abstract.

The immediate experience of time is one that preserves the pure quality of psychic states. Bergson refers to this as "pure duration": "Pure duration is the form which the succession of our conscious states assumes when our ego lets itself live, when it refrains from separating its present state from its former states" (*The Multiplicity of Conscious States. The Idea of Duration*, paragraph 14).

> Pure duration might well be nothing but a succession of qualitative changes, which melt into and permeate one another, without precise outlines, without any tendency to externalize themselves in relation to one another, without any affiliation with number: it would be pure heterogeneity.
>
> (*The Multiplicity of Conscious States. The Idea of Duration*, paragraph 15)

In pure duration, past and present are part of an organic whole, like the notes of a tune. Each represents the whole and cannot be isolated and differentiated from the rest. The multiplicity of states is holistic, the states form a succession, interpenetrating each other, whereby no single state is singled out. Bergson calls this 'succession without externality'. We stay in the moment because to single out and differentiate successive states requires stepping out of it.

To appreciate the difference between 'externality without succession' and 'succession without externality', Bergson offers the example of listening to the chimes of a church bell. In the former, in attempting to count the chimes, we step out of the immediate experience of listening (i.e. externality) and make a mental note, say a dot. But to count the dots, we cannot pile them one on top of the other – we start extending them in space. But in marking a new dot, we also retain all the previous dots because in the end we need to count them all. It is in this sense that there is no succession to the chimes: we retain them all, by means of representing them and extending them into space. In 'succession without externality', we stay within the immediate experience of listening to the chimes. They interpenetrate and succeed one another.

It is thus the position of externality that turns time from pure duration into space, with the associated line as the medium on which to record its extension. Bergson offers another interesting example of a straight line and a material point A on it. The point would see itself changing, but this change would not necessarily be in the form of a line. To see itself moving along the line, the point needs to rise above (outside of) itself and perceive different points on the line, thereby forming the idea of space. In other words, in order to perceive a line as a line, one needs to step outside of it and take account of the void around it.

Crucially, the line symbolises only the time that has passed, not the time which is passing . . . or the time that will pass.

Back to the precipice

Turning back to the example of walking along a path and approaching a turn, it is curious that I have resorted to using space – and the line of a path – to represent our movement. In this sense, we think about the corner and the turn around it as also being in space. But the concept of space is misleading here because it invites the metaphor of being able to peek around the corner, which is what we aim to do in trying to think about what lies there.

It should be emphasised that the corner – and the gulf between us and it – lies not in space but in time. If the journey up to the present moment can be represented by a line, the line cannot be extended until the moment passes. Thus, what lies around the corner will become part of the line once the corner is turned. Until then, what lies behind the corner does not really exist in the present moment; it is merely an extension of our imagination. Therefore, the gulf between us and the corner becomes such only when we seek to extend the line of our time and look to identify the other shore.

Doing this requires that we step out of the immediacy of our experience, that we see our journey stretched out on a timeline and seek to extend the line forward, to form a bridge of sorts that we can then cross. We therefore seek to define our experience before we actually experience it.

In contrast, staying with the immediacy of our experience, there is an interpenetrating multiplicity of present and past moments . . . but no future other than the vision or imagination that represent our purpose, that form a whole with our present and past and that cannot be isolated from them. This is similar to the experience of daydreaming, of present and future being one. Any other future is an abstraction and, as such, it cannot be part of pure duration. Thinking about it shuts down the immediacy of experience and gives the reins to cognition, which – with its focus on abstraction and differentiation – operates in space.

There is no uncertainty in pure duration. It arises only when we start thinking about what lies outside of it. But what prompts such thinking? Why can't we just relax and let our ego live in the present moment, taking the new experiences as part of the holistic succession of time, the ultimate freedom? Where does the worry about what lies around the corner come from? It is related to the possibility of our vision, the immediate effortless extension of the present, being exposed as wrong. It is the need to preserve that vision that creates the craving for certainty that this will be the case. This is a force that aims to work against the inevitable entropy. It becomes the source of uncertainty, and this source is internal.

A plane story in the meantime

As I was thinking about this section, I was flying from Catania, Italy, to London, with a connection in Milan. My connection time was short, 50 minutes, and I had been thinking about it ever since I left London for Catania a couple of days before. I had become fixated on making it; this became of paramount importance to me. I started thinking about it more and more.

As I was about to leave for the airport, it started pouring with rain (this was in Catania, Sicily, where it had been sunny and over 30 degrees for days, and just until a few hours earlier). My first thought at the rain was that it might cause flight delays – my 50-minute connection was firmly in my thoughts. I got the airport, the rain had stopped, and the sun was out. The boards said that the flight was on time, as scheduled at 17:05. A sigh of relief. At 16:15, as I was passing by the announced gate, I could not help noticing that there was no plane yet at the end of the bridge; the plane had not arrived yet. I immediately thought of my connection and started calculating the possibility of the plane arriving soon and still leaving on time. Just then, a plane was landing; I hoped it was mine. After a few minutes, it was parked at the end of my gate. Phew! But despite the gate opening soon, boarding did not start until 16:50. It was completed at 17:20 and as the pilot announced it, he also said the flight would be 1 hour and 40 minutes. I was calculating frantically – if we arrived 15–20 minutes late, I would have 30 minutes to get to the other flight. The plane took off at 17:35 and I was told by the hostess that our expected arrival time was 19:25. 20 minutes in between, with gates normally closing 15 minutes before . . . and I had to go through security and passport control.

I asked about my connecting flight and had to sit nervously until I got a response shortly before landing. It seemed that there was a slight delay to the flight – I had a chance after all. But another uncertainty arose: would we park on a jet bridge or on the tarmac, to be taken to the terminal by bus? The first option was clearly speedier, as I could be one of the first out of the plane, able to proceed. In the second option, I had to wait on the bus for half of the plane to disembark and then for the bus to take me to the terminal. We landed at 19:20 and . . . parked on the tarmac five minutes later. The mobile staircase took some time to come to be positioned on the plane. I was counting the minutes.

I rushed to the front and was second on the bus at 19:30. But I had to wait for the rest of the passengers. I was nervous and realised I was noticing and reacting to things I would normally be oblivious to. Gradually the bus filled with passengers. The very last people coming down from the plane were an old couple, moving down the stairs very slowly, waiting for one another. At the end of the stairs they hesitated and then took their time to choose the door through which to get on the bus. At that point, the second bus – for the passengers from the back half of the plane, who started disembarking five minutes after us – drove off. I had never seen the second bus go first. How irritating. The old couple on the bus, our driver was still not to be seen. Turned out, they were waiting for a baby stroller, unfolded it and were trying to get it through the last door of the bus. We finally drove off and reached the terminal at 19:39.

A ground agent was waiting with a London Heathrow sign. There were three of us connecting and she led us with a brisk walk through the airport and through the priority security check. The usual procedure . . . but now I was asked to open my bag to be checked (they had not done this at Catania airport). I ran on, putting on my belt on the go, through passport control. I was at the gate at 19:45, as the last passengers were boarding and getting on the second bus, waiting outside. As soon as I realised that I made it, the uncertainty disappeared and all my worries over the previous minutes, hours, and days now seemed petty and trivial. I was on the bus at 19:47. The plane was fully boarded at 20:10. By then, a strong wind had come and traffic control had to change the landing and take-off pattern. We did not take off until 21:00, over an hour late. This meant that now I would most likely miss my train to Bath . . .

There is nothing entrepreneurial in this story, but I was unnerved by the uncertainty of not knowing whether I would make my connection. Normally insignificant events took on significance as bearing on that ultimate outcome. Nine minutes on the airport bus felt like an eternity and it seemed that all sorts of small events were lining up for the purpose of slowing me down.

There were two factors that generated this experience. The first was that the outcome was outside my control: I was entirely at the mercy of circumstances. The second was that I had vested my interest in a particular outcome, of making the connection. Missing it would mean spending the night in Milan (normally not a bad thing) and disrupting my planned work the following day. It was also my children's first day at school and the plan was that I would take them to school. Disrupting that pattern felt like a loss because I had attached plans, other events to it. It had assumed a taken-for-granted status, whereby I would have images of the following day interpenetrating my many presents as the day was drawing near. Yes, these are trivial but the point is that they generated a very real feeling of bearing uncertainty. That feeling would be by order of magnitude more intensive if something much more serious was on the line. I recall the last time I had missed a connection, I had to spend the night in Amsterdam. A couple were in the same situation, on their way to their son's graduation from university, which was happening the following morning. They did not make it.

Loss, uncertainty, and vulnerability

The disruption of the image of the future in which we start living feels like a loss because of the personal value of what is tangibly attached to it. This could be emotional, such as not making it to a wedding or graduation, or material such as missing an important job interview or loosing invested money. This can also have emotional or material consequences for others, such as investors, for which we feel a burden of responsibility.

In her principles of effectuation, Sarasvathy (2001) discussed the importance of affordable loss. The insight behind comes from earlier research in which entrepreneurs and bankers differ in their approach to a new venture situation: while bankers focus on a given return and look to minimise risk, entrepreneurs focus on setting an acceptable level of risk and then look to maximise return (Sarasvathy, Simon, & Lave, 1998). In this scenario, it is actually the bankers who bear uncertainty and not the entrepreneurs. All because they have become vested in a particular outcome.

Sarasvathy (2001) discusses the bankers' approach as belonging to the realm of causal reasoning, which focused on predicting the future and setting goals. As such, it becomes the source of anxiety in a situation of uncertainty. But the discussion so far suggests that this conception may be misleading. While the situation may be objectively uncertain, it is not necessarily subjectively so. What creates the subjective uncertainty is not so much the setting of goals or focusing on a particular prediction of the future, but the pre-organisation (and pre-commitment) of our lives around a particular future scenario, to which we aspire. We do not necessarily set it as a goal driven by prediction, it is simply where we want to be; it is a purpose. And when our purpose excites others, they may make commitments behind it, such as investments of money or time. This is not driven by a causal reasoning (something that we have to suppress). It is a natural expression of human aspiration, of the future flowing into our immediate experience. Stepping outside of that experience – such as when the future feels threatened or outside of our control – we become aware of the time gap that separates us from the future and of our vulnerability to the commitments made. It is their unaffordability that generates uncertainty.

In other words, entrepreneurship – rather than acting in the face of uncertainty – entails the enactment of purpose, the attachment to which generates uncertainty. This is because the attachment takes the form of present commitments such as promises, plans or investments and, as such, goes beyond the entrepreneur to involve other people. This creates a new reality in the present that is vested in things turning out in a certain way. The image of the future can no longer remain an immediate psychic state since it needs to be communicated and 'seen' by others. By having to use the medium of language to do so, the entrepreneur inevitably becomes external to it and thus needs to project it on a spatial timeline. But as the line of time runs only to the present, the future state becomes separated by a gap, by a dotted line representing things not yet passed. It is not a line we can move on since, by attempting to move, we inevitably create another line, the solid line of actual history. The original image inevitably gets lost. And this has implications for the commitments vested in it.

Bergson offers a feel for this experience in his discussion of hope:

> What makes hope such an intense pleasure is the fact that the future, which we dispose of to our liking, appears to us at the same time under a multitude of forms. Even if the most coveted of these becomes realized, it will be necessary to give up the others, and we shall have lost a great deal. The idea of the future, pregnant with an infinity of possibilities, is thus more fruitful that the future itself, and this is why we find more charm in hope that in possession, in dreams than in reality.
>
> (Bergson, 1913, *The Intensity of Psychic States*, paragraph 8)

If the vesting in a future image through present commitments is inevitable, the question then arises of what makes such commitments affordable, so that they do not generate enervating uncertainty. These commitments can be viewed against an accumulated collateral of social and financial capital as well as self-esteem, i.e. how much disappointment we can generate in ourselves as well as in others and how much money we can lose. These collaterals and their thresholds vary across individuals. What is common among them is that crossing them creates a sense of vulnerability, i.e. a possibility of being harmed, whether emotionally, socially, or materially. Thus, the question of 'what is affordable?' can be rephrased as 'when do I become vulnerable?' Without awareness of our vulnerability, we cannot determine what is affordable. Indeed, Brown (2013), who has studied vulnerability in great depth, describes it both as the birthplace of creativity and the source of uncertainty.

Therefore, entrepreneurial action operates at the interplay of purpose and vulnerability. They can reinforce or undermine one another, as in when strong purpose can elevate one's threshold of vulnerability, or when strong sense of vulnerability can dampen one's purpose. Both of these emanate from the individual, while reflecting a number of social constraints. Because individuals vary both in their purpose and thresholds of vulnerability, entrepreneurship cannot be viewed and explained in absolute terms. What may be a bold, meaningful purpose for one, may be trivial for another. What seems a scary prospect for one, may be just an energizing challenge for another. Understanding entrepreneurial action is ultimately a quest to understand one's purpose and vulnerability.

Conclusion

Uncertainty is typically seen as the defining feature of the context for entrepreneurial action. It is undoubtedly an important concept, arising in economics, in the context of a rational decision calculus for the future, in a quest to offer a normative basis for decisions. It puts emphasis on entrepreneurship as judgmental decision making about resource deployment (Knight, 1921; Foss and Klein, 2012) that makes consideration and conclusion as the filter for action. In particular, Foss and Klein define judgment as "residual, controlling decision-making about resources deployed to achieve some objectives; it is manifest in the actions of individual entrepreneurs; and it cannot be bought and sold on the market, such that its exercise requires the entrepreneur to own and control a firm" (2012: 78).

This view leaves unanswered the question of how entrepreneurs exercise such judgment. The judgment itself is a latent construct, inferred from observations of objectives and the resources deployed. It is considered to be made under uncertainty, because there is no rational way of connecting the objectives and the deployed resources. And it is considered to be a judgment because ... how else would people act but through deliberation. There is thus a residual mystery about the experience of the entrepreneur. It feels like a dive.

This essay offers a conception of entrepreneurship resting on the experience and interplay of purpose and vulnerability. Through the former the entrepreneur acts upon the world. Through the latter the world acts upon the entrepreneur.

Note

1 There is also parallel here with Pascal's distinction of four kinds of persons: zeal without knowledge; knowledge without zeal; neither knowledge nor zeal; both zeal and knowledge (Pascal, Pensees: 867).

References

Bergson, H. (1913 [2001]). *Time and free will: An essay on the immediate data of consciousness* [Kindle version]. Mineola, NY: Dover Publications.

Brown, B. (2013). *Daring greatly: How the courage to be vulnerable transforms the way we live, love, parent, and lead*. London: Penguin Books.

Brumbaugh, R. S. (1966). Applied metaphysics: Truth and passing time. *Review of Metaphysics, 19*(4), 647–666.

Cook, T. D., & Campbell, D. T. (1979). *Quasi-experimentation: Design and analysis issues for field studies*. Boston: Houghton Mifflin.

Dewey, J. (1938 [1991]). *Logic: Theory of inquiry*. Later Works 12. Edited by J. A. Boydston. Carbondale and Edwardsville: Southern Illinois University Press.

Foss, N. J., & Klein, P. G. (2012). *Organizing entrepreneurial judgment*. Cambridge: Cambridge University Press.

Knight, F. H. (1921). *Risk, uncertainty, and profit*. Boston, MA: Houghton Mifflin.

March, J. G., & Shapira, Z. (1987). Managerial perspectives on risk and risk taking. *Management Science, 33*(11), 1404–1418.

Pascal, B. (1991). *Pensees*. Edited by P. Sellier. Paris: Bords.

Romme, A. G. L. (2003). Making a difference: Organization as design. *Organization Science, 14*, 558–573.

Sarasvathy, S. D. (2001). Causation and effectuation: Toward a theoretical shift from economic inevitability to entrepreneurial contingency. *Academy of Management Review, 26*, 243–263.

Sarasvathy, D. K., Simon, H. A., & Lave, L. (1998). Perceiving and managing business risks: Differences between entrepreneurs and bankers. *Journal of Economic Behavior & Organization, 33*, 207–225.

Venkataraman, S. (1997). The distinctive domain of entrepreneurship research. In J. A. Katz (Ed.), *Advances in entrepreneurship, firm emergence, and growth* (Vol. 3, pp. 119–138). Greenwich, CT: JAI Press.

Wiklund, J., Patzelt, H., & Dimov, D. (2016). Entrepreneurship and psychological disorders: How ADHD can be productively harnessed. *Journal of Business Venturing Insights, 6*, 14–20.

Index

Note: Page numbers in italic indicate a figure and page numbers in bold indicate a table on the corresponding page.

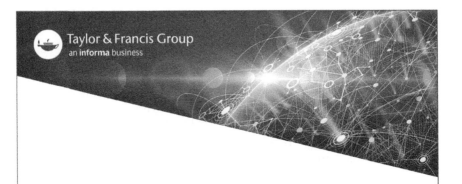

For Product Safety Concerns and Information please contact our EU
representative GPSR@taylorandfrancis.com Taylor & Francis Verlag GmbH,
Kaufingerstraße 24, 80331 München, Germany

Printed and bound by CPI Group (UK) Ltd, Croydon, CR0 4YY

01/05/2025

01858424-0002